Collecting Antique Plants

THE HISTORY AND CULTURE OF
THE OLD FLORISTS' FLOWERS

Collecting Antique Plants

THE HISTORY AND CULTURE OF
THE OLD FLORISTS' FLOWERS

Roy Genders

PELHAM BOOKS

First published in Great Britain by
PELHAM BOOKS LTD
52 Bedford Square
London w.c.1
1971

7207 0418 9

Set and printed in Great Britain by
Tonbridge Printers Ltd, Peach Hall Works, Tonbridge, Kent
in Baskerville ten on twelve point on paper supplied by
P. F. Bingham Ltd, and bound by James Burn
at Esher, Surrey

Acknowledgments

The author wishes to thank Mrs Margaret Ness for the preparation and typing of the M/S; Mr John Gledhill for his delightful photographs of the old florists' flowers; W. A. Genders, B.A. for the line drawings; and R. P. Genders for historical research.

I am also grateful to Mr William Luscombe for giving me the opportunity of writing this book on the flowers I love best of all.

ROY GENDERS

Contents

Illustrations

Photographs by John Gledhill

CHAPTER I

The Florists and Their Flowers

The show auricula – The gold-laced polyanthus – The old flower shows
– The pink and carnation – Fancy pansies – The old florists' tulips –
Decline of the florists' flowers – Where to find the old plants

In the same way that the cottage home has maintained a constant
supply of antique furniture, of china and glass and early English
water colours, so too, in the cottage garden are to be found many of
the old fashioned flowers which also have antique value. They are
collectors' plants which are eagerly sought by those who love the
quaint old flowers and do not wish to see them disappear, though
they have become as difficult to find as pieces of early Wedgwood or
a Paul Sandby drawing. They are not only appreciated for their
beauty but also for their scarcity value. They are antique plants in
the real sense of the word, many of them known to gardeners of the
first Elizabethan reign and earlier. They are plants steeped in the
history of these islands and some of them were taken up by those
who worked at home in the early days of the industrial revolution
when these lovely flowers brought interest and beauty into the home.

They are the florists' flowers which were brought to a perfection of
beauty unknown in any other flowers before or since, and for this
reason they were depicted by the early Dutch flower painters in
whose masterpieces they may be seen to this day if many are no
longer to be found in the garden. They appear in the paintings of
Abraham Mignon (1640-1679) and of Ambrosius Bosschaert (1570-
1645) in whose *Flowerpiece* in the Rijkes Museum, Amsterdam,
appears the streaked tulip which made such high prices in western
Europe at the time. The 18th century flower painters made extensive
use of the auricula as to be seen in one of the most beautiful of
paintings in the National Gallery in London. It is by Theodore van
Brussel, a Dutchman who lived between 1754-1795. At the centre is
a grey-edged auricula with its circular blooms, more than a dozen of
which make up the flower truss. It has a quality which would ensure
its earning the premier award in any flower show of modern times.

Another fine grey-edged auricula is depicted in the painting of
spring flowers previously in the collection of the second Lord Fair-
haven and now in the Fitzwilliam Museum, Cambridge. It was

painted by J. Linthorst in 1799 and shows most of the florists' flowers of the time.

Many of these flowers have been lost to cultivation but at least some remain to be rediscovered by those who would seek them out and with patience, it is possible to build up a sizeable collection of those which most please one's fancy. They were known as florists' flowers because a florist was a specialist grower or craftsman who took up the culture of certain flowering plants which in his hands could be expected to attain a degree of perfection hitherto unknown in the floricultural world.

From the old fringed pinks, the Paisley growers bred out the serrated edging and replaced it by smooth-edged petals and a bloom of perfect symmetry. Only those flowers capable of this transformation in the hands of these craftsmen growers were considered worthy of attention; thus all had this symmetrical appeal and smooth, rounded petals. The aim was to produce a flower which was completely circular and it was not long before the pansy, with its horse-shaped face had also become entirely circular in the hands of the florists.

In addition, the flowers were to have their circular appearance made more pronounced by an edging which contrasted with the ground colouring of the bloom as in the laced pink, picotée, gold-laced polyanthus and fancy pansy. Most of these plants lend themselves to pot culture in the greenhouse or garden room whilst with their neat habit, they make admirable subjects for the small garden. Here, provided they are given the cultivation they require, collections may be built up which can be expected to increase in value with each year. They are as valuable an investment as a piece of antique furniture or a water colour drawing. As they become more scarce, so do they increase in value, like any other object of art.

A few years ago, the double yellow primrose Cloth of Gold, could be obtained for a very small sum. Today, it may cost £5. Likewise the double crimson Madame du Pompadour, whilst the double white primrose, described by John Gerard in his *Herbal* of 1597, has more than trebled in value within a few years, though it may still be obtained for the price of a packet of the more expensive cigarettes.

The old plants have not become scarce because they were in any way difficult to manage or because of tender constitution. That many have survived for the last four hundred years, clearly shows them to be almost indestructible but they are plants which require care in their culture, neither do they lend themselves to modern methods of mass production. They have survived in cottage gardens because of the loving care bestowed upon them by several generations of plant lovers. They were and remain so to this day, the cottager's pride and joy, to be cherished and enjoyed, in the same way that an inlaid cabinet or a china figure which has been handed down from one generation to another, still gives pleasure and satisfaction of ownership. Those who grow the antique plants may not perhaps be aware of their monetary value but cherish them the same.

In the introduction to *Hardy Florists' Flowers,* written and published by James Douglas, gardener to Mr Francis Whitburn and later of the nursery bearing his name, the Rev. Francis Horner, Vicar of Kirkby Malzeard, near Ripon has written lovingly of the florists' flowers : 'They have been the delight of many a man in whom the love of nature was inborn and inextinguishable but whose means were very spare, whose leisure time was very scant, and whose advantages in pure air and light and garden space were poor and cramped. Little could he see, in his toiling pent-up life, the changes as they came and went across the face of the green earth . . . yet did the spring smile on him in his polyanthuses, his auriculas, and pansies, and summer visit him in the bloom of his tulips, ranunculuses, carnations and pinks. In one or more of these, his love of nature found expression, and enough to live upon.'

THE SHOW AURICULA

The auricula was the first plant to be taken up by the specialist growers. The earliest reproduction of it known to me is in the painting by Jan Bruegel the Elder ('Velvet' Bruegel) of the *Holy Family festooned with Flowers,* now at Munich. It was painted about the year 1600 and shows a magnificent specimen of a green auricula which would take first prize at any show. Though without the now familiar paste-like centre, it has an exotic beauty, which, in the words of Thomas Hogg, Florist of Paddington Green 'seems to engross our undivided attention'. Hogg wrote this in 1820 and a hundred years earlier, John Laurance in his treatise, *The Auricula,* had said, 'nature nowhere discovers her variety of colours, her shades and pretty mixtures more than in this little flower.'

The plant had been introduced into England about the year 1575, by Flemish weavers fleeing from the Huguenot persecutions and who settled in the Lancashire towns of Rochdale and Middleton. These towns were to become the centre of auricula growing and have remained so until this day, though several of the early specialists were Cambridgeshire men.

John Gerard who was from Nantwich in the county of Cheshire, was the first to describe the plant which was known to Elizabethan gardeners as Bears Ear, from the shape of the leaf which was covered in fine hairs. Gerard, who had charge of the gardens at Theobalds for Lord Burghley, Elizabeth's Lord Chancellor, published his *Herbal* in 1597 and in it he listed seven varieties, the original yellow which he called the Greatest English Garden Cowslip; and purple, blush, red, bright red and scarlet. In the *Paradisus* of 1629, which he dedicated to Queen Henrietta Maria wife of Charles I, Parkinson described 21 varieties and illustrated eight of them but the amazing 'edged' varieties, due to a covering of meal in various degrees of density, and the paste-like centres were still unknown. The structural change of the petals did not occur until more than a century later when there appeared the Black Imperial, the ground colour being of darkest red with a contrasting white centre. This was composed of minute glandular hairs which give the appearance of paste or enamel. Shortly after, appeared a bloom of almost black ground colouring and a paste-like centre but which also had a remarkable edging of green which is a replacement of the ordinary petal colour by leaf characteristics. It is shown in the auricula of Jan Bruegel's painting.

In 1757 came the first green-edged variety with a white paste-like centre. It was named Rule Arbiter and the hardy border auricula had become the show auricula for the plants had now to be grown in pots and kept under glass for the paste 'ran' when in contact with rain. The first white-edged auricula, Mortain, followed Rule Arbiter and the age of the auricula 'theatre' was about to begin. Here, the plants were arranged in tiers, one above another, like seats at the theatre and they were protected from rain beneath a glass canopy or structure.

The show auricula appeared at the time of the sedan chair and harpsichord, when Beau Nash presided over the Pump Room at Bath and George II and his Queen were regular visitors. It appeared at exactly the right moment, at the beginning of an era of elegance and achievement.

By the end of the 18th century, there were several hundred varieties and as many as 50 auricula shows were held each year, mainly in the north of England with Manchester and Sheffield the two chief centres, three shows often taking place in these towns on the same day. The Cambridge show was also prominent. Amongst the most consistent winners at the early shows were Wrigley's Northern Hero, green-edged; Lee's Bright Venus, white or china-edged; and Waterhouse's Conqueror of Europe.

The latter, a grey-edged auricula was raised by John Waterhouse of Lady's Walk, Sheffield and was first exhibited at the Sheffield Horticultural Society's Spring Show on 8th May, 1833. A coloured plate appeared in the June issue of the *Floricultural Cabinet* of the same year and it shows the flower to be of outstanding beauty. In describing its first appearance on the show bench, one said that 'each flower was as large as a crown piece.' It was priced at 30s, a large sum in those days but M'Intosh, gardener to H.M. the King of the Belgians in his book *The Flower Garden* (1838) names many famous varieties which cost 4s. each which is considerably less than the price asked for the show auriculas of today.

Of such importance had the plant become by 1800, that it was found necessary to determine the 'points of a flower' suitable for the show bench and which have persisted, almost unchanged until the present day.

The beginning of the century saw the formation of many florists' societies, one being that formed by the Cambridge florists who in 1836 presented a 'neat silver cup' to John R. Stubbings in appreciation 'for his unwearied exertions as their Hon. Secretary for many years'. At this show, held at the Hoop Hotel on 29th April, the Rev. Lascelles won 1st prize for Green-edged auriculas with Hunt's Conquering Hero and Richard Headley, first in the Grey-edge section with Oliver's Lovely Ann which was judged Premier auricula of the show. His auricula, George Lightbody, introduced in 1860, shortly before his death was possibly the finest ever raised and is still exhibited after more than a century. Gold Laced Polyanthuses and double hyacinths were also exhibited at the show. At about this time, the Show auricula had reached a perfection which, the older enthusiasts have said has never since been equalled.

At the Leeds Florists' Society's Show held on 25th April, 1836 Wm. Chadwick was first of his class in the Green-edged section with Lee's Colonel Taylor and the same exhibitor took the premier award for Grey-edges with Grime's Privateer, introduced (with Wrigley's Northern Hero) in about 1780. It is shown in all its glory in one of the plates for Thornton's *Temple of Flora*, published in 1807 and for which it was painted by Philip Reinagle.

The following week at the Hull Floral Society's Show, the same two varieties were again successful in their respective groups and in the White-edged group, the celebrated Dr Horner took 1st prize with Hugh's Pillar of Beauty. He was also 2nd for Green-edges with Pollet's Standard of England. What delightful names they gave to the old auriculas and those who raised and exhibited them were not then ashamed of their country and its achievements which seems to be a trait of modern times.

How the auricula was able to attain such a degree of perfection so soon after it appeared was surely because the descendants of the Flemish weavers, in whose hands the growing of these plants was almost entirely concentrated, had not only a vast knowledge of the culture of the plants handed down to them from a previous generation, but, being their own bosses, were able to give that attention to detail so necessary for the plants to attain perfection. In the Heavy Woollen district of Yorkshire the cricket bat then reigned supreme; to the silk weavers of Lancashire and Cheshire and the cutlers of Sheffield, the auricula took pride of place, and there were few distractions 150 years ago.

The Show auricula was rarely a success with the wealthy, who would invariably delegate the tasks of looking after the plants, to paid servants. With the plants demanding attention to detail from the beginning, only those who were prepared to give them unlimited care and who had the plants close to their heart could hope to achieve success. The Show auricula could be linked in this respect to the Show pansy, which demanded the same care for it to be successful. They are plants which were happier in the back garden, under the constant observation from the kitchen or spinning room window, than in the large garden of the country mansion, far removed from the watchful eye of the owner.

The Rev. Francis Horner has charmingly written of the conditions under which the old craftsmen weavers worked and tended their plants during the early days of the Industrial Revolution and which by 1870 had been absorbed in urban development. 'There stands many an old house,' he wrote, 'now deeply embedded in a town, that used to have its garden, oft-times a florist's. Here, for instance, is the very window – curiously long and lightsome – at which a hand-loom weaver worked behind his loom, able to watch his flowers as carefully as his work, his labour and his pleasure intermingled, interwoven as intimately as his silken threads.' And the same could be said of the small craftsmen cutlers of Sheffield, a city which was famous for its auricula and carnation growers until after the second world war.

It is of interest that the centre of auricula growing has persisted, from earliest times until the present with but one or two notable exceptions, in that relatively small area of Lancashire which adjoins the Yorkshire border. The most famous auricula growers of both olden and modern times have mostly been concentrated within an imaginary circle drawn with its centre equidistant from Burnley in the north, and Manchester in the south; with Halifax, in Yorkshire, to the east; and to the west, Chorley. Sheffield, just outside the circle, is no longer famed for its auriculas, the chrysanthemum having taken its place, though only in quite recent times. Playing as great a part in the success of the Lancashire growers as did their knowlege of the plants handed down by succeeding generations, was the cool, moist climatic conditions, which prove ideal for the rearing of the blooms. And just as the auriculas continue to flourish, so do those who grow them, auricula growers being the longest living of all people. One of the earliest enthusiasts was James Fitton of Middleton, who passed away at the age of 86, likewise his son, who carried on his father's famous collection until the mid-nineteenth century, during the golden age of the Show auricula. Another Middleton grower was Joe Partington, who won first prize at Eccles show at the age of 16, and was exhibiting his beloved auriculas 80 years later. And so to that great enthusiast of modern times, the late Mr Dan Bamford of the same town which still retains its traditions for growing auriculas, though with the ever-growing worries of smoke pollution, this becomes more difficult with each year.

Only a short distance away, across the bleak moorland country, beyond Rochdale and Blackstone Edge, one reaches Halifax in the neighbouring county of Yorkshire, where the Midgeleys have raised and exhibited Show auriculas for more than half a century. W. H. Midgeley, contemporary with such famous auricula growers as the Rev. Horner and Samuel Barlow, raised the fine grey-edged variety named after himself; whilst his son J. W. Midgeley, one of the premier auricula judges in the country, raised the white-edged variety which also bears his name. In the possession of Mr J. W. Midgeley is a photograph, reproduced in the *Year Book* of the Northern Auricula Society, which shows more than two dozen plants of Show auriculas grown by his father. The year was 1902 and the quality of the bloom is such as to leave no doubt as to the ability of the auricula enthusiasts of that time. It may be said that this was the culmination of the golden age of the Show auricula which began more than a century before. With the auricula growers of Lancashire and Yorkshire, the quality of their flowers went hand in hand with that of their cricketing prowess, both attaining a peak of perfection at the turn of the century which has never since been equalled, before a craftsman culture and its inherent pride gave way to shoddiness and mass production.

Many of the old show auriculas may still be obtained but with each year become more difficult to find. As recently as 1950, that grand auricula George Rudd introduced in 1880, won the Premier Award at the Northern Auricula Society's Show for Mr Lewis Ambler of Halifax, but with the death of Mr Ambler the following year, the variety has since been less prominent and may soon be lost to cultivation. The old growers had their favourites and knew exactly what the plants required to bring them to their best.

Samuel Barlow of Castleton was for long one of the most respected of the old auricula growers. His father, raiser of Barlow's King, was a friend of Thomas Buxton the pansy breeder, and Samuel's first love was the Show pansy. Those who visited his gardens during the mid-1850s have recorded the quality and wide variety of plants to be found growing there, for his garden was ringed by tall chimney stacks, which, even in those days, belched forth their injurious smoke over the surrounding countryside. Barlow raised tulips and gold-laced polyanthuses in addition to his pansies and auriculas, working on so large a scale that he would generally raise 500 auricula seedlings every year from which he would select no more than one which he considered worthy of propagation and naming. Together with Rev. Horner and Ben Simonite of Sheffield, who was the raiser of the fine Green-edged auriculas Henry Wilson, Shirley Hibberd and Mrs Henwood, which he introduced in 1904, Samuel Barlow was one of the founder members of the Northern Auricula Society in 1873, happily still flourishing.

In extolling the qualities of the north-country auricula growers, those known as the London group – Hogg, Emmerton, Glenny and Maddock – must not be forgotten; not only as raisers of some fine new varieties, but as writers on the subject they exerted considerable influence on the florists' flowers and particularly the auricula during the first half of the nineteenth century. They preceded the northern growers as specialists and were able to put into words, interesting details of their culture which were to prove of inestimable value to the mid-nineteenth-century growers. It was surprising that almost nothing was set to print by the northern growers, and all we know of the auricula during the early nineteenth century is almost entirely from the pens of the London growers, though several were of northern extraction. They were practical nurserymen, James Maddock, a Quaker of Walworth, being a native of Warrington who moved south in 1770, whilst Hogg who published his famous *Treatise* in 1822, was a Scotsman.

James Maddock was the first of the florists to write on the subject and published his *Florists' Directory* in 1792. In it, he describes only eight flowers as being worthy of the florist's attention, the hyacinth, tulip, ranunculus, auricula, anemone, pink, carnation and polyanthus. The sweet william and pansy were added later to make ten in all and these remained the 'florists' flowers' for more than a century, during which time they reached a perfection not seen in any other flower since the end of the 19th century.

Hogg's *Treatise* appeared in 1822 but seven years before, Isaac, Emmerton, a nurseryman of Barnet had published his *Treatise on the Culture and Management of the Auricula* which he dedicated to the Marchioness of Salisbury. Later, Emmerton moved his nursery to Paddington Green to become a neighbour of Thomas Hogg, but the two never became friends for they were entirely different in temperament. Emmerton's *Treatise* was the first important work devoted entirely to the Show auricula and it was thorough in the extreme. Besides giving in some detail, at times revolting, various composts suitable for auriculas, there are also chapters on saving and sowing seed, conveying plants to shows, and monthly cultural instructions. He concludes with a catalogue of the best named varieties listing nearly a hundred, which by the end of the century had grown to 400 or more. Emmerton certainly practised what he preached, for his bitter rival Hogg said 'Glenny and Emmerton have not been surpassed (as auricula growers) by any florist of the present day,' which must be considered generous in the light of the rivalry between the men, and Hogg by no means 'pulled his punches' when on the subject of the auricula. In his *Treatise* Hogg wrote : 'Almost all (growers) pride themselves in that they are in possession of some infallible nostrum . . . yet after all this mystery and boasting, the state and condition of the plants too often belie their pretended skill'; which revealed all too plainly Hogg's opinion on the art and mystery of auricula cultivation when in the hands of rival growers.

It is said that both Hogg and Emmerton carried their ideas to extremes, yet the older generations of auricula growers firmly believe that the quality of the plants was never so high as during their time so we are in no position to criticise the methods of the old growers.

The writings of Hogg and Emmerton were followed, in 1834 by some excellent advice on auriculas in *The Flower Garden,* a large book written by M'Intosh, and it was not until 1860 that George Glenny published *The Culture of Flowers and Plants.* He begins his writings on the auricula by agreeing that it is the most difficult of all florists' plants to grow well. Glenny backed his advice by a great practical knowledge and his writings carried enormous influence at that time. His description of what he considered to be the perfect Show auricula was still accepted as the requisite standard by the Royal Horticultural Society, a century later. But though we have had handed down through the nineteenth century a vast store of cultural knowledge of the auricula, unlike the sweet pea and the pansy and other florists' favourites, the Show auricula has remained unaltered for 200 years, as the picture in *Thornton's Temple of Flora* (1807) clearly shows and in which the two green-edged Show auriculas, Pott's Eclipse and Grime's Privateer, are revealed in a form greatly superior to most varieties exhibited today. Certainly the plant has remained unchanged since that time, and if anything the Show auricula has tended to lose vigour, due possibly to pollution of the atmosphere and to there being so many more ways of utilising one's spare time than in giving Show auricula the detailed attention it requires.

THE GOLD-LACED POLYANTHUS

At the time of the appearance of the first Show auricula, a coloured illustration of a polyanthus appeared in John Hill's famous work, *The Vegetable Kingdom.* It was published in 1757 in 25 volumes and had taken Hill 16 years to write. In the author's own words, the flower was 'of a beautiful crimson with an eye of yellow'. In reality, the flowers are of purple-crimson with a yellow eye, around which is a striking circle of white which gives the bloom an auricula-like appearance. Careful inspection also reveals a thin wire edge of gold from which we may deduct that the polyanthus had also taken on a new characteristic upon which its fame was to rest for the next hundred years. This was the brilliant golden centre and a lacing or edging of the same pure gold on a ground of darkest crimson. The yellow polyanthus did not appear until 1880 when Miss Gertrude Jekyll discovered a chance seedling growing in the garden of her home at Munstead Heath in Surrey.

By 1760, the Gold-laced polyanthus had become one of the most widely grown of all plants for none responded more rewardingly to the skill of the craftsman (or workman) and grower. Several years later, Rev. William Hanbury said that in his garden at Church Langton in Leicestershire there grew 'more than a thousand varieties and nearly the same number of auriculas'. In 1780, Abercrombie wrote that the gold-laced polyanthus had become 'one of the most noted prize (Show) flowers amongst florists!'

The first recorded exhibition of the Gold-laced polyanthus, and indeed of any of the florists' flowers, was held in 1769, at the home of one, John Barnes of Lichfield in Staffordshire, a county which has always been associated with the craftsman-florist. In 1792, James Maddock described the Gold-laced polyanthus in his *Florists' Directory*. 'The beautiful yellow of the cowslip,' he wrote, 'which it did not formerly possess in the same degree of perfection as it now does, has in the opinion of some been communicated to it within the present century . . .' The yellow however, is of true gold colouring, very different from the pale yellow of the cowslip and primrose, being similar to that of the gold-centred Alpine auricula. It is as if the centre and petal edges had been treated with gold-leaf. Here then was a flower worthy of the craftsman's care and attention and during the first half of the 19th century, it reached a zenith of perfection and popularity along with all the other florists' favourites.

Although the industrialisation of Britain had begun, many workers continued to use their craftsman's knowledge by working at home. The worker was still his own boss and could combine his love of flowers with the love of his work. Each house had its tiny garden where the plants could be grown in stock beds, to be planted and grown on in small pots, to bloom indoors in a sunny window at the appropriate time.

THE OLD FLOWER SHOWS

The extent to which the Gold-laced polyanthus and other florists' flowers were exhibited during the early years of the 19th century is revealed in a small book which recently came to light. It is '*An Account of the Different Flower Shews held in Lancashire, Cheshire*

and Yorkshire and in other parts of the Kingdom in the year 1826'
and it was printed by Thomas Cunningham of Ashton-under-Lyne.

The shows usually took place in the local public house and the
auricula and gold-laced polyanthus were exhibited together. The
first of the spring flower shows took place early in April; the last
about mid-May. Then would follow the tulip meetings, until the
month end. In June would come the ranunculus shows, then the
pink and carnation shows which lasted until almost the end of July
to be followed by exhibitions of dahlias and chrysanthemums.
Almost every day there was a show somewhere. The florists of
Paisley, famed for the lacing of their pinks, met every Thursday,
'from the flowering of the gold-laced polyanthus to the disappearance of the carnation' and the dahlia shows continued until the end
of autumn.

In *'An Account of the Different Flower Shews'* (note the spelling)
there is a record of 50 shows held in the counties of Lancashire,
Cheshire and Yorkshire between 17th April and 6th May 1826, the
last being the great show which took place each year at the Cutler's
Hall, Sheffield on the first Saturday in May. Here were exhibited
auriculas and gold-laced polyanthuses. The report of the Show of
1826 said 'the Polyanthuses were excellent. The whole gave great
satisfaction to the company present'.

Many of the shows were of considerable size and were a great
social occasion. At the London Horticultural Society's show held on
Saturday, 6th June, 1835 more than 5,000 people attended, and
there was an even larger attendance at the show of the Metropolitan
Society of Florists held in Regent's Park ten days later. To provide
the music was Wieppert's Band; also the Band of the Blues and a
Brass Band. The report said that the 'tents and coverings were of
no use except to afford shade' for the weather was most favourable.
Amongst the company present was the Marchioness of Tavistock,
the Duchess of Sutherland, the Marchioness of Westminster, the
Countess of Jersey, Lord Amherst and several Ambassadors 'of
whom the Turkish Minister was most conspicuous'. Half a crown
was the entrance fee if tickets were purchased at seed shops or
florists beforehand, otherwise the cost was five shillings. It is worthy
of mention that 'the majority paid this demand without hesitation
but a large proportion of persons, of the respectability, objected to
so great an augmentation of charge over the previous year and
declined to become spectators of what was going on in the gardens'.
The prize for the best twelve ranunculuses was won by Mr

Alexander; for the 12 best heartsease, by Mr Glenny who also won a prize for 36 varieties of cut flowers. Mr Hogg of Paddington won the award for the 12 best pinks and Mr Salter for his collection of roses. The prize for the finest coxcomb went to Mr Fleming and for the best nosegay, to Mr Hopwood of Twickenham.

The following week was held the famous Cambridge Florists' Society's Show, in the Assembly Rooms at the Red Lion Inn. In the report in the *Florists' Magazine,* the Secretary was to be congratulated on the arrangements whilst 'the flowers were in great profusion and finely grown'. There were 21 classes for the ranunculus alone, the 'best of any colour' being awarded to Mr Catling for his bloom of Bartlett's Charlotte.

The report is concluded by saying that 'the military band enlivened the evening show, and we observed improvement in the softened tone of their instruments!'

But most shows were held in the village public house and were open to all-comers; 'Free to all England' was how the invitation was worded, and a special prize was given by the landlord for the best flowered plant for it must be remembered that most flowers on display were of pot grown plants. Generally the prize was a copper kettle, possibly because it was so durable. Rarely was an award made in cash. As it is frequently reported that it was usual for more than a hundred people to dine at the inn after the show, the landlord could well have afforded his generosity.

Most of the florists of old transported their plants to the shows on foot and many an old grower would walk 20 miles or more carrying a dozen pots as a milkmaid would carry her pails. From a yoke or wooden support fixed across the shoulders there would be suspended (on either side of the person) two wooden boxes, each capable of holding half a dozen small pots which, filled with compost, meant that there was a considerable weight to carry. But the journey was not considered a toil, it was an event of great expectancy and reward. After the meal, the growers would set out to cover the 20 miles home in the cool of the evening, happy with the day's proceedings and especially so if a prize had been won.

Thomas Hogg in his *Treatise* on the florists' flowers presents the reader, by way of an appendix, with the Rules and Regulations for the Islington and Chelsea shows 'for encouraging the cultivation of Auriculas, Pinks and Carnations'. Hogg tells that the rules were drawn up by 'several amateur gentlemen florists and the most eminent public florists around the metropolis.'

RULE I : stated that any person desirous of becoming a member of the Society must be proposed by one of the members and seconded by another.

RULE II : That a president and the secretary be chosen annually, on Carnation Show day, by ballot.

RULE III : That the names of members and their residences be shown in the articles.

RULE IV : That subscription be £1.11.6; 10s. 6d. for auriculas; 10s. 6d. for pinks; 10s. 6d. for carnations.

RULE V : All absentees from meetings to forfeit 2s.

RULE VI : Each member must pay for a dinner ticket for auriculas, pinks and carnations.

RULE VII :That each member provide, at his own expense, a pan to show his carnations in.

RULE VIII : That all flowers on show-days shall be in the room by one o'clock, precisely by the house clock, or they shall not be admitted.

RULE IX : The committee, three in number, to determine the prizes, to be chosen by members present on show days who shall declare that they have not seen or assisted in dressing any blooms present.

RULE X : Members showing flowers to declare that they have been in their possession the last four months.

RULE XI : That the value of prizes to be presented to successful candidates on show-days.

RULE XII : That prizes be limited to six in number for named flowers; two for seedlings.

RULE XIII : That each member showing flowers shall return to his seat as soon as he has carried them into the show room and shall not leave it until the flowers have been brought into the dining room, and have passed round the table, beginning on the president's right and returning to his left, in order that each may view them. The flowers not to be taken away until dismissed by the president.

RULE XIV : That if any member shall call the judgment of the censors in question after the prizes are declared, he shall for such offence forfeit 1 guinea or be expelled from the society.

RULE XV : If any member shall create a quarrel so as to disturb the harmony of the company on show days, his conduct shall be considered at the next meeting and if a majority decide on its impropriety, shall expel him from the Society.

RULE XVI : That if any member refuses to pay any fines or

attempt to evade the rules, he shall be expelled from the Society.

RULE XVII : That all forfeits be appropriated to the seedling prizes.

RULE XVIII : That no member be allowed to show flowers on the day he is admitted.

RULE XIX : That no person be allowed to touch or handle the blooms on show-days without consent of the proprietor, under forfeit of 20s.

The rules were rigorous but fair and in an age noted for strength of character, they were expected to be observed. In the same way were the properties of a florist's flower precisely drawn up and the judges would allow no deviation however slight. As most florist societies were open to all England, the rules were the same for all who took part.

Important shows incuded separate classes for the gold-laced polyanthus which was exhibited with the auricula and of the 63 varieties listed in the table of prize winners given in *An Account of the Different Flower Shews,* the most successful were Pearson's 'Alexander' in the dark ground classes; and Cox's Prince Regent in the red ground classes. Pearson, who was possibly the most famous of all gold-laced polyanthus breeders, also raised many famous auriculas, including the grey-edged Liberty, a frequent winner in its class. He was also an expert on 'flaked' carnations, his Madame Moira being the greatest show winner of the time. Cox, was a specialist grower of several plants and raised the champion green-edged auricula, Duke of Bridgwater.

Amongst other successful gold-laced polyanthuses of the time was Parke's Lord Nelson (Trafalgar had not long been won); Turner's Emperor Bonaparte (a generous gesture so recently after Waterloo); Billington's Beauty of Iver (frequently wrongly called Beauty of Over); Collier's Princess Royal; Crownshaw's Invincible; and Waterhouse's Incomparable. A later introduction, Conqueror of Europe was also outstanding. All were listed in *A Concise and practical Treatise on the Culture and Growth of (amongst other florists' flowers) the Polyanthus,* published in 1820 by Thomas Hogg. The colour illustration in Hogg's book (reproduced on the jacket) conveys something of the beauty of the gold-laced polyanthus. The most famous prize winning varieties of the time were well established by 1820 and shortly after, came Eckersley's Jolly Dragoon (1822) and Revell's Othello (1824), both of which were included in M'Intosh's book *The Flower Garden.* Also of the period was Buck's

King George IV which was a winner at the Northern section show of the National Auricula and Primula Society as late at 1909 and appeared on the show bench until the end of the first world war.

It is told that John Revell was one of the most experienced of florists and specialised in pinks and carnations as well as in gold-laced polyanthuses. M'Intosh quotes him freely and informative articles by Revell, who grew his plants at Pitsmoor, Sheffield, appeared from time to time in the *Floricultural Cabinet,* a monthly journal of the time devoted to florists' flowers and edited and published by Joseph Harrison, then gardener to Lord Wharncliffe at Wortley Hall. Later, Harrison set up his own nursery in partnership with his son at Downham, in Norfolk. It is of interest that from Revell's time and until the beginning of the second world war, pinks and carnations continued to be the speciality of a number of Pitsmoor gardeners, in the same way that the culture of pansies and violas has remained in the hands of the Cheshire and Staffordshire growers, and auriculas with Lancastrians, the Northern Section of the National Auricula and Primula Society still holding its annual show on the first Saturday in May each year in Manchester as it has done for almost a hundred years.

One of the most respected of the Pitsmoor growers of pinks and carnations from about 1880 until 1940 was the late Mr Jack Elms for many years cricket professional to the Sheffield United Club at Bramall Lane. Each day during June and July he would arrive on the ground with a bloom of exhibition quality in his buttonhole and never did he twice wear the same variety in any one summer. He was always as ready to give hints on the culture of his favourite flowers as he was on how to play his favourite game and many a young gardener and cricketer obtained great benefit from his wisdom and kindly instruction. 'Jack's carnations' were famous throughout the north and with his death ended more than a hundred years of specialist culture of pinks and carnations with the Pitsmoor growers but a number of those plants which were raised to perfection during that time still flourish in allotments and gardens in this district of Sheffield though with the continual encroachment of new housing estates, they have become more difficult to find with each year.

It is interesting to compare the prices obtained for varieties of the gold-laced polyanthus during their heyday. In *The Flower Garden,* M'Intosh priced Collier's Princess Royal at half a guinea, though in those days, florists flowers were usually sold in pairs. Crownshaw's Invincible cost 5s. but apart from these two, almost all varieties could be obtained for a shilling or so and this included Cox's Prince Regent, considered by the old florists to be the finest red ground polyanthus ever raised. *The Florists Cultivator,* edited by Thomas Willatts and published in 1837 confirmed these prices though here, Crownshaw's Invincible was priced at half a guinea. 1837 was indeed a vintage year. Queen Victoria ascended the throne; the P. and O. Steamship Company launched its first ship; and Dickens' *Pickwick Papers* appeared. It was also the year in which John Constable died and with his passing, the great period of English landscape art which started with Richard Wilson almost a century before, began its decline. Likewise the florists' flower though by 1844, a publication appeared called *The Polyanthus* and in it was listed 96 varieties as being of outstanding merit and by 1860, there were well over a hundred varieties but by then, interest was on the wane.

THE PINK AND CARNATION

Sharing equal popularity with the auricula and gold-laced poly-anthus was the pink and the carnation, the first having reached England at the time of the Norman invasion. The earliest form of *Dianthus plumarius* may be found to this day on the stone used in the building of the great Norman keep at Rochester and on the ruined nave of Fountains Abbey in Yorkshire. And because of the rich clove scent of its companion *Dianthus caryophyllus,* the flowers were in great demand by keepers of ale-houses to impart the spicy fragrance of their blooms to ale and wine, hence its ancient name of 'sops-in-wine', the 'sops' being the wet flowers.

A plant of this name still survives and may well be the original for the story is told that it reached England during the 14th century from a monastery garden situated near Orleans. It may be found this day in a number of cottage gardens in Berkshire where it is called by its ancient name and where many of the old pinks are to be found.

In early times, pinks were known as Gillyflowers, to distinguish them from carnations. In his *Prologue* to the *Canterbury Tales,* Chaucer, whose father was a wine merchant in the City, wrote of

> . . . many a Clove Gilofre,
> And nutmeg to put in ale,
> Whether it be moiste or stale.

27

The pink was the favourite flower of Queen Henrietta Maria and she obtained seed from the Dutch growers and began the vogue in this plant. Parkinson, who dedicated the *Paradisus* to the Queen wrote : 'What shall I say to the Queene of delight and of flowers, carnations and gillyflowers, whose bravery (hardiness), variety and sweete smell joined together, tyeth everyone's affection with equal earnestness both to like and to have them?'

One famous pink of the period was The Painted Lady. It was re-discovered in 1950, growing in a cottage garden in Monmouth-shire and resembles in every detail an illustration of a pink known by the name of 'Ye Gallant's Fayre Lady' which is illustrated in a book of garden flowers of the first year of James I's reign. The flower was known to Elizabethan gardeners. It is semi-double with fringed petals and is white with purple flashes. In his book *Old Carnations and Pinks,* the Rev. Oscar Moreton tells that it grows in his garden in Oxfordshire and has 'the strongest and sweetest clove scent of all pinks'.

Others of the same period are Queen of Sheba and Unique, both bearing single flowers of Painted Lady type and still obtainable. The latter bears red flowers, covered all over with flashes of black and pink. Even older is Caesar's Mantle which is Bloody Pink of early Tudor days. The crimson-red flower is shaded almost black at the centre with a grape-like 'bloom' and it possesses a powerful clove scent.

Chaucer's mention of 'many a clove gilofre and nutmeg to put in ale' may well be a reference to the Nutmeg Clove carnation which dates from the early 14th century. It later came to be known as Fenbow's Nutmeg Clove for it had been grown in the garden of one, Julian Fenbow near Leeds since the 17th century, to impart its powerful nutmeg flavour to his home-made wines. It was believed to be lost to cultivation until re-discovery by Mr Sanderson of Leeds in 1960, actually growing in the same garden of which records pre-served since the 17th century, tell of its growing there. It bears a small but fully double flower of crimson-red and has bright blue-green foliage.

But it was the early years of the 19th century that were to become the Golden Age of the pink and its fanciers were situated in more northerly areas than those of the auricula and gold-laced polyanthus. The pink was already well established in the Pitsmoor district of Sheffield when the miners of Durham and Northumberland took up its culture and from there it spread into Scotland where the weavers of Paisley toiled to introduce the intricate patterns of their shawls to the flower.

It was the double black and white or Laced Pink, Lord Stoverdale with its smooth-edged petals that first attracted the attention of the Paisley weavers. Though not the first laced pink, it had been raised by James Major in 1774 and it began a cult in the flower that continued until the middle of the 19th century. To those south of the border, the pinks of Paisley became known as the Scottish Pinks but it was difficult to obtain plants away from the gardens of Clydeside. There is no record of them being exhibited in London, though they appeared occasionally in shows as far south as Oxfordshire.

Hogg in his *Catalogue of Pinks* (1882) listed 121 varieties and in addition, a dozen Scottish Pinks, one of which had the charming name of Robertson's Gentle Shepherd. By the mid 19th century, it is said that there were at least 80 varieties of the Laced Pink grown at Paisley and a reproduction from *The Florist* (1848) shows the degree of perfection to which the flower was capable of attaining.

The object of the weavers was to impart the characteristic of rounded or smooth-edged petals to the blooms, thus eliminating the serrated edges of *D. plumarius*. At the outer edge was to be a band of black, purple or crimson with which colouring the blooms were also marked at the centre. The ground was to be pure white. The example in *The Florist* of two varieties of the time, Young's Double X and Mr Edwards clearly shows this perfection of marking. By 1860 however, conditions in Paisley had so changed as to make it no longer possible to cultivate plants, the reasons for this being the same as those which brought about the demise of most of the other florists' flowers in industrial Britain.

FANCY PANSIES

Long before that time however, in 1820, William Richardson, gardener to Lady Bennett, daughter of the Earl of Tankerville, had raised a number of pansies which were a great advancement on our native heartsease. At about the same time, and less than ten miles away, at Iver in Buckinghamshire, William Thompson, gardener to Lord Gambier, obtained the first all-blue pansy, working with a 'blue' variety brought over from Holland. Though Thompson succeeded in raising several new colours besides the blue, he has said that the blooms were 'as diminutive as the originals' and 'as lengthy as a horse's head'. But he charmingly adds, 'nevertheless, his Lordship was pleased and thus I was amply rewarded'. One was a yellow named Lady Gambier and from it was raised the first large flowered pansy, King George IV, though Thompson's King which followed soon after, was equally fine.

In 1840, came Medora, a chance seedling discovered amongst some heathers. It was, in Thompson's words 'like a cat's face gazing up at me'. In the following year, the Hammersmith Heartsease Society was founded, to be followed four years later by the Scottish Pansy Society. The first bronze flowered pansy appeared at the same time. It was named King of the Beauties and was described by Thompson as 'the best flower of its kind ever submitted to public inspection'.

These blotched pansies as they were called, made their way to Belgium where for a decade they were greatly improved upon. They were then taken up by William Dean, one of three brothers who raised many new plants from their garden at Shipley in Yorkshire. He named his new strain, 'Fancy' pansies, from which time they have retained this name. As the cooler temperatures of the north proved more suitable than the south in obtaining top quality bloom, it was to Scotland and the north that the raising of new varieties was entrusted.

Foremost as an exhibitor in those early days was John Downie of Edinburgh, who in 1852 exhibited six new fancy pansies at the Botanic Gardens in London and within a few years, Alex Lister of the now famous nursery of that name and Dobbies of Edinburgh were exhibiting their new pansies. But the plants still retained their weak, straggling habit of *V. tricolor*, the wild heartsease, and were not suitable for bedding, though Richard Dean, at the Viola and Pansy Conference held in Birmingham in 1895, told that John Fleming, head gardener at Cliveden, was using the white variety Great Eastern, raised at Bath by Harry Hooper and Magpie, discovered in a French cornfield and introduced by John Salter of Hammersmith, for bedding. The bedding displays of these pansies at Cliveden were given much publicity and in 1867, James Grieve of the firm of Dicksons of Edinburgh – and after whom the famous apple is named – began his great work on the improvement of the bedding habit of the pansy.

He collected plants of *V. lutea* in the Pentland Hills, *V. amoena* at Moffat and made use of *V. cornuta*, the recently introduced Horned Viola of the Pyrenees. To each species Grieve crossed the Show and Fancy pansies, taking pollen from the pansies and applying it to each of the species in turn. From the crossing with *V. cornuta* Perfection, which had previously been introduced by Mr B. S. Williams, head gardener at Rotherfield Park in Hampshire, Grieve obtained The Tory and Vanguard and from a crossing with *V. striata,* came the magnificent yellow Bullion which is still in cultivation. These were pansies of compact, tufted habit with short-jointed stems and fibrous roots. They were ideal for bedding and came to be called violas.

In addition, the plants were of more perennial habit than the pansies.

At the same time that James Grieve was raising his new violas, John Baxter, head gardener to Col. M'Call at Daldowie was working on similar lines, perhaps inspired by Grieve's work. Baxter was the first to adopt the now familiar method of exhibiting blooms on the show bench as individual blooms rather than in bunches. Probably the best known of his introductions was Duchess of Fife, a plant of almost prostrate habit, with primrose-yellow blooms strikingly margined with pale blue. It achieved instant popularity, being the first of a series of margined or belted pansies which have retained their popularity with exhibitors. Duchess of Fife is still in commercial cultivation, likewise Richard Dean's White Swan, probably the best pure white viola ever raised.

It was the miners of north Staffordshire who took up the specialised cultivation of pansies and violas and in his *Hardy Florist's Flowers* (1880), James Douglas gives a list of the outstanding varieties of the time, given him by a Mr W. Miller of Leek. The outstanding Selfs were Alexander Watt (purple); George Rudd (yellow) and True Blue; and in Fancies he gives us the best, Jas. Grieve, Mrs Shirley Hibberd and W. H. Miller, the latter possibly raised by himself. The culture of these plants has remained in the hands of the north Staffordshire growers until the present time, for almost a century and for this reason, many of the old varieties, the collectors' plants are still obtainable. That they have survived is possibly because they came later, when the Show auricula and gold-laced polyanthus were passing from the scene though in *Hardy Florist's Flowers,* there is an advertisement to the effect that Richard Dean, Florist of Ranelagh Road, Ealing was still able to offer :

New high-coloured Primroses.
New double and laced Alpine Auriculas
Named Fancy and gold-laced Polyanthus
Named Show and Alpine Auriculas

If anyone could now offer a similar selection, they would be fortunate indeed.

Two other florist's flowers which reached the zenith of their popularity shortly after the middle of the 19th century were the ranunculus and the tulip. At this time, the number of named ranunculuses must have been numbered in their thousands for the plant was readily raised from seed and no two seedlings were exactly alike. The flower captured the imagination of the florists for its almost perfect symmetry whilst it was obtainable in almost every conceivable colour with the petals of many edged or spotted in widely contrasting shades.

Like the tulip, the ranunculus was introduced from Turkey and Persia during Elizabethan times. It quickly became popular for by planting every fortnight from early March until the end of July, there would be a succession of bloom from early May until late October. By 1820, Mason's catalogue included four hundred varieties and twenty years later, M'Intosh listed almost as many. Amongst the more expensive were Midas (yellow); Lord Byron (white edged); Groom's Duke of Wellington (yellow edged); and Gunn's Crimson, each being priced at half a guinea. But from 1860, like almost all the florist's flowers, they quickly lost popularity and by the end of the century, scarcely a single named variety was to be obtained anywhere.

THE OLD FLORISTS' TULIPS

It is fortunate that a number of the old tulips, several dating from the middle of the 17th century, are still obtainable and are offered in the 1970 catalogue of Messrs. P. de Jager and Sons of Marden, Kent. They are priced from 10p. to 25p. each which compares favourably with prices asked for the tulip when at its peak of popularity. Introduced from Turkey about 1570, it is recorded in *The Florists' Magazine* that in 1637 at a sale at Alcamaer in Holland, one variety named Viceroy was sold for 4200 guilders (about £400) and in England, Semper Augustus made 4600 florins at auction, 'together with a new carriage and a

Green-edged auricula – Lancashire Hero

Grey-edged auricula – George Lightbody

pair of horses and their harness', the whole of which could be valued not less than £600 at the time and this for a single bulb. But it was not the self coloured tulips that made such high prices. Those so eagerly sought after were marked with streaks of colour produced by the mysterious process known as 'breaking'. This is due to a virus but the strange thing is that these tulips attacked by the virus not only retained much of their vigour but also bred true from offsets after the 'breaking' had taken place. This striping caught the mood of the Regency period, famous for its striped furnishings and wall decorations.

The florist's divided the striped tulips into three groups :

  i. Bizarres. Yellow ground colour shaded with scarlet or purple.

  ii. Bybloemens. White ground shaded with violet or purple.

  iii. Roses. White ground shaded with rose.

Each was carried a stage further in that it was classed either as 'feathered' or 'flamed'. When only the petal edges are streaked with colour, it is 'feathered' but when the centre of each petal is also pencilled with the same colouring, it is said to be 'flamed'.

The Dutch masters made frequent use of their flamboyant beauty as in *Flowers and Lizards,* painted in Utrecht in 1629 by Jan Baers.

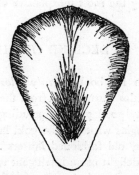

Fig. 1. Tulips: 'feathered' (left) and 'flamed'

Such was the demand for these 'broken' tulips from the time of their introduction that it is recorded that in 1827, a Mr Davey of Chelsea gave £100 for one bulb and two offsets of Fanny Kemble, a feathered bybloemen; and 10 years later, M'Intosh priced Groom's King George IV at 50 guineas a bulb and Edmund Kean at 15 guineas, these being considered two of the outstanding varieties of the time.

The most important of the tulip breeders were situated in Derbyshire and around the Wakefield district of Yorkshire and it is pleasant to be able to mention that the Wakefield and North of England Tulip Society, founded in 1836, is still active. At their annual meeting held in Wakefield each year, many of the old 'broken' tulips continue to be exhibited and create considerable interest. One variety still in cultivation is Lord Stanley, raised in 1860 by Tom Storer of Derby who was perhaps the most experienced of all the old tulip fanciers. Lord Stanley is a yellow and chestnut 'breeder'. Another of Storer's tulips was Sam Barlow, still obtainable and named after the famous Castleton florist. It was Barlow who, in 1878 instigated the introduction of a class for the gold-laced polyanthus in the National Auricula Society's show, though by then the flower had almost passed into obscurity. Two years later, Barlow was to write that the greatest of all gold laced polyanthuses, Pearson's Alexander was already extinct and when it is realised that this variety had been grown in its thousands by the leading enthusiasts since its introduction, the decline of the florist's flowers must indeed have been rapid. The variety was at one time so common that in M'Intosh's book where it was included in 'A Select List of Named Polyanthuses', it was priced at only 18d, being the most inexpensive of all.

DECLINE OF THE FLORISTS' FLOWERS

In his book, *Hardy Florists Flowers* which he dedicated to Charles Turner who from the Royal Nurseries in Slough sent out so many good plants (including Cox's Orange Pippin apple), James Douglas wrote: 'The gold laced polyanthus has shared the fate of many old fashioned flowers . . . it is found that the old varieties, the delight of an intelligent section of our predecessors, cannot now be purchased. A guinea a plant is considered cheap for some sorts and others are only to be obtained by the influence of friends. . . .' The plants already had an antique value.

As late as 1854, John Groom of Clapham Rise catalogued his tulips at enormous prices. Duchess of Cambridge sold for 100 gns. a bulb and others were listed at prices ranging from 10 gns. upwards. The following year, his entire stock of more than a quarter of a million was sold as the plants stood in rows, at very low prices for almost overnight, the old florist's tulip had declined in public esteem to an unprecedented degree. Yet why was the decline so rapid and so complete?

The decline began when the mill, in the words of the Rev. Francis Horner, 'supplanted the patient hand machine and brickworks took up his (the florist's) garden'. In about 1860 or shortly before, the village craftsman began to leave his home to work in the mill. No longer was he his own boss, who in spite of low wages, could find sufficient time to lavish on his beloved plants when working at home. This he did by operating his looms at hours most convenient to the demands of his plants and to enable him to earn sufficient money to support his family, which often meant working long hours far into the night. But the plants were his delight, his only contact with nature's beauty. As the years passed, the weavers tended to leave their village homes to be nearer their work; the shift of the rural worker to the towns had begun. In 1860, the proportion of rural and urban workers was about equal; twenty years later, the urban population had so increased as to be almost double that of rural dwellers. During that time, in the mill towns of the north and midlands, and on Clydeside, where the florist's flowers had for almost a century reigned supreme, long rows of houses with nothing more than a back yard of cobble stones began to replace the cottage with its well-kept garden, however small it may have been.

As early as 1846 the change in conditions had been noticed by a writer in *The Horticultural Magazine*. 'Those who look upon the thousands of houses which already cover the space that used to boast of the gaudy tulip beds of the working man would scarcely think it possible to have seen so great a change. Yet there are many small gardens even now, in the Mile End Road with their canvas houses looking, in the season, like an encampment, which are doomed at no short distance of time to give way to brick and mortar dwellings (and to factories).'

It was in the small back gardens, usually after church on a Sunday morning, that neighbours gathered for a chat about the flowers of their raising and many a deal, often involving £100 or more would take place whilst the lady of the house was indoors cooking the Sunday lunch.

Soon, new interests began to cater for the leisure of the rapidly expanding urban population. In 1871, the Football Association Cup Competition was inaugurated and seventeen years later, the Football League came into being. One of the founder members was the

Accrington Stanley Club which in 1952 itself had to withdraw from the League as television and other interests had replaced it in the affections of local supporters. But the rapid decline of the florist's flowers was also due to other reasons. Mr Geoffrey Taylor in his delightful book, *The Victorian Flower Garden* suggests that 'the florist's flowers were the product of an urban-peasantry, groups of town-dwellers who had a sense of intimate community, such as you still find in country villages. The gradual absorption with the townsman, with his new pleasures and means of recreation, brought about the almost complete extinction of the florists' clubs within a period of twenty years'. The decline began about 1855 and was almost complete by 1875, a major contribution being the smoke laden atmosphere which did great damage to plants and crops in the industrial areas. This had become troublesome as early as 1840 when mills and factories were belching their obnoxious fumes over the countryside and those plants still growing in cottage gardens found it difficult to survive in the polluted atmosphere. Mill owners were not blind to the situation and many did much to alleviate the trouble, the dangers of a polluted atmosphere being appreciated at the time just as it is today.

In 1843, Mr Joshua Major, florist of Knosthorpe, Leeds, has told of his passing through Bradford in the company of a Factory Inspector when he observed the chimney of a mill (belonging to a Mr Billesley) from which there was almost no smoke emerging. Upon making enquiry Mr Major was assured that the mill was working and that the chimney had been fitted with apparatus which enabled the smoke to be consumed. As the cost was only a few shillings, hope was expressed by the writer that we could now look forward 'to an improvement in the health and cleanliness of the inhabitants, and that the cottager, gardener and horticulturist could pursue their vocations with confidence and pleasure when the great and common enemy is annihilated'. But this was not to be and the mills continued to pour out their deadly fumes against which the florist had no answer.

A new era was beginning, not only in the affairs of the nation but of gardeners too. Writing in 1850, George Glenny (who in his *Properties of Flowers*, published in 1836, had done so much to set the standard for the florist's flowers) said, 'It is now much the rage to obtain new plants and neglect old ones.' At this time, Joseph (later Sir Joseph) Paxton was experimenting with his glasshouses at Chatsworth which resulted in his obtaining the contract to build the Crystal Palace and soon those who had achieved great wealth from the new industries were eager to install a conservatory or glasshouse on their estates or in their gardens so that for the first time it was possible to raise new and half hardy plants for summer bedding. The flowers most in demand were the begonia, calceolaria and pelargonium which at about this time had reached Britain from the warmer climes. Their flowers had a brilliance of colour, a brashness which appealed to the Victorian taste and were more suited to an era of pomp and splendour. They were also entirely new and created much interest. The result was that the old hardy florist's flowers, developed during a more leisurely age, quickly lost popularity and many have survived only in country cottage gardens, usually remote from the industrial areas.

WHERE TO FIND THE OLD PLANTS

It is here that the old florist's flowers, the collector's plants, are still to be found, and they may be discovered in many parts of the British Isles. One recalls the wonderful double primrose Rose du Barri found in a Wiltshire cottage garden in sight of Salisbury Cathedral. There the plants grew to be as large as cabbages and each spring they bore masses of bloom one inch across and of a deep pink colour flushed with orange, exactly the colour of Picture rose. And the ancient Painted Lady pinks, Queen of Sheba and Unique. They were known to Tudor gardeners but with their gaudiness and richness of colour would have appealed to the French Impressionists. They flourish in a garden near Chipping Norton in the Cotswolds where they have been growing since earliest times. The Rev. Oscar Moreton has told in his book *Old Carnations and Pinks* of finding the old Scarlet Flaked Carnation (mentioned by Parkinson) at Hawkshead and at Dungeon Ghyll in the Lake District. Parkinson also mentioned the Granaldo Gilly flower. A carnation of Stuart times, it was white, flaked and striped with purple. The Rev. Oscar Moreton tells of having received flowers and cuttings of it from a Mrs Hutt of Norwich who first saw the flowers in a vase on a grave in a Norfolk churchyard.

The ancient pink Bat's Double Red still grows in the Botanic Gardens at Oxford as it has done since the end of the 17th Century, and in the cottage garden of his ancestor, the laced pink Paisley Gem, raised by John Macree in 1796, flourishes to this day.

37

Another fine laced pink, raised in the days of the Paisley silk weavers, was discovered in a Berwickshire cottage garden by the late Mr A. J. Macself and as its name was lost, he re-named it Dad's Favourite for the old cottager told him that it was always his dad's special favourite amongst the many loved pinks which grew there.

Murray's Laced is another striking example of these pinks – raised to such beauty by the Paisley weavers – which still grows in many northern gardens.

It was the late Mr Montagu Allwood who found the Old Fringed pink growing in a cottage garden in Lincolnshire. He was to cross it with a perpetual flowering carnation to raise a new race of perpetual flowering pinks he named *Allwoodii* and which now grace our gardens with their beauty.

In several cottage gardens of the ancient Yorkshire town of Beverley exist to this day, a dark red pink flaked with white and known as the Beverley pink. It probably dates from the early years of the 18th century, possibly much earlier.

The diligent searcher after the lovely old plants will be amply rewarded, for almost every cottage garden has at least one of the old plants flourishing in its protective care, though each year they become scarcer as more and more land is needed to house the ever expanding urban population. Look especially for the old plants in the Cotswolds and in cottage gardens of north Yorkshire and in Scottish and Irish gardens. Many of the old tulips may be obtained around the Heavy Woollen district of Dewsbury, Cleckheaton and Heckmondwyke, towns as rich in name as in the Yorkshire dialect, whilst the old pansies enhance many a Staffordshire allotment garden and many are still grown in the west of Scotland. Probably more of the old florist's flowers – and those of even greater age – exist to this day in Scotland than elsewhere. Pinks and double primroses are common plants in gardens of the N. East coast; in that part extending from Stonehaven to Aberdeen and in the south west, the old Show dahlias and fancy pansies are grown by a number of well respected nurserymen. These plants have survived from the time of the passing of the hand loom, about a hundred years ago but unless they can be nurtured and a new interest taken in them, they must gradually cease to exist. Yet for those who would build up a collection, the pleasure will be enormous, the financial rewards considerable.

CHAPTER II

The Auricula

Its introduction – The florists' auricula – The show auricula – Characteristics of the auricula – The qualities of a show auricula – Tube, ground and paste colour – Growing auriculas – Composts for pot plants – Growing auriculas in pots – Bringing the plants into bloom – Propagation – Varieties of the show auricula – The alpine auricula – Qualities of the alpine auricula – Varieties of the alpine auricula – Border auriculas – Double auriculas.

Amongst the most exotic of flowers, the auricula belongs to the mountainous regions of Europe, which extend from the Pyrenees to the Caucasus. The plant first reached this country by way of Holland and Belgium towards the end of the sixteenth century, and so may be said to have been grown in English gardens for about 400 years. Though today few attempt to cultivate the Show auricula, and great is our loss, it has never lost its unique position of being the most prized of florists' flowers. Its exotic beauty never ceases to thrill those who come into contact with it. In the words of Thomas Hogg, 'it seems to engross our undivided attention', and this was written in 1820 before the auricula had reached the height of its popularity. A hundred years earlier, John Laurance in *The Auricula* had written, 'nature nowhere discovers her variety of colours, her shades and pretty mixtures more than in this little flower', to which should be added its almost overpowering fragrance, like honeysuckle on a calm July evening after a shower of warm rain.

The auricula was introduced to England about the year 1575 by the Flemish weavers fleeing from persecution, and was first known to gardeners as the Bear's Ear, which name it retained for several centuries. The botanical name of the plant from late fifteenth century reference books was *Primula ursi*, for it was rightly believed to be a member of the large primula family. Clusius, gardener to the Emperor Maximilian II of Austria during the sixteenth century, called the plant which we now know as *Primula pubescens*, the miniature Alpine auricula, *Sanicula alpina*, which later became *Auricula ursi*, from the Latin meaning 'the external part of a bear's ear'.

39

A more suitable name for the plant is that used by Parkinson in his *Paradisus* of 1629. He called it the French Cowslip, whilst Gerard describes it as the Greatest English Garden Cowslip. 'They are without all question kinds of Cowslips, wrote Parkinson. Both writers also referred to the auricula as the Mountain Cowslip, for it was the common yellow Alpine, *P. auricula,* which was introduced into England only a decade before Gerard began his writings. The auricula of that time bore little resemblance to the Alpine and Show varieties of today, for the unique edging and paste-like centre was not to appear until another 150 years had passed. Indeed, the blooms were more like those of the cowslip, being small with almost no eye or centre, a dozen or more being held on a long stem to form the head.

It should be said however, that in the thirty-two years which elapsed between the publication of Gerard's work and Parkinson's *Paradisus* the auricula had already made headway in its development. Whereas the illustrations in Gerard's work show plants with only four or five blooms to a truss, Parkinson's illustrations show plants with two and three times the number and larger in size.

By 1659 Sir Thomas Hanmer, an ardent supporter of Charles I, had forty varieties growing outside in his garden in Wales for it must be remembered that the Alpine auricula was a hardy plant, and he sent several plants to a learned Shropshire gardener by the name of Dr John Rea, who was to publish his *Flora* in 1665. Here a number of beautiful varieties are described, amongst them being the almost black-flowered auricula called Black Imperial, said to have been raised by Rea but which may have been sent him by Hanmer. Rea also described a striped auricula, and one bearing a double bloom. It was possibly the 'black' auricula which was to give the attractive black ground colouring to the show varieties of a later date.

THE FLORISTS' AURICULA

John Rea was to publish his second book, *A Complete Florilege* in 1702, when the Border and Alpine auricula was so well established as to permit rules to be formulated as to the merits of the flowers.

Rea also described that which is possibly the first named florists' auricula, called the Fair Downham. It was purple with a large white eye and was named after Mr John Downham, 'from whom many years since I had this (variety)'. Eighteen years after the appearance of Rea's *Flora*, his son-in-law, Rev. Samuel Gilbert, of the same county, published his *Florist's Vade Mecum*, in which more detailed descriptions of the auricula are to be found. One he especially mentions as bearing a bloom of intense scarlet with a large brilliant white centre is interesting, for the centre may have been of a similar 'mealy' nature to Green's famous crimson with its 'well produced centre' of 1728, which was the forerunner of the paste centre. Gilbert's Scarlet may also be Mistress Austin's Scarlet, mentioned by Rea and which was raised in Oxford by Jacob Roberts, whom some believed to be the raiser of the famous Black Imperial. Gilbert also mentions striped single and double auriculas valued at £5 each, but which were soon lost to cultivation.

Of perhaps greater interest, however, is Sir Thomas Hanmer's description of several varieties which he classes as 'haire coloured'. Exactly what colour this describes is impossible to determine with any degree of accuracy, possibly pale yellow or brown, but the important point is Hanmer's description of the foliage of the plants : 'They have a larger, whiter, mealyer leafe than the purples have.' These plants must have been descendants of *P. auricula*, which bears yellow blooms, for the crimson and purple flowered *P. hirsuta* carries no meal on its foliage. This he wrote almost 100 years after the first auriculas reached this country, and it is the first reference to the qualities of the two chief species or groups then in cultivation.

But apart from this reference to the foliage, it was not until 1728 that any further reference was made to the bloom taking on different characteristics. In *The Garden* of January 1902, a Mr Samuel Perry gave a number of interesting references to the auricula taken from the minutes of the Spalding Gentleman's Society, for 28th March, 1728 when it was recorded that a 'Dr Green brought an *Auricula ursi* with a truss of forty-five peeps (flowers) of a deep crimson colour, with a white eye well powdered'. This plant must have contained 'blood' of both *P. hirsuta* and *P. auricula*, and must surely be the first reference to the amazing structural change of the petals, which a few years later was to produce that unique edging and paste-like centre we now know so well. It also appears that the auricula had come to be grown in pots, for the meal of both bloom and foliage would be spoiled if in contact with rain outdoors. Four years later a manuscript, whose writer is unknown, in describing the striped auriculas says, 'they (the blooms) are covered with a fine white powder, which being laid very thick renders them most distinguishably brilliant.' So that the process would appear to be carried a step further.

Thus by 1732 the auricula had reached a very high standard. There was the famous Black Imperial, another bearing a bloom with a paste-like centre, and one covered throughout in white powder. Add them all together and there is some semblance of the white and grey edged auriculas with their paste centre, black ground colour and petals covered with meal. By this time the auricula had become so popular in Europe that special 'theatres' were built, in which the plants were arranged in tiers so that they could be exhibited for their dazzling beauty, to be seen by all. At Tournai and at Douai the monks had as many as a dozen of these 'theatres', and lavished an almost unbelievable care on the plants, yet the exotic beauty of the Edged auricula had not yet appeared. Theatres were built in the homes of the wealthy in England during the Regency period, the pot-grown auricula being then the most fashionable of all plants. The auricula theatres were on a most elaborate scale, black velvet being draped over the shelves or tiers to show off the blooms to advantage, whilst ornate mirrors were often placed at the back and sides of the staging, so that the beauty of the plants was magnified many times. Though the Edged auricula did not appear until 1750, there was a great diversity of colouring. Not only were there double flowered auriculas, but some were striped. There was a crimson-and-white striped variety, and one striped crimson and yellow which was valued at £20 a plant. The doubles too could be obtained in the most glorious shades of sky blue, peach pink and crimson, and were even more beautiful than the Edged auriculas.

Perhaps that amazing transformation which was to occur about the year 1750, was not so remarkable after all, for the ingredients were already apparent and were only carried a step further. Soon, a bloom appeared having a thick paste-like centre, a shining white 'meal', a black ground and an edging of green (or grey). This edge colouring is a replacement of the ordinary coloured petals by leaf characteristics, representing the foliage and its stages of mealiness, whilst the peculiar paste of the centre also appears at the base of the leaves which form the calyx of the flower. There was now a combination of the Black Imperial, Dr Green's 'powdered eye' and the mealed bloom, and from the crossings the Edged auricula was born, in which the structural transformation of the petals took place.

The first green-edged variety was called Rule Arbiter, introduced in 1757, and the auricula at once took on a new popularity. The hardy border auricula now became a florist's pot plant for indoor display, for as the paste 'ran' when in contact with rain, it was no longer suitable for garden culture.

It is a disappointment to the auricula lover that there is no known record of where and to whom the first Edged flower appeared. It seems strange that no details have been recorded of this amazing happening, when we know so clearly how and where the first waved sweet pea appeared, and the first rayless viola. But of the structural change in the auricula nothing is known until the appearance of the green-edged Rule Arbiter in 1757, and ten years later there were dozens of these Edged auriculas and a completely new concept of this plant had been evolved. All that can be said, however, is that the Show auricula first appeared about the year 1750. Where and to whom we do not know, but the old Border auriculas had now taken on these unique characteristics and it was the Edged varieties which now received the greatest attention.

Such was the enthusiasm amongst the weavers of Lancashire and Yorkshire, who, like the lace makers of Paisley and their edged pinks, had an eye for unusual beauty, that by the turn of the nineteenth century as many as fifty auricula shows were being held each year in the North of England.

THE SHOW AURICULA

The auricula may be divided into two main groups, those which are grown under glass and those grown in the open. This is not because the Show auricula, which should be given protection, is in any way tender, but it is necessary to protect the blooms from the rain, otherwise the paste-like centre will 'run' so badly as to spoil the bloom entirely, whilst some protection should be given against the damp conditions of winter. The Show auriculas are themselves divided into three sections :

(a) the Edged varieties
(b) the Self colours
(c) the Fancy varieties

Each has a paste centre and so demands protection from rain. They are therefore grown almost entirely for decorative purposes in the home, in the greenhouse or conservatory, or in frames. The enthusiast may exhibit his best plants, for the auricula as an exhibition plant is in a class to itself. Though the plants may be grown in a cold frame to be taken indoors at regular intervals for decoration, a cool greenhouse or cold frame enables them to be displayed in such a way as to reveal their full beauty. Though requiring protection from rain, the plants require no artificial heat. They are grown quite cold throughout.

They are descended from the hardy alpine species, whose only protection from the severe frosts and cold winds of winter is the covering of snow the plants receive. The culture is in no way difficult, excessive temperatures and humidity playing no part, whilst any structure which admits light will prove satisfactory, provided it gives protection from the rain. The plants do, however, require attention to detail, and for this reason those who have achieved success with the auricula are those who have devoted considerable time to it. The Show auricula is not a plant which can be expected to look after itself like the polyanthus, or even the Border auricula; it demands care throughout its whole life. The rewards are great for the colourings and velvet-like quality of the blooms are unlike those of any other plant. The Show auricula as a florist's flower has no rival.

MEAL AND GROUND COLOUR

Whilst all of the Show auriculas have that unique paste-like centre, not all have the interesting edging. Those with edging, or outer zone colouring, which may be of green, grey or white, are unique amongst flowers, for this edge colouring is made up of thousands of minute hairs, which seen through a microscope are structurally identical with those to be found on the mealy leaves of the auricula. The late Sir Roland Biffen discovered that when segments of the edging of a green-edged auricula and a part of a leaf of the plant were mixed together, it was impossible to make any distinction between them. The blooms may be said to have mutated by which the petals have been replaced by leaf structures. This, as has been shown, first occurred two centuries ago and was in no way due to the ability of the hybridist. The same thing occasionally happens with the yellow primrose, the petals being replaced by small crinkled leaves which is recognised as the 'green' primrose, the flower having taken on a new form or 'mutation'. This is quite different from 'sporting', which may be said to occur when a variety 'throws' a new colour but which retains the same form. The dahlia and chrysanthemum provide more 'sports' than any other flower.

The degree of mealiness determines the colour of the edging. All the Edged varieties are green in colour, but the density of the minute hairs changes the edge colouring either to grey or white, whilst there are blooms of intermediate shades, difficult to classify. At the end of each hair is a small globe from which wax or resin is secreted; the denser the concentration of these hairs, the whiter their appearance, hence where the concentration is heaviest the edging appears to be pure white. Sir Roland Biffen has shown that there are both large and small hairs, a concentration of the latter at the centre of the bloom forming the enamel-like paste to be found on all Show auriculas. These same hairs are to be found on the foliage of a number of auricula species; the more dense they are, the more frosted is their appearance. This has led to the conclusion that the mealy *P. auricula,* used for hybridising, gradually led to the appearance of the paste centre, which was known to have existed in a less defined form some years before the plant 'mutated'. The meal covering may be found in less clearly defined form on the old Border auriculas, where it covers the foliage, stem and blooms, presenting a most attractive frosted appearance, though here the plants have shown no signs of that interesting 'mutation' which characterises the Show auricula. To add to the interest of the Edged auricula is the colouring which separates the paste-like centre from the outer edging, and is known as the body colour. If a bloom is closely examined it will be noticed that this coloured band is composed of cells filled with a deep red sap, whereas the cells of the outer edge are devoid of colouring. Again, with the green-edged varieties, their foliage and flower stems are completely free of meal, whereas plants of the grey and white-edged varieties are heavily coated with meal throughout. Another point worthy of mention is that the more mealy the bloom, the smaller it is. Of the Edged varieties, the green form bears the largest blooms, the white the smallest, but whereas the whites are the first to open in spring, the green are the last to open. The green-edged varieties may sometimes reveal a greyish appearance which may be repeated when the plant is reproduced. This is, of course, due to a greater density of the glandular hairs, in the same way as there are dark and light grey blooms, blooms which appear quite white and those which are of a dirty or greyish-white colour. The old variety Shirley Hibberd frequently produced greyish blooms, and a number of its offsprings have the same quality. A green-edged auricula should show no signs of meal, and it frequently happens that a slight mealiness will spoil an otherwise perfect bloom. The bloom should be of brilliant jade green, which will be accentuated by a smooth enamel-like paste of purest white.

Both the Edged and self-coloured varieties possess the same paste centre, which badly 'runs' when in contact with moisture and thus makes it essential for the Show auriculas to be grown under glass. This paste or white meal is to be found at the base of the leaves forming the calyx of the flower, and though it appeared in its more pronounced enamel-like quality with the first Edged varieties, it became accentuated by degrees rather than by first making its appearance with the 'mutation'. It is the paste which distinguishes the self-coloured Show auricula from the white-centred Alpine type and is to be found in no other flower. So easy is it to spoil the paste of a perfect bloom by careless handling, or watering, that the greatest care must be exercised with the plants when once the blooms or pips begin to open.

Fig. 2. A white-edged auricula

Nowadays, there is a tendency for the paste centre and the edging to become wider, with a result that the body colour zone diminishes, thus giving the bloom a brighter appearance than in the past. The body colouring may be black, dark brown, deep crimson or violet, which are generally so deeply coloured as to be indistinguishable from black. With the meal-free petals of the green-edged varieties this gives them a pronounced, clear-cut appearance which the grey and white-edged varieties do not possess, and which makes the green-edged auricula the most prized of all. With the more extensively mealed grey-edged varieties, the body colouring appears to be in greater variation, there being intermediate shades of red and brown.

What is remarkable about the Edged auriculas is that the mealiness is not fixed. For example, with the white-edged variety, J. W. Midgeley, though the bloom is heavily covered in meal, the foliage of the plant is entirely free of any farina. Some varieties have six petals, others seven, eight or nine, whilst on the same truss the blooms may vary in their number of petals. All of which adds to the interest of the plant.

With the white-edged auriculas, the mealy deposit is most pronounced, giving the edge almost as white an appearance as the paste, and so it is important for the body colour to be as dark as possible in order to provide the desired contrast. It has been said that it was the dark, particularly the black, colouring of P. hirsuta which so fascinated the old weavers, in the same way as did the black lacing of the pinks so beloved by the Paisley shawl makers, the contrast accentuating the colouring of the bloom. The Show and Fancy pansies, with their black faces and bright-edged colouring, also achieved a similar prominence with Victorian gardeners and became florists' flowers of similar popularity.

The selfs are highly valued Show auriculas, for their brilliant petal colours contrasting with the dense pure white paste provides an appearance of indescribable richness. In their diversity of rich colouring no flower is their equal. Unlike the Alpines, which do not have uniformity of petal colour, the selfs have uniform colouring extending from the paste to the edge of the petals. The colours include pale yellows, which may have originated from the yellow ground Fancies, for the selfs were recognised very much later than the Edged varieties. Other colourings range from the almost black of Freda to the brilliant Scarlet Prince, the colours being similar to the body colourings of the Edged varieties, particularly the grey-edges, for excellent selfs of these colourings may be raised from the seed of grey-edges, which has been self-pollinated.

The colourings of the selfs may be divided into two groups, those which follow the parent *P. auricula* which produces shades of yellow, from pale primrose to golden-bronze; and those derived from *P. hirsuta* which range from mid-blue to crimson-black. The pigment of the latter species is known as hirsutin and is of a rosy-red colour, which changes to crimson if in contact with acid and to mid-blue if treated with an alkali. Varying degrees of acidity and alkalinity in the cell sap brought about a variation in the pigment colouring. Where acidity is more pronounced, the crimson colouring would become almost black; and where more alkaline, the mid-blue colouring would become deeper. The possible colour range is thus large and it becomes even more so when 'blood' of *P. auricula* is introduced. For instance, crimson colouring over a yellow ground becomes brilliant scarlet. This richness of colouring appears in the same way in the Alpines, but here the colouring is not uniform whereas with the Show varieties it is so. The paste-like centre also adds to the beauty of the Show selfs which, on account of this, must be given protection when coming into bloom. It should be said that the selfs should possess no meal or farina.

CHARACTERISTICS OF THE AURICULA

So much for the various groups of the Show auricula. What of the plant itself? All members of the auricula family are of perennial habit and where grown undisturbed in the open ground will form large plants with broad ear-shaped leaves, some having a beautiful silvery appearance due to the coverings of meal, whilst others have a luminous grass-green quality. The tapering main root, from which new fibrous roots are continually formed, is called a 'carrot', for it is shaped exactly like a small carrot. Above soil level the plant forms a 'neck'; with established plants this may have a diameter as large as a ten pence piece. From here offsets are formed by which the plant is propagated. From the 'neck', the plant forms a rosette of leaves from which the flower stem arises and which may be from 4 to 10 inches in length, depending upon type and variety. From the top of this are borne, on short stems called footstalks, the pips or individual blooms, which vary in number from five to twenty or more. The flowering season extends from early April until mid-May, depending upon variety and situation. The bloom is generally made up of six petals, though there may be as many as nine, which are slightly overlapping and arranged symmetrically so that the bloom is as flat as possible. The individual pips should be placed so as to form a rounded, well-shaped truss, when the plant will be seen to best advantage. All Show auriculas possess the paste-like centre, and with the Edged varieties this is surrounded by a coloured zone which irregularly merges into the edging. With the selfs, this body colour extends to the outer rim of the petals. The reproductive organs are contained in a tube at the very centre of the plant, which is yellow. This is surrounded by the paste. So much for the make-up of the bloom.

THE QUALITIES OF A SHOW AURICULA

No florist's flower has been more clearly defined as to those qualities which make up the perfect bloom than the Show auricula. These characteristics were first laid down towards the end of the eighteenth century and they have remained almost unchanged until the present day. There are more points which go to make up a good Show auricula than for any other flower. Indeed, not only the individual pips or blooms must measure up to a certain standard, but also the quality of the foliage. Every part of the Show auricula must attain the required standards in order to satisfy the judges, and no other plant is ever put through so searching a test.

The most exacting test of all is that given to the green-edged varieties, which must reveal a complete absence of any meal on the petal edging. Where occasional mealiness is observed there are various methods of removing this without damaging the petals, but the really good green-edge should appear entirely free of farina. Thomas Hogg, writing in 1820, said that 'every part of the bloom must be in exact proportion; the stalk must be proportionate to the leaves, the pedicles and truss to them both; the ground colour must be clear and bright, the eye circular and of a clear white; with the border or edging of a lively green, the petals or pips nearly of a size, perfectly level and disposed in regular order, the eye, the tube and the rim must correspond one with another showing an exact symmetry throughout'.

The actual size of the individual bloom is given little attention, and whilst some varieties naturally make larger pips than others, the proportions of the bloom, the eye, the ground colour and the edging are of more importance than size. It may be said, however, that the greater the density of meal on the bloom the smaller will it be. Thus the green-edged varieties, having no meal, make the largest blooms, whilst next in size are the greys. The whites, with their densely mealed blooms, bear the smallest pips. Not all auricula blooms possess the same number of petals, and whilst the average number of petals per bloom is six, that fine green-edged variety Linkman often bears a bloom with nine petals which so overlap as to give it a more circular appearance than of any other Show auricula. The number of individual pips to each truss will be governed as much by the characteristics of the plant as by its culture. Certain varieties, Tinkerbell being an example, will rarely bear more than five pips to a truss, whilst those other fine greens, Longdown and Green Woodpecker, may be expected to produce twice that number. Sometimes a variety will tend to bear most of its pips on one side of the stem, thus giving the truss an unbalanced effect with the bloom overlapping, whilst the rest of the truss will be sparse. Much can be done to correct this by careful coaxing, but any variety which is prone to the trouble is better discarded.

The *Show Handbook* of the Royal Horticultural Society lays down that the pips should be perfectly flat, smooth-edged and round, the six or more petals being without notches or serrations. According to Maddock, the bloom should be as round as possible, though he says 'it is rare to find this roundness perfect', whilst it should be flat. In certain cases, too many petals give the blooms a frilled appearance which may be delightful with certain of the Border varieties, such as Broadwell Gold and Celtic King, but which detracts from the qualities of the Show auricula. Too few petals gives the bloom a sparse appearance, the bloom being as if 'winged' rather than circular. A bloom having seven petals seems to be the ideal, though the multi-petalled Linkman forms a most attractive circular bloom. Occasionally the petals of certain varieties are pointed, 'mouse-eared' as they are called by auricula growers, a factor which again prevents that much desired circular appearance and goes against a good auricula. Less frequently seen is that slight indentation at the edge of the petals, not so noticeable as with the Alpines, which also detracts from their circular appearance. This, as with the pointed petals, is a fault of the green-edged varieties. The grey and white-edged auriculas generally have a more circular bloom, petal placement and texture being so much better than with the greens. Certain varieties also form a bloom which is either slightly cup-shaped or reflexed, both of which faults spoil the appearance. This is often the case where there are too many petals to a bloom, thus preventing them from opening flat. M'Intosh, writing more than a century ago, tells us 'that when the flower does not come flat naturally, florists use an implement called a "flattene", made of ivory, which is pressed upon a cupped flower until the disc is made flat,' but though a bloom may be so treated, flatness is an inbred characteristic of a plant, likewise where the petals are pointed.

TUBE, GROUND AND PASTE COLOUR

The old growers were most critical about their auricula bloom and those plants not bearing a bloom of perfect proportions would be eliminated. M'Intosh describes the perfectly proportioned bloom when 'the tube is one part, the eye three parts, and the whole disc six parts,' and this may be said to appertain to this day. The tube, that part which contains the reproductive organs, should be quite circular and should be of a good mid-yellow colour. Modern show requirements agree with M'Intosh in that the diameter of the tube should be one-sixth of that of the bloom. Sometimes the tube reveals an edge which appears as if finely chiselled all the way round; a 'notched' tube as it is called by auricula breeders. This is considered a fault, for the edge of the tube should be quite circular, likewise that part of the paste surrounded by the ground colour. The more circular the bloom, from the tube to the outer edge of the petals, the nearest approach to perfection will it be, provided the various sections are in exact proportion, or nearly so. The stigma should not protrude beyond the edge of the tube, indeed it should not be visible. If it should appear at the end of the tube, or extend beyond, the bloom will be called 'pin-eyed' and will not be of show standard. The anthers which surround the stigma should, however, be bold and almost fill the tube, terminating just above the rim.

Surrounding the tube is the paste, which should be pure white, without any traces of grey, whilst it should be dense and smooth. Blooms having granulated paste will present a poor appearance. The paste area should be quite circular. Where it has an angular appearance, the perfect circular proportions of the bloom will be absent. The diameter of the paste should be the same as that of the ground colour and edge combined. Again, where the paste covers either a too small or a too large area, the appearance is spoilt. The ground colour which separates the paste from the edge perhaps causes more discussion than any other point of the auricula bloom. The old breeders said that this should be rich and of an equal amount on every side. Where it joins the paste it should be distinct. The following is the scale of points to be awarded to an Edged Show auricula :

	Points
For foliage, stem and truss formation	7
For pip	2
For tube	2
For paste	3
For ground colour	3
For edge	3
	20

With selfs, ground colour and edging become one – that is, they form a border of self colouring which should be equal in width to the paste. The colour should be uniform thoughout, without any shading as is permissible with the Alpines. Apart from an occasional tendency to shading, the selfs reveal few faults though the paste area may occasionally be larger than required. Of the selfs these are obtainable in various shades of yellow, crimson, scarlet and blue, though buff and bronzy shades are not so popular on the show bench. Though the true yellow selfs reveal few faults, one is their thinness of petal, they seem to lack the velvety substance of the crimsons and blues. Petal formation, however, is well-nigh perfect, for with most varieties they overlap beautifully, giving the pip a flat, circular appearance of a perfection rarely to be found in the Edged varieties.

GROWING AURICULAS

Those of the Golden Age of the Show auricula, grew their plants under tall glass jars, originally containing bleaches and dyes, used in the Lancashire cotton industry. The base was removed before using. They were inexpensive and acted in the same way as the glass bell jar or the more modern barn-type cloche, providing winter and spring protection whilst the plants were in bloom. Four small pots could be placed under each – the modern barn cloche will take six – and these were half inserted into the soil, which prevented the compost from drying out too quickly. During the summer the plants were repotted and allowed to occupy a semi-shaded position until removed to a more open position in late autumn, when they were again covered with the jars. Today the plants may be grown in the same way by using cloches, which will provide adequate protection from cold winds and winter rains and fogs. During severe weather, straw is placed around the glass sides and held in position by soil, or sacking may be placed over the glass and removed on all sunny days. Auriculas must never be completely dried off during winter, as for example geraniums growing in pots in a cold greenhouse, though pot-grown plants must never be allowed to become water-logged during the dormant period, or the roots will decay.

A garden frame will prove equally suitable, and owing to the ease in removing the lights may be easier to manage than cloches. The frame should not be too large or the lights will prove difficult to move and may be impossible for the ladies of the household, who usually attend to the plants at midday, to open and close. A light 4 feet x 3 feet is quite large enough. Construct the frame so that as far as possible it will slope towards the north or east, away from the midday sun, which can be very warm during April and May when the plants will be in bloom.

Fig. 3. A suitable garden frame

The use of a greenhouse will permit the plants to be tended with greater ease and efficiency whilst enabling them to be displayed in such a way as to reveal their full beauty. Those who have no greenhouse, nor available space in which to erect one, need not be discouraged, for until about 1840 and the appearance of the first glasshouse of Joseph Paxton at Chatsworth, auriculas were grown entirely under makeshift lights and glass jars. They were grown without a greenhouse and grown well too, some of the best growers using no method of protection othen than covering the plants where they grew in the open. A number of the Derbyshire growers made use of the entrance to the caves at Cresswell and elsewhere to protect their Show auriculas from Christmas until they finished blooming in May, and very successful they were; whilst Hogg has told that a number of the Lancashire florists protected their plants during the same time by means of boarding reared against a wall, the plants being covered only during severe weather, otherwise the stems would be too 'drawn' to support the truss. An auricula enthusiast of my acquaintance had built into the wall of his living room, a window which projected 18 inches from the wall, the sides of the window also being of glass. Here the plants were grown from mid-October until mid-May on plate glass shelves. In this way the plants received all the light they required and were shaded during April and early May by a small, but efficient, outside sunblind released from the top of the window. The auriculas provided a display which it would be difficult to better and which could be enjoyed from all parts of the room, strip lighting being fixed above the plants to provide evening pleasure.

Few, however, will be so enthusiastic as to go to so much expense, but equally good results may be obtained by constructing a shelter of wood and Windolite, using stout 2 inch x 2 inch timber for the supports, which should be from 6–7 feet high to permit ease in tending the plants. The door may also be made of Windowlite, and the most inexperienced carpenter will be able to erect a shelter capable of accommodating a hundred or so plants. Though the shelter may be of any length, it should be about 6 feet wide with benches 2 feet wide along either side, allowing 2 feet between each to enable one to tend the plants. The roof should be made with a slight slope from which rain and snow may escape. Owing to heavy falls of snow being experienced in the north, it will be advisable to make the roof of glass, which may be whitened to provide shading. Hessian canvas may be tacked along the sunny side so as to shield the plants from the midday sunshine of spring. The Windolite used for the sides may be tacked on to the wooden frame with the greatest of ease and will prove extremely durable. Equally suitable is polythene sheeting which is so strong as to withstand hard kicking, whilst for those living close to a jet aerodrome, it will not splinter as will glass whenever the planes pierce the 'sound barrier', neither will hailstones cause damage. One need not fear loss of quality in the plants where polythene is used, for it has been found, after exhaustive tests, that it will allow the maximum of ultra-violet rays to penetrate. Ample ventilation must be provided and this may be done by placing two window vents, one at each end of the structure.

COMPOSTS FOR POT PLANTS

Being slow to reproduce themselves, auriculas, with the exception of the Border varieties, are always more expensive to obtain than most hardy plants and so should be afforded the greatest care with their culture. If those fine old varieties such as Fanny Meerbeck and George Lightbody had been treated with contempt, they would have ceased to exist long ago, for a century is a long life for any plant and particularly where grown entirely in pots.

Almost every ingredient known as suitable for making up a compost has been used for the auricula. Hogg tells that one of the best known breeders of the late 18th century, Matthew Kenny of Totteridge in Middlesex, used a sandy loam, to which was added sheep-dung and hay litter which had been composted together for at least twelve months. The manure and loam were used in equal quantities, to which was added a little coarse sand, and this was the compost used for all his auriculas. For top dressing he used a mixture of sheep's blood and poultry manure mixed with an equal quantity of his potting compost, repotting the plants every year. He was a most successful grower, being a partner of George Lee who introduced the famous variety Bright Venus. Such a compost as used by Kenny would appear to be satisfactory to the auricula grower of today, but what of Isaac Emmerton's repulsive concoction? Taking a medium-sized barrow as a measure to make up his compost, he used two parts of goose dung steeped in bullock's blood, two parts of baker's sugar scum, two parts of night-soil, three parts of yellow loam to which was added two pecks of sea sand. It is said that he was so particular he would use only soil of a yellow colour : that cast up by moles.

Hogg's description of Isaac Emmerton and his composts which appeared in *The Floricultural Cabinet* of 1st September, 1833 makes interesting reading. He writes, 'Though Emmerton certainly grew his auriculas well at Barnet, with his "hot" manures of sugar scum, night soil, blood, etc., yet notwithstanding his vain boasting, they were never long lived with him; he was sending for fresh plants from the country almost every year to keep up his stock. He never sold any at that time; he might perhaps exchange one occasionally but he grew them entirely to gratify his own fancy. He was obliged to leave his nursery at Barnet, in consequence of his having libelled the parson of his parish, a magistrate withal, by hanging him in effigy on a tree in his garden near the public road, for which offence he was indicted and suffered a year's imprisonment in the King's Bench.

'He afterwards moved to Paddington and occupied a small nursery and flower garden near me; where he continued for a while to grow auriculas for sale but he was far from being successful with them. He complained by way of excuse that he had not got his compost right and that the London air did not suit them. He at last gave it up as he was not likely to gain either credit or advantage by the pursuit. . . .

'Emmerton, after he had published his *Treatise*, was looked upon as a professor, as one well qualified to give instruction in the art and mystery of auricula growing, and was invited by some beginners, to superintend the management of their flowers, that they might benefit by witnessing his practical skill, his dexterity in mixing composts, in trimming the roots, in potting them as well as thinning out the pips and flattening them in the truss. He considered himself a perfect adept in this process and fully entitled to his fee of a good dinner and a glass of "grog".'

Hogg has told of the difficulties of obtaining the correct loam for his auriculas. 'From the enclosure of waste and common lands and from the prohibition of the Lords of the Manors of others not yet enclosed as Old Oak Common and Wimbledon, there is great difficulty in procuring pure native loam around London.' He continues 'I, as well as many other florists have been lately under the necessity of sending for it as far as Waltham Flats and Wanstead Common at considerable expense. This loam is of a yellow cast, of too free and unsubstantial a texture for carnations and tulips; yet very suitable for auriculas. It seems free from any sour quality. . . . There is this advantage arising from auriculas being grown in moderately manured soil, that they are more easily kept in a healthy state. Only conceive for a moment what the effect would be, of turning a fat stall-fed ox into a barren pasture, or of restricting a London Alderman to the plain and frugal diet of a poor citizen.

'Experience has taught those florists who are in the habit of keeping auriculas to exhibit for prizes and of forcing them forward when coming into bloom in rich and stimulating composts to cause them to throw up large trusses, that they never can depend upon the same plants for the succeeding year, for vegetation over-excited, like the human body, must decline afterwards. Those plants they generally dispose of, with the recommendation attached to them of having won a prize, and select others, to prepare and train in like manner for next year's contest.' Hogg continues : 'Strong stimulative manures, however beneficially they act for a time in producing large flowers and vivid colours, too frequently leave the plants in a state of exhaustion, if not of premature decay. By forcing them so much, the constitution is impaired; for we all know the injurious, if not fatal effects, that opium, laudanum, brandy, gin and even wine, taken in excess, produce upon the human body. Mr Bailey of the Clapham Nursery some years ago, produced at the Islington Flower Show as fine an auricula of Lee's Colonel Taylor and in as fine a flower, as ever was exhibited perhaps in all-England; and for which he sold the same day to Mr Brooks of Ball's Pond Nursery, for the sum of 5 guineas. But this plant, having been forced in the manner described, began to decline after it had been freshly potted and never lived to bloom again!' Shades of a 'Gainsborough' painting with the signature added at a later date!

From Hogg's writings, it may be concluded that the artificial doctoring of the florists' plants with the sole object of winning a premier award at a major show, contributed more than anything to the rapid extinction of the plants for with the supplanting of the hand operated loom of the cottage by the machines of the mill, it was not possible to give them the detailed attention necessary for their survival. A plant which has been unduly forced and subjected to all manner of artificial aids is not able to take care of itself and the florists' time was now severely limited.

Again, from Hogg, it is possible to compare the preparation of the plants with the sole object of winning a prize and making a sale at an attractive price, with the way in which many antiques are brought to the salesroom in modern times with a signature added to a picture of dubious authority, whilst a damaged piece of furniture may be made to appear of high quality by a coating of paint and varnish.

It was the opinion of most of the early nineteenth-century growers that the potting compost should be as rich as it was possible to make it, and it was not until the publication of Robert Thompson's *Gardener's Assistant,* in 1859, that the dangers of over-feeding were first put forward. It was Thompson's opinion that undue stimulation led to a weakly plant, followed by disease and premature death, and for a suitable compost he suggests that used by Mr George Lightbody of Falkirk, after whom the famous Show auricula was named. This consisted of a barrowful of leaf mould, one of light loam from an old pasture and two barrow loads of cow-dung at least two years old. To this he mixed a small quantity of coarse sand to assist drainage and he allowed the composts to become weathered by leaving it in the open throughout the winter.

The *Midland Florist* of 1853, describing the successful methods of Mr Cooke of Coventry, mentioned that he always used a small quantity of charcoal and wood ash in his compost instead of sand, 'which not only kept the soil open and therefore sweet, but also helped to fertilise it'.

So the modern idea of using charcoal has been in use for over a century! Thompson's ideas about suitable auricula composts and the matter of over-feeding took a considerable time to influence growers, and even today there are would-be enthusiasts who fight shy of potgrown auriculas simply because they believe it almost impossible to obtain the necessary ingredients for their compost. A remark overheard at a recent show, that the auricula 'was no good to a town gardener, for only the countryman could get the right stuff', was indeed wide of the mark, for quite half of the best auriculas grown in Britain today are grown within sight of the factory chimney, in the same way as they were in Sam Barlow's day.

The compost used by the late Mr James Douglas, at Edenside, consisted of four parts fibrous loam, one part well-decayed horse manure and one part of leaf mould, to each bushel of which was added a pint of silver sand. It was the opinion of this great auricula grower that a good loam was able to supply the plants with almost all the food they required. This compost has not been varied by the House of Douglas for over half a century.

Peat was not used by James Douglas, but was always included in the diet provided for his auriculas by the late Mr G. H. Dalrymple, of the old Bartley Nurseries, Southampton, where the potting compost conformed almost to the formula suggested by the John Innes Institute today. Whereas this contains artificial fertilisers, it was the opinion of Mr Douglas that these should be strictly avoided. The controversy continues, and in the *Year Book* of the National Auricula Society (Northern Section) for 1956, Mr F. Faulkner, a grower of repute, attributes the failure of more than a hundred of his auriculas to using the John Innes composts. It was his belief that the chief trouble was caused by the use of peat in the compost, and it is of interest to read that when he substituted decayed leaf soil for the peat in the J.I. compost, the losses were entirely eliminated. Mr Faulkner explains his experiences in more detail, believing that the use of peat, containing little or no food value, resulted in a half-starved plant, for it has to occupy the same pot for at least twelve months. The compost now used by this well-known grower consists of three parts fibrous loam, one part coarse sand, one part half-rooted leaf mould, to which is added a sprinkling of superphosphate and steamed bone flour, which is almost the John Innes compost except for the substitution of the peat by the leaf mould.

That the Show auricula required a supply of plant food over a long period led Thomas Hogg to write : 'If you put your plants at an early period of summer into pots in which they are to remain until they flower next spring, a space of nearly twelve months, the strength of the compost will be greatly reduced before that time, especially with so much watering during the hot months of June and July.' For this reason he recommends potting during the first week of August, not before. There is no denying that the Show auricula enjoys a liberal diet, for it must be remembered that constant repotting as with chrysanthemums, or where large pots are used as with tomatoes, which they occupy for only six to eight months, is a very different matter to growing auriculas in the same pots for almost twelve months. The need to supply the plants with food which will be slowly released over a long period is therefore important. At the same time it is important to provide a compost which is able to retain as much moisture as possible during summer, yet an excess about the roots during the dormant period will bring about root decay. To strike the happy medium is not easy and calls for experience, for even where auriculas grow well in open-ground soils of a known quality, this does not mean they will do so where growing in the same soil when in pots. Sir Roland Biffen has told how his Show auriculas remained vigorous for nearly half a century growing in a heavy clay soil in the open ground entirely unprotected, yet when grown in the same soil in pots the plants died of water-logging in less than two years.

As with all things the old adage 'horses for courses' would appear to be applicable to the auricula, though this is a fact which is rarely heard mentioned. A well-known Sheffield grower of my acquaintance kept a stock of George Lightbody in a condition of the utmost vigour until his death, at a ripe old age. His small greenhouse was as perpetually covered with soot as are the seats at nearby Bramall Lane cricket ground, and yet his auriculas remained supreme to the end. He would tell that his plants were divided into three groups, each of which he had found to require a slightly different compost from each other – a little more bone meal, a little less dried cow manure, or a little more leaf mould as the case may be. Notes were carefully made of the exact requirements of each group and these were strictly adhered to, but it was the grower's belief that if every variety could be given its individual compost he would have enjoyed even better results. His opinion may be confirmed when it is realised how large a number of varieties remain healthy and vigorous only when in the hands of one or two growers, who generally lived in the same district as each other. One famous grower had a small frame always completely filled with plants of that fine green-edged variety Henry Wilson, yet upon the owner's death the plants were taken over by friends who were enthusiastic growers, yet all had perished within two years.

It has been said that the late Mr Lewis Ambler could grow the fine grey-edged George Rudd better than any other person, and since his death the plant appears to be on its way out, though taking Premier Award for Mr Ambler as recently as 1952. Where certain plants have flourished when in the hands of one or two growers, they must have been provided with a compost which was made up to their exact requirements. Perhaps that basic ingredient, loam was of the correct texture, or maybe it contained minerals in the right proportions. That certain varieties have for long continued to flourish in certain districts, but not in others, must confirm such a belief and many instances can be provided. It was in Halifax that the grey-edge George Rudd was introduced by Thomas Woodhead, in 1882, and it was there that it continued to flourish in the hands of Louis Ambler for 70 years. George Rudd never proved so vigorous away from its native district, where it remained happy in spite of the factory chimneys in ever-increasing numbers.

The loam should be given the utmost care in its selection, for Sir Roland Biffen has written that a compost with a fertile loam as its basis requires little or no reinforcement with artificial manures, and it is significant that Mr R. Loake, who in recent years has achieved greater success on the show bench with his auriculas than anyone, grows his plants at Kettering, famous for its loam from earliest times. Not only is this soil of the right consistency as to the proportions of clay and sand, thus ensuring adequate drainage, but the pastureland around Kettering has been renowned for its fattening qualities for years, with the result that the manurial value from the droppings of sheep and cattle has been continually washed into the soil, making it extremely fertile. This has also resulted in the stimulation of the grass roots, so that Kettering loam is of a particularly fibrous nature. It is in fact, about as ideal a soil as it is possible to obtain and will require augmenting by only limited supplies of manure or fertilisers.

Where possible, Kettering loam should be used, even if it has to be transported a distance. As an alternative, obtain a pasture loam of a fibrous nature from land which is well drained. This should be stacked under cover for several months, when it will be ready for breaking down by rubbing through a sieve of a mesh of sufficient width to enable as many of the fibrous roots as possible to penetrate. Sufficient quantities of soil should be obtained to last for two years, for after that time the quality will deteriorate. A good-quality turf loam which will bind together when tightly squeezed in the hand will prove ideal for all pot-grown auriculas. A top-quality loam will have a slightly greasy 'feel'. Besides its texture, it will be free from the deposits of soot and sulphur of most town garden soils, which are not only acid but generally of an inert nature, due to constant use without the addition of organic fertilisers. Such a soil must be avoided when growing auriculas, and for that matter any plants which have to occupy the same pots for any length of time.

The greater the fertility of the soil the less fertiliser will be required, but the ability of the soil to provide correct drainage and yet retain moisture in sufficient quantity to promote healthy plant growth, must be ensured. A soil which is badly drained, whereby excess moisture is continually retained about the roots, may quickly cause them to decay, whilst a soil of too sandy a nature from which the moisture all too quickly drains, will cause the few fibrous roots formed by the plants to shrivel and die back. If the roots dry out, the plant will take a considerable time to recover, if at all.

Old mushroom bed compost, which will be friable and free from weed spores and which should just bind when tightly squeezed is excellent for auriculas. It is similar to the 'old hot-bed dung' used by Samuel Curtis, a lecturer in botany at the beginning of the 19th century and co-editor, with Maddocks of the *Flower Directory*. Curtis used no loam in his auricula compost which was made up of two-thirds hot-bed manure and one-third peat and sand in equal parts. If the soil is light and sandy, use more manure than where it has a higher clay content. Two parts by bulk to eight parts of fibrous loam of medium texture will prove satisfactory, using slightly more where the soil is of a sandy nature and where no additional sand or drainage material will be required.

The John Innes Institute recommend using seven parts of loam, three parts of peat and two of sand. It must, however, be remembered that the peat is almost sterile, devoid of plant food, whilst old mushroom bed compost, and to a less extent leaf mould, will contain valuable plant foods. Where leaf mould, which must be thoroughy decayed, is substituted for the mushroom compost, then this should be augmented with a quantity of decayed manure, preferably cow manure, which may also be used in small quantities to make up the two parts by bulk of the mushroom bed compost.

The addition of powdered charcoal has been widely used through the years, a small quantity being mixed into the compost just prior to its use. It acts as a sweetener, and being black attracts and retains the sun's heat to a great extent, an important factor where it is desirable for the plants to receive the maximum warmth for growth to recommence during the last days of winter. Charcoal is also able to absorb ammonia gas in the compost and convert it into nitrogen required by the plants. It also helps with drainage, though for this purpose alone coarse sand will be less expensive and prove equally successful. Charcoal also helps in the rooting of young plants and offsets, but here again sand is just as good. However, for maintaining soil sweetness over a considerable period, and in other respects, a small quantity of charcoal could be added to auricula composts with advantage.

To sum up, the compost should be friable and free from any stickiness and should be sweet smelling, not too richly fortified with food, yet should not contain too large a quantity of useless fibre.

Certainly there is nothing difficult or mysterious abouts its preparation to dissuade auricula lovers from taking up their culture.

GROWING AURICULAS IN POTS

The auricula having to remain for 12 months in the pot, it will
be obvious that some attention should be given to the pot before
any planting is done. The old growers used a slightly larger pot
than is popular amongst growers today, one having a diameter of
$4\frac{1}{2}$ inches, which we call a small 60 size pot, they being made and sold
60 to a cast. The old pots were glazed either red or light brown on
the outside and so gave the plants a more pleasing appearance
when staged. After the first world war, unglazed pots were considered better able to promote healthy plant growth and so the
glazed pot is now rarely used. However, experiments recently
carried out both in this country and America have led to the
discovery that plants will grow equally well in any type of recept-
acle, proving as happy in jam jars or tins as in hand-made
unglazed earthenware pots, provided that drainage is adequate.
Perhaps, too, with the old growers, the use of a larger pot, thus
making it possible to provide more plant food for the auriculas,
contributed towards the magnificent quality of the plants which
prevailed as we know from photographs, during the 19th century.

M'Intosh also recommended that the pots should be glazed 'to
prevent their sides absorbing too much moisture from the compost
with which they are filled', which seems sensible advice. Today we
saturate the pots by placing them in a tank of water for 24 hours
before using them, and though this goes some way to prevent loss
of moisture in the compost, the pots quickly dry out in summer
long before the plants have become established in their new
quarters. The porous pot makes for more frequent watering, with
the result that the food value of the compost is washed out more
quickly. Possibly the non-porous pot was the secret of success of
the old growers, for with all our modern scientific knowledge
growers, speaking generally, cannot compare with their counter-
parts of 50 or even 30 years ago, when a hundred growers grew
superb auriculas in every small town of northern England.

As a rule, a rooted offset or seedling will be first potted into a
$2\frac{1}{2}$ inch or 'thumb' size pot. Then after six months the plant will be
moved to a $3\frac{1}{2}$ inch pot, finally moving to the 4 inch pot in which it

will bloom, and no larger pot need be provided; indeed it is not advisable. Controversy also continues as to how often an established plant should be repotted, for whilst it is now usual to repot every year, many older growers preferred to do so only in alternate years. George Glenny in his *Culture of Flowers and Plants* (1860), in which he devotes more space to the Show auricula than to any other garden plant, suggests repotting only once in two years for 'the check is much greater than is desirable'. Almost a century later Sir Ronald Biffen agreed with this, for in *The Auricula* he wrote : 'There is some difference of opinion about the repotting of older plants. It used to be the practice to do this annually, but if the plants are growing strongly, repotting in alternate years is now considered to be all that is necessary.' On the other hand, another famous auricula grower of the last century, Dr Horner of Hull, said, 'Neglect of yearly repotting is a great evil'; so there is much to be said for both opinions, and if a plant gives every appearance of being quite healthy, then it may be advisable to leave well alone and resort to top dressing and feeding. Potting every year, however, not only enables the plant to be provided with a supply of fresh food, but permits the roots of the plant to be inspected for pest or disease so that it may be treated before taking a hold.

Yet another point of controversy with auricula culture is the correct time to repot. Maddock would repot immediately the plants finished flowering, during the last days of May, and he repotted his auriculas every year. It was his contention that by potting towards the end of May the plants did not remain inactive during the summer months when the warm weather would tend to bring about disease where there was little root activity. On the other hand, Hogg recommended potting much later, during the first week of August, his reasons being that those plants repotted late in May would commence activity again and so tend to come into bloom during autumn, to the detriment of spring flowering. Again, it was Hogg's opinion that by repotting in May, not only would the plant food of the compost become washed away by constant watering through the summer months, but with the plants remaining almost 12 months in the same pots before coming into bloom in spring, the compost would tend to become sour and devoid of food when they should be sending up flower stems. There now seems to be a happy medium, repotting generally being done some time in June, though some growers prefer to wait until early July. As each method grows good auriculas, as Hogg surely did,

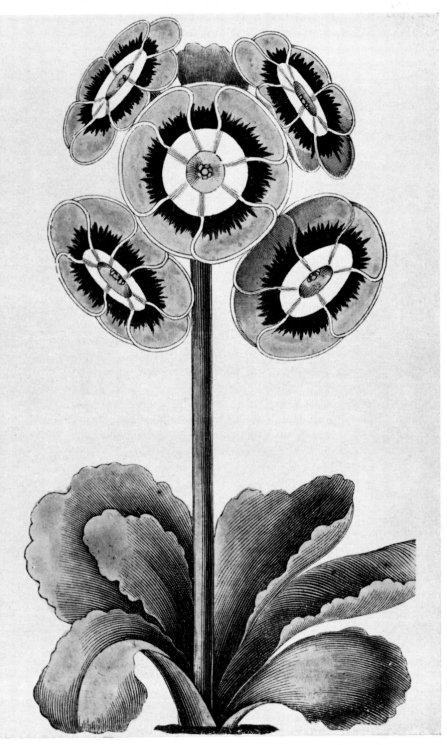

Grey-edged auricula – Conqueror of Europe (from a coloured engraving
of 1833)

Green-edged auricula – Buckley's Chloe

repotting should depend upon conditions during summer. If a well-ventilated and shaded greenhouse or frame can be provided, then the plants should not require undue applications of water at this time. The plants will be as happy in a shaded corner of the garden, but some gardens, however, are unable to provide such a position. They have to rely upon home-made contraptions, and under these conditions repotting should possibly be delayed until the end of July.

The main root of an auricula is known as the 'carrot' and from around it the fibrous roots radiate. If the lower portion of the 'carrot' is unduly long, remove with a sharp knife and rub the cut with sulphur.

To plant, first 'crock' the pots then add a little compost before introducing the plant. Then add more compost, making it firm around the plant with the fingers. The 'neck' of the plant should be just covered with compost. Give a thoroughly good soaking, then shade from the direct rays of the sun until re-established.

From mid-October, the plants will require very little moisture apart from that which they obtain from the atmosphere, and never at any time should the foliage be splashed by careless watering. To allow moisture to lodge in the centre or crown of the plant will be to cause decay of the most important part, and though the plants should never be completely dried off, they will require only an occasional watering, given around the sides of the pots. Nor must there be any indiscriminate damping of the floor of the greenhouse. To prevent the plants from being exposed to excess moisture, they should be taken indoors or placed in a frame early in October. Water only when the compost appears dry on top, or when the pots upon tapping, give a ringing sound. Never water by rule-of-thumb, for during a damp, foggy period, frequently experienced during November and again in January, little or no water will be required. Indeed, during a damp period it will be advisable to withhold all water and to provide as much ventilation as possible. Whenever fog or continued rain is experienced close the ventilators and open again as soon as conditions improve, to allow a free passage of air over the plants to dry up any surplus moisture on the foliage.

Whilst the trouble so often experienced with auriculas is to under-water the plants during summer, a winter-time worry is generally that of over-watering. It must be remembered that the roots will be dormant or inactive from early November until early

March and so will not be able to use up more than the smallest amount of moisture in the compost. To give too much, even though drainage may be satisfactory, will be for the compost to become sour, whilst the roots and 'neck' of the plant will tend to decay.

During winter, water only when necessary and give just sufficient to keep the plants alive. For this reason the plants should not be left outdoors unprotected so late in autumn that the compost will have become saturated so that when the plants are taken under cover it will take a considerable time to dry out, with the risk of serious harm to the plants. Throughout winter, provide conditions as near as possible to those the plants would receive when growing in their original surroundings, where they are kept almost dry by their covering of snow and ice throughout winter, yet at the same time are protected from ice-cold winds and excess moisture. Under such conditions the plants will remain healthy and will reawaken in spring with the utmost vigour.

As soon as plant growth recommences, which will be visible from about 1st March, any decayed leaves should be removed with scissors, and after the soil has been stirred the pots should be given a slight dressing of finely sifted leaf mould. This is given because a number of the young and most important roots may have become exposed, or almost so, due to constant application of water throughout the previous summer. If the plants have been frosted this may tend to force them out of the soil. An excellent top dressing will be to mix with the leaf mould, a small quantity of decayed cow manure or old mushroom bed compost. Or loam stored under cover and mixed with a small proportion of manure may be used to a depth of about half an inch.

From early March, regular judicious feeding will benefit the plants and increase the size of the bloom whilst the Selfs and Alpines will respond by a greater richness of colouring. Over-feeding, however, will do more harm than good, and if the plants have been grown from the beginning in a rich compost and have been given a top dressing, they will require only diluted applications of dried blood or manure water, which may be obtained from most sundriesmen in concentrated form. Dilute to use and only once each week, watering in the fertiliser with clean water so that it penetrates to the roots before evaporation can take place. Care should be taken to ensure that the manure water does not come into contact with the foliage, so apply around the sides of the pots.

66

Dried blood, or fish meal, may be given in granulated form, a pinch to each pot, which should be well watered in. Though these organic fertilisers are quick-acting and safer to use than those of an inorganic nature, there are those who use sulphate of ammonia or nitrate of soda during March to help the plants come into new growth as quickly as possible. Where these inorganic fertilisers are used, give only a small pinch to each pot, taking care to keep it away from the foliage, otherwise it may cause burning. The fertiliser should be watered in immediately after applying it and should be given early in March and again towards the month end, but no more frequently. Watering with manure water, or dried blood in liquid form, may continue until the plants come into bloom towards the end of April, or ten days earlier in the south.

From the end of March until the plants come into bloom great care must be exercised not only with watering but with ventilation and shading. As the flower truss is formed, more and more water should be given, care being taken to ensure that the mealy foliage is not splashed, likewise the bloom when it commences to open. During April especially, watering should be done with greater care than at any time during the life of the plant. Where plants are grown in cold frames, the lights should be kept in position from 1st April, when the first of the pot-grown auriculas, the Alpines, begin to open their bloom. Though the Alpines have no meal or paste on the bloom, their bright white or gold centre will be spoilt if splashed with rain, especially in the soot-laden atmosphere of industrial areas where deposits will be left on the bloom. Keep the lights over the plants, but ventilate freely by raising the lights throughout the day and closing them at night. If hard frost is still being experienced it will be advisable to cover the lights with sacking or canvas each evening, or tissue paper should be draped over the trusses where growing in a greenhouse. The protection should be kept over the plants until about 10 a.m., for following frost the sun's rays should be only gradually admitted. Too rapid exposure of a frosted plant may cause the stem to collapse, whilst the pips, if frosted when on the point of expanding, will never open flat, which is the hall-mark of a good Show auricula. The lights may be raised two hours earlier whilst the frost protectors are still in position, for the plants should be given as much air as possible.

BRINGING THE PLANTS INTO BLOOM

Show and Alpine auriculas grown in pots for exhibition will generally be confined to a single flower truss, any secondary shoots being removed as soon as observed. Where the plants are grown for home display a number of these secondary growths may be allowed to remain, though everything should be done to direct the full energies of the plant into bringing the main truss into as perfect a form as possible, and to allow secondary growths may reduce the size of bloom. If the plants have been grown as hardy as possible from the time of repotting, and provided ventilation and shading have been correctly managed during early spring, the flower stem will grow sturdy and will be able to support a very large truss. The Alpines and certain of the green-edged Show varieties will form a much larger truss or flower head but it is important to build up a truss of pleasing proportions, and in some cases it will be necessary to disbud so that each pip is given room to expand.

First remove any damaged or badly formed pips, removing them with the full length of the footstalk to which they are attached. Footstalks without a bloom give the truss a most untidy appearance. Only where there is overcrowding should any disbudding be done, yet all too often plants are exhibited with only three or five blooms when it is obvious that a number have unnecessarily been removed for no other reason than for the full energies of the plant to be directed to the remaining blooms. Size, which is so often the criterion of a good bloom on the show bench, is therefore preferred to form. Occasionally the pips may be unevenly arranged on a truss and to correct the balance one or possibly two pips should be carefully removed from that side where there is overcrowding, but to disbud just for the sake of it has little reasoning and cannot be recommended. M'Intosh suggests disbudding to not less than seven pips and not more than 13 to a truss, and adds, 'they should be taken out with such nicety that those which are left may grow in an equidistant form, causing a common spectator to suppose the truss to be quite naturally grown without any thinning'. Where there are few pips and these are bunched together, the truss may be made more attractive by very carefully 'persuading' the footstalks into a better position by placing between them small rolls of cotton. These may be made from an old handkerchief, cutting strips less than 1 inch wide and tying into rolls with thread. These rolls may be slipped between the footstalks with ease and should be removed with a pair of tweezers when the blooms are half expanded. This is done with the greatest of care. Certain varieties of the Show auricula naturally tend to form their pips on one side of the stem, and here little can be done to correct things, for it is a fault which has been bred into the plant and which in turn will be passed on to their seedlings.

Maddock has shown that with the Show varieties 'crown' stems, those produced at the very centre of the plant, are rarely as well formed as those which appear from the side of the crown. Sometimes this is so, sometimes it is not, and whereas certain varieties tend to produce a side stem which is often borne at an angle, others will produce a centre or 'crown' stem which is quite perpendicular. Most varieties possess a different habit in the formation both of the stem and of the pips, and where flowering seedlings for the first time, the quality of bloom should not be judged by that borne on the 'crown' stem, which may be of coarser quality than that produced on a side stem.

It will be found that Alpines bear a larger truss than the Show varieties and care will be needed so that the individual blooms do not greatly overlap.

PROPAGATION

Auriculas are propogated from offsets which form at the point where the soil surface is in contact with the 'neck' or collar. If the compost at the surface is allowed to dry out during summer, no offsets may form. They are removed by tearing in a downwards direction with the thumb and finger, taking care that only the smallest possible wound is made on the 'neck'. The offset, if large and vigorous, should be removed with a sharp penknife and as neatly as possible. Most of them will be found to have a few fibrous roots attached and so should present no difficulty with their rooting. After all the offsets have been removed – and this is best done before the plants are turned out of their old pots – the point of severing should be well rubbed with sulphur, which may be done at the same time as the 'carrot' is trimmed, and after the roots have been washed clean of soil.

Border auriculas should be lifted and divided every third or fourth year to prevent them becoming 'woody'. The offsets are pulled away from the main root (the 'carrot') and re-planted into freshly prepared ground. This is best done in October or in April and as the offsets will have numerous fibrous roots, they will soon become re-established if the soil is kept moist.

Border auriculas should be planted 12 inches apart and will benefit from a mulch of decayed manure and leaf mould each year which should be worked up to the crown of the plant.

A PRICE LIST OF SHOW AURICULAS OF 1825

Name	Raiser	Type	£	s	d
Alpine Shepherdess	Ackerley	Grey edge		7	6
Apollo	Dickson	Self		10	6
Britannia	Hodge	Green Edge	1	1	0
Colonel Taylor	Lee	Green Edge		4	6
Conqueror of Europe	Waterhouse	Grey Edge	1	10	0
Delight	Wood	White Edge		10	0
Early Grey	Eaton	Green Edge		5	0
Fair Rosamond	Laurie	White Edge		5	0
Favourite	Taylor	White Edge		10	0
Lord Collingwood	Yates	Green Edge		5	0
Lord Dacre	Troup	Grey Edge		5	0
Lord Dudley	Hogg	Grey Edge		5	0
Lord Nelson	Howard	Green Edge		5	0
Metropolitan	Redman	Self		10	0
Ne Plus Ultra	Fletcher	Grey Edge	1	1	0
Newton Hero	Ashworth	Green Edge		10	6
Pillar of Beauty	Hughes	White Edge		4	6
Ploughboy	Taylor	Grey Edge		5	0
Privateer	Grime	Grey Edge		5	0
Regulator	Potts	White Edge		5	0
Ringleader	Kenyon	Grey Edge		10	0
Robert Burns	Campbell	Grey Edge	1	5	0
Ruler of England	Pollett	Green Edge		7	6
Trafalgar	Partington	Green Edge		5	0
Venus	Leigh	White Edge		4	0
Waterloo	Ryder	Grey Edge		5	0

PREMIER WINNING VARIETIES FOR 1932 AT THE LEADING SHOWS WAS AS FOLLOWS:

Grey Edged	Firsts	Total Prizes
Grime's Privateer	20	36
Kenyon's Ringleader	14	31
Fletcher's Ne Plus Ultra	4	4
Taylor's Ploughboy	3	14
Thompson's Revenge	2	13
Ryder's Waterloo	2	10
Green Edged		
Booth's Freedom	9	17
Lee's Colonel Taylor	7	12
Pollit's Highland Laddie	4	13
Moore's Jubilee	3	5
Warris's Blucher	3	5
White Edged		
Hughe's Pillar of Beauty	10	25
Lee's Bright Venus	8	24
Taylor's Glory	5	20
Popplewell's Conqueror	3	13
Pott's Regulator	3	9
Selfs		
Grime's Flora's Flag	11	30
Redman's Metropolitan	7	31
Berry's Lord Leigh	5	20
Netherwood's Othello	5	13
Cox's Bishop of Lichfield	3	6
Schole's Ned Lud	2	19

VARIETIES OF THE SHOW AURICULA

Green Edged

ABRAHAM BARKER. Though now little grown, it is a fine green, striking with its smooth paste, well-defined black body colour and wide edging of dark green. Around the petals is a wire edge of

71

silvery meal, which does not please everybody but which greatly accentuates the deep green edging.

ANTONIA. A good green for the beginner, for it is a strong grower and makes a good fair-sized truss. The blooms are nicely rounded and have a dense, smooth paste and an edging of vivid green.

BROCKENHURST. One of the late Mr Haysom's introductions. It forms a truss of six or seven pips which open together, and though the placement is not ideal, the individual blooms are outstanding. The six petals are nicely rounded, the paste being dense and smooth, the tube perfectly round, whilst the ground colour is not overdone. The edging is of the most brilliant green.

COPYTHORNE. Both its foliage and petal edging are of bright, medium green. The medium-sized blooms, with their rounded petals, have a circular golden-yellow tube and dense, smooth paste.

GREEN PARROT. A fine variety bearing large, rounded blooms of deep green. The tube is bright gold, the paste dense, the black body colouring being clearly defined and not overdone.

GREEN WOODPECKER. It may be expected to open seven pips to a truss, the nine-petalled blooms having a circular appearance. With the round tube, dense paste and wide green edging, this variety would attain almost perfection but for the tendency of an occasional petal to be pointed.

HOUNSDOWN. Of robust habit, the large rounded blooms have an edging of brilliant green, a well-shaped tube and dense paste. The body colour, too, is clearly defined and well proportioned.

LINKMAN. This variety is readily distinguishable by the thin edge of black appearing round the outside of the tube. The paste is smooth but irregular, whilst the jet-black body colour reaches almost to the edge of the petals, which often number as many as nine. These overlap beautifully and give the bloom a completely circular appearance. The plant is of sturdy, vigorous habit, making it one of the easiest of the greens to manage.

LONGDOWN. Raised, like so many of our modern Edged auriculas, by Mr Cyril Haysom, this is likely to be a favourite for some years to come. It forms a large, well-shaped truss, the blooms having the paste dense and well defined with a deep yellow, rounded tube. The body colour is black, the edging being of dark green with beautifully rounded petals.

TINKERBELL. Raised by Mr Clive Cookson, it is one of the finest of all the greens, but is difficult to manage and should not be asked to open more than five pips to a truss. The paste is smooth, the body colour black and the green edge wider than usual. The tube is deep yellow and perfectly round.

Grey Edged

GEORGE LIGHTBODY. A magnificent variety but now rarely seen. With its smooth paste, jet-black ground colour and beautifully mealed edging it was always popular on the show bench, and though introduced in 1860 won premier award when exhibited at the Northern Auricula Society's Show a hundred years later. It was raised by Richard Headley of Stapleford.

GEORGE RUDD. Raised at Halifax by Thomas Woodhead, and introduced in 1882, this together with George Lightbody, has remained amongst the best of all Show auriculas until the present day. Bearing a bloom of exquisite form, it really is a grey edge, as distinct from those which tend to lose their identity with the white edges. The petals are so placed as to form the most perfectly shaped of all auricula blooms, its one fault being that the tube is not all that could be desired.

LOVEBIRD. The best grey to come from Edenside. The seven-petalled pips are smaller than with most greys, but the bloom is refined, the paste, body colour and edging being evenly defined. One of the most prolific varieties with its offsets and should be in every collection.

MARMION. One of the best in this section, the medium-sized blooms having beautifully rounded petals. The tube is bright yellow and free of notches, the paste smooth, whilst the ground colouring is clearly defined.

NUTHATCH. One of the best greys with a beautifully rounded tube, smooth dense paste and well-proportioned black ground colouring. Both petals and foliage are nicely covered with meal.

SEAMEW. A fine grey which will open as many as nine pips on a truss. The medium-sized blooms are rounded and the golden-yellow tube free of notches; the paste smooth, with a smaller amount of body colour than most varieties.

SHERFIELD. One of the best varieties to come from the Bartley Nurseries, and now possibly the premier grey, though it is not an easy plant to grow well. The bloom is so densely covered in meal that it almost comes into the white-edged category. The tube is deep yellow and rounded, the paste smooth.

White Edged

ACME. Though introduced almost a century ago, this variety has remained the most popular white-edged auricula of all. The petals are heavily mealed, the tube being golden yellow and quite round. The paste is dense and smooth, whilst the body colour is well defined.

DOROTHY MIDGELEY. Raised by Mr J. W. Midgeley, this variety is outstanding for its well-nigh perfect outline and rightly received an Award of Merit. The pip is large, the seven petals overlapping to provide a beautifully rounded bloom, the truss numbering from five to eight pips.

HINTON ADMIRAL. Probably the best white-edged of recent years. The nicely mealed petals are beautifully rounded, likewise the tube, whilst the paste is smooth and dense. The body colour is outstanding, being black and well defined.

J. W. MIDGELEY. Though easy to grow to perfection and propagate, it does not make a large plant and carries only four or five pips to a truss. For refinement of bloom, however, it is one of the best of all white-edged auriculas. Though the petals are well covered with meal, the foliage has none.

SILVERLEY. Now the premier white, possibly because it is one of the easiest of the Shows to manage. The tube is perfectly round and of deep yellow, the paste dense and the body colour black. The heavily mealed petals are nicely rounded. The plant forms a large truss.

WHITE ENSIGN. A white of vigorous habit and easy growth, both bloom and foliage being heavily covered with meal. Paste, tube and petals are beautifully round, whilst the body colour is black and well defined.

Self Coloured

ALICE HAYSOM. One of the best crimsons since Harrison Weir, its red colouring is even brighter, but it has not quite the same smoothness of paste as the older variety. The tube is bright gold and perfectly round, whilst the foliage is densely mealed.

BLOXHAM BLUE. From seed sent out by Mr C. Cookson of Hexham, raiser of the green-edged favourite Tinkerbell and said to be saved from a Bluebird cross, this auricula was raised by the Rev Oscar Moreton when at Bloxham, Norfolk. With its dense pure white paste and body colour of rich violet-blue, this is a

74

striking plant and rightly received an Award of Merit.

BLUE FIRE. Until the introduction of Bloxham Blue, this was the best blue self. It was raised during the early years of this century by the late Mr James Douglas, and bears blooms of bright mid-blue which are rather small in size. The pips are held on long foot-stalks at the top of the main stem and are heavily mealed. Unless grown quite cool, the bloom tends to slight purple shading. It is easily grown and propagated.

FANNY MEERBECK. One of the oldest of the selfs, raised by Ben Simonite of Sheffield, it is a strong grower and forms a bloom of seven or eight petals which are well rounded to give the pips great substance, though the large number of petals often cause 'ridging'. The colour is brilliant crimson-red and with the smooth paste is most showy.

FREDA. This is a strikingly beautiful old variety which may be described as almost black, the contrast with the dense, pure white paste being most marked.

HARRISON WEIR. Raised by James Douglas at Edenside towards the end of the last century and named after the famous animal painter and cat breeder of that time. For 50 years it has remained the finest red self and has won more honours than any other self. The paste is smooth and clearly defined, the body colour being bright crimson-red.

INNOCENCE. This is a delicate pale yellow self of exquisite form. The paste is smooth and clearly defined, the tube free from notching, whilst the six-petalled blooms are large and circular and make up a well-shaped truss.

MARY WINN. Raised by Mr T. Sheppard it is one of the best yellow selfs, being more satisfactory than that other fine yellow Edith Winn, which rarely produces any offsets. Mary Winn forms a beautifully shaped pip, the paste being smooth and regular, the tube round, whilst the colouring is a deep primrose yellow, having the similarly coloured Daffodil for a parent which was the premier yellow self of the 1920s.

OWER. Raised by C. G. Haysom, it is a robust grower and makes a large rounded truss. The blooms are of excellent form, the paste being clearly defined, the tube free of notches, whilst the body colour is of pale golden yellow. The beautifully mealed foliage has a silver-grey appearance.

ROSEBUD. The beautiful rose-pink colouring of the well-formed circular bloom is unique amongst Show auriculas. Of vigorous habit, the plant is easy to grow and to propagate. The paste is dense and clearly defined, likewise the tube.

SCARLET PRINCE. One of the finest of the crimsons, being easier and of more vigorous constitution than Harrison Weir or that grand old crimson J. H. Watson. It forms a bloom of perfect shape, whilst the colour is bright crimson-scarlet, free from any tawny colouring. Both paste and tube are well defined.

THE ALPINE AURICULA

The Alpine auriculas, readily distinguishable from the Borders and the Show Selfs in that their bloom is free from meal, are possibly the finest of all the auriculas for the beginner, combining the beauty of the Selfs with the extreme hardiness and vigour of the Borders. It was the rich colouring and beautiful symmetry of the Alpines which made them so popular with the early 19th century painters of quality china. Their blooms must figure on more pieces of fine china than any other flower and they were mostly depicted in shades of crimson. A Coalport fruit service dated 1825, in my possession, has the Alpine auricula exquisitely painted on each piece, whilst a number of Coalport door plates of the same period are adorned with auriculas of similar colouring to that most popular of all Alpines, the purple flowered Gordon Douglas.

The Alpines or 'Pures' as they were called by the old growers, to distinguish them from those with meal, are extremely hardy, and though like the Shows they are generally grown in small pots so that their beauty may be enjoyed to the full, they are sufficiently hardy to withstand the coldest of weather and so may be used in much the same way as the Borders. When grown in pots, the plants are better able to withstand excess moisture about the foliage than will the Shows, whilst they are more tolerant of fogs and a smoke-laden atmosphere. Provided the plants are given protection from strong sunlight during summer, and are not allowed to suffer from lack of moisture about the roots, they will present little trouble. With their more vigorous habit they should not be given so rich a compost as the Shows, otherwise the stem and footstalks may grow too 'lanky' and be unable to support the large blooms which are half as large again as those of the grey and white-edged Shows. With their lack of farina on both the blooms and foliage and forming an enormous truss, the plants present a picture of

76

the richest colouring imaginable. Whilst the edged Show auriculas may be said to possess a more refined beauty, the Alpines may be described as being sumptuous; they possess a richness unknown in almost any other flower. The plants may be grown in a cold greenhouse or alpine house, or in frames from which they may be taken indoors when the pips are beginning to open. There, in a bright room, their beauty may be appreciated to the full, and particularly when under artificial lighting. Or they may be set out in window boxes, their pots being buried in soil to retain moisture. The Alpines are also most suitable for a rockery where they may be left in position throughout the year, a cloche being placed over the plants, which should be in groups of two or three, from early November until the end of February to protect them from excessive winter moisture. But frost and snow will cause them no trouble. They may also be used, in the same way as the Borders, to edge a path but they do prefer to be away from the full glare of the summer sun and a well-drained soil is essential. The beauty of the blooms when flowering outdoors may not be enjoyed to the full, but if a sufficient number can be brought on in pots to bloom indoors in all their glory, surplus plants may then be used to advantage in the open. When grown outdoors they should be given the same treatment as for the Borders : when in pots they will receive the same culture as given the Shows, though they will tolerate rather less attention to detail.

It was Charles Turner of Slough, who achieved fame by introducing Cox's Orange Pippin apple in 1855, who did so much to improve the Alpine auricula about the same time. After the appearance of the Show auricula 100 years previously, all other auriculas gradually fell from popularity. For a century the Edged varieties reigned supreme, and during that time the doubles and striped auriculas as well as the pure Alpines, the 'pures', almost passed out of cultivation. Indeed, but for Charles Turner's interest in the Alpines between the years 1850 and 1870 they would almost certainly have been lost to cultivation. Turner was to improve these plants in several ways. He obtained a larger pip and richer colourings and was so successful that at the General Meeting of the National Auricula Society in 1889, the Turner Memorial Trust was created. This offered £5 in prizes for pairs of Show and Alpine auriculas, and gradually the number of classes for Alpine auriculas was increased until today they receive equal recognition with the Shows.

James Douglas at Great Bookham took over where Turner left off, and no one has done more for the auricula during the past half-century than the Douglas family. Their world famous business of growing Border carnations and auriculas was commenced in 1892 by Mr James Douglas, who may be said to have taken over from the Sheffield and Lancashire 'school' in the breeding of auriculas, especially the Alpines upon which they have since concentrated. James Douglas's son also called James, later carried on his father's great work and for his raising of the wonderful Show auricula Harrison Weir, would have achieved everlasting fame if for nothing else. Now the business is in the hands of the founder's grandson, Gordon Douglas, after whom the well-known Border auricula was named. The House of Douglas are the only firm ever to have won three Gold Medals for their auriculas at Royal Horticultural Society shows, and since 1912 they have exhibited regularly at Chelsea, a record which they may regard with pride.

The first auricula to be sent out by the founder was the fine green-edge Abbé Liszt in 1894, and this was followed two years later by the equally fine Prince Charming. Later came the grey-edge Marmion, and Harrison Weir already mentioned. The firm also introduced dozens of fine Alpines: Gordon Douglas and Bookham Firefly being outstanding and unsurpassed in their respective colours. It is worthy of mention that, although the auricula cannot be considered to be anything like as as popular as it was 50 years ago, there are now more than 12,000 plants being raised at Great Bookham each year, all of which find a ready market.

It is interesting to recall that in a recent letter to the author Mr James Douglas, father of the present owner, gives unselfish praise to several of the older Show auriculas which were not raised by his firm. Of George Lightbody he writes, 'this variety has never been excelled unto this day; it was easily the finest grey-edge ever raised'. He gives equal praise to the white-edge, Acme, and to Barlow's blue self, Mrs Potts. In the opinion of Mr Douglas there have never been any varieties to be their equal in their respective groups.

QUALITIES OF THE ALPINE AURICULA

The Alpines are of more robust habit than either the Shows or the Borders, the foliage is larger, the stem longer and the bloom is the largest of all the auriculas. The plants may be divided into two main groups, those which bear a bloom with a white or light centre and those which have a gold centre. There are also those which have the intermediate cream colouring at the centre, but these are generally included in the light centre group. The blooms have either six or eight petals, which overlap better than those of many of the Show varieties, thereby producing an almost completely circular bloom, and whereas the body colour of the petals, which is darkest around the eye, shades out to the edge, with the Show selfs it is uniform or should be so. The gold-centred varieties are especially showy, for the centre is large and its brightness is made more pronounced by the deep body colouring which surrounds it. The Alpines may be likened to the charming *Primula pubescens* group from which it is now believed they were evolved. The *P. pubescens* may also be divided into those having a white-and-cream centre and those having a gold centre. Sir Roland Biffen has pointed out that *P. pubescens,* which bears a large number of blooms of varying shades of mahogany and crimson, has passed on this quality to the Alpines. This colouring is reached by combining the bright yellow of *P. auricula* and the carmine red of *P. hirsuta*, which are thought to be the parents of *P. pubescens*. Apart from their paste or mealed centre there is little difference between the Show selfs and the light coloured Alpines and both must have a large proportion of the same 'blood', probably of *P. auricula* and *P. hirsuta* in varying amounts. The tube, in which the anthers should hide the stigma, should be yellow both for the light and gold centre varieties. The centre should be free of meal, whilst the petal colouring should be rich and shade out to a paler colouring. The following points are awarded to an Alpine auricula :

	Points
For foliage, stem and truss	8
For pip	4
For tube	2
For centre	3
for edge	3
	20

VARIETIES OF THE ALPINE AURICULA

Gold Centre

BASUTO. A striking variety, the large refined blooms being of rich crimson-maroon shading to wine-red. The habit of the plant is vigorous.

BOOKHAM BEAUTY. A fine variety, the large well-formed blooms make up a large rounded truss and are of a striking shade of burnt orange shading to pure orange.

BOOKHAM FIREFLY. From the House of Douglas, this is one of the most popular of all Alpine auriculas though introduced in 1913. Then it cost 2s. 6d. now 50p! The blooms have a bright, well-defined centre, whilst the glowing crimson colouring shades to maroon. The petals vary from five to seven, whilst the truss is somewhat irregular. Where it does well, however, it is unbeatable.

CAROLINA. This grand old variety with its exceptionally good centre is a plant of vigorous habit. The colour may be described as being deep crimson shading to rich apricot-bronze.

CICERO. An excellent variety for a beginner's collection, for it forms a large truss and is of vigorous habit. The rich maroon blooms with their velvety texture shade out to crimson-red.

CLOTH OF GOLD. An outstanding new variety of easy, vigorous habit. The blooms are of rich old gold, shading to pure golden-yellow.

DORIS PARKER. It makes a large truss, the medium-sized bloom being of excellent form and of deep crimson-maroon colour shading to bright flame-red.

FORESTER. Both tube and centre are of perfectly rounded form. The blooms, with their velvety texture and rounded petals, are of deep maroon shading to a pale brick-red colour.

FRANK FAULKNER. Carrying the name of its raiser, this is a fine crimson, of velvet-like appearance, described by many as the best gold-centred Alpine seen for a long time.

GOLDEN GLEAM. One of the best Alpines ever raised. The blooms are are of rich golden-yellow, shading to mahogany-bronze, the footstalks being sturdy, the pips well placed.

GOLDEN GLORY. Raised by Mr R. H. Briggs, under whose guidance the Northern Auricula Society flourished during the post-war years, this lovely variety is likely to become the premier plant of its colour in this section. The colour is rich golden-brown shading to almost an old gold colouring at the outer edges of the petals. Unlike a number of the 'browns' it has no trace of the crimson to be found in Golden Harvest and others.

KINGCUP. Crimson shading to medium brown is possibly a fairly accurate description; it is one of the best gold-centred auriculas ever introduced. The trusses are held well above the foliage, the pips being large and beautifully formed. Raised by C. G. Haysom.

LADY DAMASK. A variety which is both easy to grow and to propagate. The well-shaped blooms make up a large truss and are of deep maroon shading to pale red.

MIDAS. A variety which form a large truss, the blooms being of rich brown, almost the colour of brown ale, shading out to an attractive golden-bronze.

NEWTON ABBOT. Of vigorous constitution, the blooms with their large golden centre are of deepest crimson, shading to red.

PRINCE JOHN. One of the best, the centre is larger than most and is of the brightest gold accentuated by the maroon colouring and almost complete lack of shading.

SPARKLE. A magnificent variety, both tube and centre being almost perfect, whilst the body colour is an unusual shade of rich golden-bronze shading to gold.

Light Centre

ARGUS. A fine old variety raised by the late Mr J. Keen at Southampton in 1895. It forms an extremely large truss and though the white centre is not as clearly defined as with some, its rich plum colour shading to crimson-red is unique and has won for it many premier awards during the past sixty years.

BLUE BONNET. A fine blue Alpine, but with the continued popularity of Gordon Douglas is not so well known as it deserves to be. The pure white centre is perfectly round and clearly defined, the colour being deep violet-blue shading to mid-blue. Of sturdy constitution, it is easy to grow and to propagate.

BOOKHAM GLORY. Carrying the well-known Douglas prefix, it may be relied upon to produce a well-formed truss, the colour being rich royal purple shading to pale heliotrope.

GORDON DOUGLAS. With its creamy-white centre and deep violet-blue flower, this is one of the easiest of all Alpine auriculas to manage and propagate, but it must be well shaded when opening its bloom. It is one of the hardiest and most popular of all Alpines and a constant winner on the show bench.

JOY. Raised at Altrincham by Mr Percy Johnson, this may be considered to be the premier Alpine of its section, being a rich velvety crimson so delicately shaded that is has the appearance of a Show self. It is of vigorous habit and strong constitution.

LADY DARESBURY. This is one of the finest white-centred Alpines ever raised. The very large blooms have eight petals and are of beautiful form. The pips are so freely produced that they form a large truss. The colour is rich wine-red, shading to pale cerise, whilst the plant is of strong constitution. Raised by Mr C. Faulkner of Hale, Cheshire.

MRS HEARN. One of the most beautiful Alpines ever introduced, it may be described as grey-blue, shading to Cambridge blue. The centre is pale cream, whilst the well-shaped bloom possesses a strong honeysuckle perfume.

PINK LADY. It forms a lovely truss, the blooms being of an attractive wine-pink colour shading to rose-pink.

BORDER AURICULAS

They are plants of great antiquity and with their hardy constitution, freedom of flowering, the rich 'old master' colouring of the blooms and their exotic fragrance, they are amongst the loveliest of all flowers, in bloom from April until mid-June. So powerful is their scent that quite a small bed of plants will be almost overpowering when the early summer sun shines down upon them whilst they impregnate the sun-baked soil with their perfume. They are plants which, like the honeysuckle which their perfume so much resembles, give of their richest scent only when warmed by the sun. Since their introduction into England about the year 1575, the border auriculas have come to be cherished in garden of cottage and manor alike. In the garden of Hardwick Hall in Derbyshire they grow where they may have been since the time of their introduction the same year in which this gracious house was built by Bess, Countess of Shrewsbury and the rich colours of their flowers match those of the tapestries with which the magnificent Presence Chamber is hung. Here Mary, Queen of Scotland and France was held prisoner and she may well have seen auriculas in the walled gardens of the old house. Auriculas are also to be found in the tiny garden of Shakespeare's boyhood home in Stratford-on-Avon for they are flowers beloved by all and they have been with us for well-nigh four centuries. Parkinson wrote that 'auriculas do seem every one of them to be a nosegay alone of itself . . . their pretty scent doth add an increase of pleasure in those that make them ornaments for their wearing'.

They were the flowers of James Thomson's *The Seasons*, when :

> 'fair-handed spring unbosoms every grace' with
> . . . auriculas, enrich'd
> With shining meal o'er all their velvet leaves

And of Thomas Fuller's *Antheologia or The Speech of Flowers* (1660) : 'And now in the springtime earth did put on her new clothes . . . For there was yellow marigolds, wallflowers, auriculusses, gold-knobs and abundance of other nameless flowers.'

Not having been confined to pots under glass as have the show auriculas, the older border varieties have in no way lost their vigour and if they can be given a sunny situation and a soil which does not readily dry out they will prove adaptable to almost every garden, quickly growing into large vigorous clumps above which they bear on 9 inch stems, irregular heads of large velvety blooms. This irregularity adds to their old-world charm. There is nothing stiff about them and when cut and placed in small vases indoors, they will remain fresh for days and scent the house with their warm sweet honey fragrance. Plant in spring or in autumn and top dress each year.

VARIETIES

ADAM LORD. A variety of sturdy habit with serrated foliage which forms into numerous rosettes above which in large trusses appear the navy-blue flowers with their creamy-white centre.

AMETHYST. It forms a large truss of bright wine-purple flowers with a clearly defined white centre and is densely covered in farina.

BLUE MIST. Now rare but an outstanding variety and so well named for the medium-sized blooms are of pure sky blue with the farina providing a silvery, mist-like sheen.

BLUE VELVET. Of vigorous habit, it forms a symmetrical head of purple-blue flowers with a clearly defined creamy-white centre and emits a rich honey perfume.

BROADWELL GOLD. A superb variety found by Mr Joe Elliott in a

Cotswold cottage garden but it is now rare. It bears large blooms of brilliant golden-yellow with beautifully waved petals and they diffuse a musk-like fragrance. All parts of the plant are covered with farina.

CELTIC KING. A strong grower, its foliage is without farina whilst its flowers are of a lovely shade of lemon-yellow with attractively waved petals.

CRAIG NORDIE. The flowers are of burgundy-red with a golden centre and are almost free of farina whilst the foliage is grey-green.

GOLDEN QUEEN. It forms a large truss of pale sulphur-yellow flowers with a white centre and which carry a rich sweet perfume.

LINNET. An old favourite which now seems to have been lost. It is late into bloom and is well named for the blooms are of a combination of green, brown and mustard, the colours of the now almost equally rare bird of that name.

MCWATT'S BLUE. Raised by the late Dr McWatt in Scotland, the rich mid-blue flowers with their white centre carry a delicious honey perfume. The foliage is heavily mealed.

MRS NICHOLLS. A most attractive variety, the pale yellow blooms have a golden centre around which is a circle of white. The blooms have a pronounced musk scent.

OLD IRISH BLUE. A most beautiful auricula, with serrated foliage above which it bears large trusses of rich mid-blue. The flowers have a white centre and are heavily mealed whilst the perfume is outstanding.

OLD PURPLE DUSTY MILLER. Also known as Blue Dusty Miller but the flowers are really of purple colouring, with pronounced perfume and are held on 12 inch stems. All parts of the plant are heavily mealed.

OLD RED DUSTY MILLER. Of great antiquity, it is so heavily mealed as to appear as if covered in flour. The flowers are not large but the colour is unique, being of crimson-brown, wallflower colouring and with a heavy scent.

OLD SUFFOLK BRONZE. A most interesting variety more Alpine than Border for it is quite free from farina. It makes a plant of robust habit and over a period of at least ten weeks bears large trusses of flowers of dollar size and of shades of gold, bronze and buff, almost impossible to describe. The scent is almost intoxicating and can be detected for a considerable distance. The plant was obtained by the author from a garden in Suffolk where it has been growing through the centuries.

OLD YELLOW DUSTY MILLER. The powerfully scented blooms are of deep golden yellow, whilst all parts are covered with farina.

DOUBLE AURICULAS

Little is now seen of these delightful plants which achieved great popularity during the mid-17th century. I know of only two – The Bishop, which bears a fully double fragrant bloom of deep purple-blue; and The Cardinal, a deep blood crimson, and said to have originated in the garden of the Cardinal Richelieu. Its bloom is not as large as that of The Bishop, nor is it of such robust habit. I have seen, but never owned, the Old Double Green auricula, a glorious plant, opening six or seven pips on a truss held on a 5 inch stem. The fully double green blooms are covered with meal, also the foliage, which gives the plant a most attractive appearance. Mr Sacheverell Sitwell in *Old Fashioned Flowers* mentions the Double Red Rufus which I have neither seen nor grown but which may still be obtained in shades of red and bronze. In Mr Sitwell's words, 'the flowers are small and attractive but, in the writer's opinion, unimpressive'. There is also a double yellow which one would think would be more common, and a double brown, neither of which I have seen. As the doubles do not readily set seed they remain extremely rare, though there is a class for them at the National Auricula Society's Shows where the odd plant occasionally appears, a delightful reminder of a bygone age.

CHAPTER III

The Gold-Laced Polyanthus

The first polyanthus – Parentage of the polyanthus – The polyanthus illustrated – Famous show varieties – Preparation of the soil – The time to lift and divide the plants – Dividing the plants – Exhibiting – Methods of the old florists – The polyanthus in pots – Preparing plants for exhibition – Merits of the gold-laced polyanthus.

Of the plant now grown by the million each year to provide the flower garden with rich colour in springtime, nothing was known until about the year 1660. The great Elizabethan writers on plant lore, Turner, Lyte, and Gerard, make no mention of any plant which remotely resembles the polyanthus; neither does Parkinson in his *Paradisus*. Parkinson does, however, mention the Primrose Cowslip which from the description one must take to be the hybrid oxlip (*P. veris* x *P. vulgaris*). He describes it thus : 'The leaves of this cowslip are larger than the ordinary field cowslip and of a darker yellowish green colour; the flowers are many, standing together on the tops of the stalks, to the number of 30 sometimes upon one stalk . . . and sometimes more, every one having a longer footstalk than the former, and of as pale a yellowish colour, as the field primrose with yellow spots at the bottom of the leaves (petals) as the ordinary hath and as sweet a scent.'

Later, in his *Theatrum Botanicum,* published in 1640, Parkinson writes that the red-flowered primrose (*Primula vulgaris rubra*) had 'recently' been introduced from Turkey. He describes this plant as being John Tradescant's Turkie-purple primrose (from the Caucasus) from which it would seem that it may have been this primrose which, when crossed with a native yellow hybrid oxlip (*P. veris* x *P. vulgaris*), was to produce a red polyanthus or 'big oxlip', first described by John Rea in 1665. Rea was a nurseryman who lived near Bewdley in Worcestershire and his *Flora, Ceres and Pomona or the Complete Florilege* was published in 1665 by Richard Marriott, 'to be sold at his shop in Fleet Street, under the King's Head Tavern, over against the Inner Temple Gate.' It was dedicated to that great gardener and patron, Sir Thomas Hanmer. In it, Rea not only mentions the red colouring of cowslips and primroses 'which are more esteemed than those of our own country', but he describes a plant which may well have been similar in form to the polyanthus we now know so well.

He writes: 'The red cowslip or oxlip is of several sorts, all of them bearing many flowers on one stalk, in fashion like those of the field but of several red colours; some deeper, others lighter; some bigger like oxlips; others smaller like cowslips.' Those he described as being 'bigger', like oxlips, must surely have borne a flower resembling a polyanthus. Since he describes the red colouring of cowslips and primroses as being 'more esteemed than those of our own country', it would appear that the plants had been introduced from abroad where, incidentally, most primroses and cowslips are red or reddish purple like the popular Primula Wanda, plants bearing yellow flowers being the exception. Included amongst these plants would surely have been the Turkie-purple primrose described by Parkinson; for when writing about the cowslips and primroses growing in his garden, Rea says 'the red primrose is of a newer date, more beauty and greater variety (of colour) . . . the tops of the shoots and bottoms of the stalks are of a reddish colour but the greatest differencee is in the colours of the flowers, there being almost twenty diversities of reds . . . the scarlet is the rarest of all'.

Though the first mention to be made of any plant resembling the polyanthus had red flowers, it is certain that the hybrid oxlip was used in the crossing; yet it is difficult to understand why no such crossing had taken place before the introduction of the red primrose from Europe. One would have thought that the natural crossing of our native hybrid oxlip and our native primrose, both, in most instances, bearing a yellow bloom, would have resulted in the appearance of a plant similar to our modern yellow garden polyanthus and growing in the wild state, like the plant I had the pleasure of finding, of perfect polyanthus habit and identical in colour to the yellow primrose. It was growing on a bank covered in wild primroses at Combe Down, Bath. This may have occurred in the past but only with the introduction of the red colouring did the plant receive the attention of the florist and only then was any attempt made at reselection and improvement. However, it has been found that the red gene proves dominant where a red polyanthus is crossed with one bearing a white or yellow bloom, hence a plant bearing a red flower would be more readily noticed. It would account for the red colour persisting for more than two centuries, proving difficult to breed out. This is confirmed in a letter dated

18th May, 1842, and which appeared in the *Floricultural Cabinet* for July of that year. 'By your leave,' began the writer, 'I beg to call the humble and simple cowslip into notice which by accident I have lately found capable of producing, without cultivation, several interesting and pretty varieties. Being a great admirer of the Polyanthus (Gold-Laced), I met with what I considered one . . . not appropriated to flowers. I carried it to another part of the garden where I planted it amongst my Polyanthuses; but behold when blooming time came, it turned out to be nothing, but a field Cowslip. . . . As the ground was shaded by filbert trees, I suppose (it) shed its seeds undisturbed until in course of time it produced the most beautiful varieties (chiefly inclining to crimson) of the Cowslip imaginable.' Thus, the yellow field cowslip when crossed with the crimson and gold-laced polyanthus, produced a plant bearing flowers like Rea's 'red cowslip', the red colour predominating as always.

Sir Roland Biffen has told of the crossing of the yellow *Primula auricula* with *P. hirsuta* which bears magenta flowers, and which resulted in the appearance of flowers of a colour similar to burnt sienna or crimson-brown. A crimson flower crossed with one of bright yellow would produce one of a vivid scarlet colour and just such a colour could be obtained where mixing paints of similar colours. The pigments contained in the flowers would give the same results, with the red colouring predominating throughout. To breed out this muddy magenta-brown colouring in the modern polyanthus strains has occupied the hybridisers for a very long time, and not until this was achieved by hand pollination were the brilliant clear colourings to be obtained. This has completely changed the appearance of the polyanthus today and has greatly added to its popularity.

John Rea has written that he knew well the 'red cowslip' and there may (about 1660) have taken place a natural crossing between a red-flowered cowslip and a primrose; for, surprising as it may be to lovers of the cowslip, it is to this day to be found in the red form growing wild in parts of south-west England and in Wales. The result would be a red hybrid cowslip as described by Rea. This, in turn, when crossed with the Turkie-purple primrose mentioned by Parkinson, would carry the evolution a stage further, when a plant appeared bearing large, loose umbels of rich red primrose-like blooms, held on inch-long footstalks and having a long sturdy stem. In other words, Rea's 'red oxlip' or polyanthus.

PARENTAGE OF THE POLYANTHUS

That the polyanthus has both the primrose and cowslip as its progenitors is certain, for characteristics of both appear in the polyanthus. There are two forms of the wild oxlip to be found growing in Britain, the true oxlip, *P. elatior,* and a hybrid form derived from a crossing between the cowslip (*P. veris*) and common primrose (*P. vulgaris*). This first cross hybrid is a handsome vigorous plant and it is of interest to note that, like the polyanthus, the first flowers of the spring appear singly on short stems, in the manner of the primrose which is the first to bloom, whilst later they appear in umbels like those of the cowslip, which blooms later and on a stout stem. This, the hybrid oxlip, a parent of the polyanthus, is the plant described in detail by the French botanist Clusius (or De L'Ecluse) in his important work, *Rarorium Planta-rum Historia,* published in 1601 and written while he was holding a Professorship at Leyden University. He describes it as *Primula veris pallida flore elatior* or the Larger pale-flowered Cowslip. The bloom is also illustrated, the large individual flower pips and loose umbels (like those of the polyanthus) readily distinguishing it from the true oxlip and from the cowslip. The Elizabethan, Gerard, also identifies this hybrid oxlip when he says that the flowers 'are not so thick thrust together (as the cowslip) . . . and do not smell so pleasantly'. How right was Shakespeare when he wrote :

> I know a bank where the wild thyme grows
> Where oxlips and the nodding violet blows

for the true oxlip enjoys conditions similar to those loved by the violet.

The hybrid oxlip may be said to have rather more of the cowslip in its make-up than of the primrose, hence its liking for a more open situation than the true oxlip, which is a lover of shade and is to be found only in woods and about thickets and hedgerows. It is seldom found in open fields. *P. elatior* is a plant native only to parts of Essex, particularly around Great Bardfield, hence it often is given the name 'Bardfield Oxlip'. The flowers are of a dull, pale buff colour and are readily distinguished from those of the hybrid oxlip by their funnel-like corolla. This is entirely without the five bosses to be found in both the cowslip and primrose as well as in the hybrid oxlip and polyanthus, appearing in the throat of the flower. In the case of the Bardfield Oxlip the stems are long and elegant.

Yet another method of distinguishing between the hybrid oxlip and the true oxlip is that in the former the eye is folded, whereas with *P. elatior* it is trumpet shaped. The leaf of the hybrid oxlip is short and somewhat rounded like that of the cowslip; that of the true oxlip is longer, growing as it would seem from a short stem. Both are to be found growing best in a stiff clay soil retentive of summer moisture and both carry the delicate perfume which characterises the whole family, though that of the true oxlip is more pronounced. Finally, close comparison of the polyanthus with the two forms of the oxlip convinces us that it more closely resembles the hybrid form from which it is undoubtedly descended, with the red forms of both the cowslip and primrose playing a dominant part in the evolution of the first polyanthus.

FIRST USE OF ITS NAME

The name 'polyanthus' (from the Greek Polyanthos – 'many flowered') so used to describe the plant which, twenty years after the publication of Rea's book had become well known to gardeners, appeared first in *The Florist's Vade Mecum*, written by the Rev. Samuel Gilbert and published in 1683. He writes 'There are several oxlips or polyanthuses; I have a very large hose-in-hose of deeper or lighter reds.' Note that always the plants bore red flowers. 'All these,' he goes on, 'I had of the generous Mr Egerton.' But it is most likely that some of his plants had at one time belonged to John Rea, for Gilbert had married Rea's daughter, Miranda, and it was she who had inherited her father's nursery-garden on his death in 1681. Rea may, in fact, have been the first person ever to raise a true polyanthus bearing red blooms by artificial methods, which would be but a short step beyond the plant he described as a 'red oxlip'.

Gilbert's description of a hose-in-hose polyanthus is of interest, for more than a hundred and fifty years later Charles M'Intosh, then gardener to H.M. King Leopold of the Belgians, writing in *The Flower Garden* (1839), reports that a Mr Herbert 'raised from the natural seed of one umbel of a highly manured red cowslip, a primrose, a cowslip, oxlips of the usual and other colours, a black polyanthus, a hose-in-hose cowslip and a natural primrose, bearing its flowers on a polyanthus stalk. From the seed of that hose-in-hose cowslip, I have since raised a hose-in-hose primrose'. From this it will be seen that so great has been the degree of hybridisation amongst members of our native primula family throughout the years that to obtain a strain of polyanthus seed which would come true to type and colour, has required a considerable degree of skill on the part of the breeder in re-selection and hybridisation. This has come about only through long and careful study of the theory and practice of pollination.

Shortly after the publication of Gilbert's work, John Evelyn made reference to the polyanthus, using the word in the modern form. Evelyn was a close friend of Pepys and was founder of the Royal Society. In 1647 he had married Mary, daughter of our Ambassador in Paris, his bride being but a child of twelve years who was soon to inherit Sayes Court in Kent. Here Evelyn devoted much of his time to improving the gardens. In Evelyn's *Directions for the Gardener at Sayes Court* (1687) mention was made of the polyanthus and of its uses, for by then the plant was widely grown for spring display.

In 1728, the poet Thomson wrote in *The Seasons* of the 'Polyanthus of unnumbered dyes', this being the first reference to the plant by a poet of repute, and one making known that the colour range, though still red, was then considerable.

Philip Miller, then Curator of the Physic Garden in Chelsea, mentioned the polyanthus in his monumental *Gardener's Dictionary*, first published in 1731, describing the plant as having 'large red flowers'. Thirty years later he wrote that 'there are a great variety at present in the gardens, such as the hose-in-hose, double cowslip and all sorts of polyanthus which have been so much improved during the past fifty years as to almost equal the variety of the auricula; and in some parts of England are so much esteemed as to sell for a guinea a root'. Yet although the polyanthus now appeared in so many forms, they bore no flowers but those of various shades of red.

THE POLYANTHUS ILLUSTRATED

In 1688 appeared the first illustration of a polyanthus. This was in the *Catalogue* of the Leyden Botanical Garden in Holland and was of a plant obtained from the Botanical Garden at Oxford in the year in which the Pilgrim Fathers set sail from Plymouth. Shortly after the publication of the *Gardener's Dictionary*, there appeared the first illustration of a polyanthus in colour, and here again the flower was of a red colour. This was in John Hill's famous work, *The Vegetable Kingdom*, published in 1757, and which appeared in twenty-five volumes. This had taken Hill nearly sixteen years to write and left him so impoverished that he took to acting as a profession and later became a quack doctor to earn a living. A coloured illustration shows the polyanthus as being, in the author's own words, 'of a beautiful crimson with an eye of yellow'. In reality, however, the flowers are a purple-crimson, due to fading of the colouring, and with a yellow eye, around which was a striking circle of white which gave the bloom an auricula-like appearance. Careful inspection also reveals a thin wire edging of palest yellow from which we may deduct that the polyanthus had now taken on a new characteristic, on which its fame was to rest for the next hundred years. This was an edging or lacing of the petals of either silver or gold, which was to make the polyanthus as highly esteemed with the florists of the early nineteenth century as the auricula, the laced pink and the ranunculus. A new era in the history of the polyanthus had begun.

Exactly when the old red-flowered polyanthus took on its golden lacing is a piece of information lost in obscurity. The red colouring persisted without deviation until about the year 1750 when the blooms took on the striking golden lacing, first revealed in the illustration in John Hill's work. The golden centre may well have been passed on by crossing a red-flowered polyanthus with *Primula pubescens,* a natural hybrid of the crossing of *P. auricula* with *P. hirsuta,* and which is believed to have produced the Alpine auriculas which were known to Parkinson. Plants of *P. pubescens* are known to have been collected by the botanist Clusius towards the end of the sixteenth century and were grown in the gardens of the Emperor Maximilian II in Vienna. The modern variety 'Kingscote' has flowers of glowing scarlet-cerise with a large, clearly defined golden centre, exactly the same gold as the centre and edging of the laced polyanthus; and similar plants may have been grown in European gardens during the seventeenth century, eventually finding their way to England. The readiness with which almost all members of the primula family hybridise with each other might well have resulted in a hybrid of *P. pubescens* passing on the golden centre to the polyanthus: though this is merely conjecture, there being no record of this having taken place.

By 1760, or perhaps a year or so earlier, the gold-laced polyanthus had become one of the most widely grown of all plants. In 1759, James Justice, who introduced the pineapple to Scotland, wrote from his home at Dalkeith that 'the varieties (of the gold-laced polyanthus) which are obtained every year by the florists who save and sow these seeds, are very great'. At one time Justice was supposed to have had the finest collection of auriculus and poly-anthus in the whole of Europe but he was later forced to sell his home at which he had spent nearly forty years of his life. Several years later, the Rev. William Hanbury said that there were in his garden, at Church Langton in Leicestershire, more than a thousand varieties and 'nearly that number of auriculus'. Abercrombie also wrote in 1780 that the polyanthus had become 'one of the most noted prize (show) flowers among florists'. This was, of course, the gold-laced polyanthus, a particular variety being recognised by the ground colour and degree and quality of the lacing. Rarely is any mention made of the 'gold' lacing by writers of old; it was always 'yellow'. Mrs Jane Louden wrote, in *The Ladies' Companion to the Flower Garden* (1840), 'the colour of the flower of the poly-anthus is always yellow and brown'. It is recorded that in 1769, an exhibition of the plants was held at the home of John Barnes at Lichfield, Staffordshire, this being the earliest reference to the showing of the gold-laced polyanthus.

In 1792, James Maddock, a Quaker and a native of Warrington in Lancashire, then living at Walworth, London, published his *Florist's Directory* in which he mentions and describes in great de-tail only eight flowers as being worthy of the florist's or specialist's attention. Included among these is the gold-laced polyanthus which had, by that time, become firmly established with the most famous florists of the time. With every year from about 1750 until the end of the eighteenth century, the laced polyanthus achieved greater popularity and this was to become intensified until the second half of the nineteenth century when, for various reasons, the florist's flowers rapidly sank into obscurity. But when Maddock was writing his *Florist's Directory*, the peak of the gold-laced poly-anthus's popularity was still in the future. 'The beautiful yellow (gold) of the cowslips,' he wrote, which it did not formerly possess in the same degree of perfection it now does, has in the opinion of some been communicated to it within the present century ... thus the sorts known fifty years ago are not now in cultivation ...'

This statement by Maddock would seem to confirm that the gold lacing first appeared about 1750, but it was, of course, a true gold colouring, very different from the pale yellow of the cowslip and primrose and similar to that of the gold-centre alpine auriculas. It was as if the centre (and petal edges) had been treated with gold leaf.

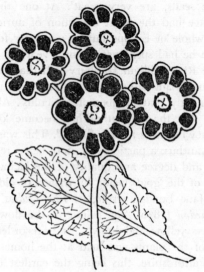

Fig. 4. The gold-laced polyanthus

Year by year the popularity of the laced polyanthus continued to increase and a little publication called *The Polyanthus* which appeared in 1844, listed ninety-six varieties as possessing outstanding qualities. By 1860, several hundred varieties could be obtained and the cult had reached its peak, about a hundred years after the laced polyanthus first appeared. Yet within twenty years, the greatest of all show winners, Pearson's 'Alexander' had completely vanished, due as we have seen to the mill with its methods of mass production, taking the place of the hand machine which was tended in the home of those who sought a little relaxation at various times of the day, in tending their pots of auriculus and gold-laced polyanthuses. When working at home, the weavers could give their plants that attention to detail which they demanded. They could leave off many times a day to give the plants water or shade them from sunlight which was not possible when the time came to work long hours in the mills away (often at a considerable distance) from home.

FAMOUS SHOW VARIETIES

Though we may never see their like again, those who are
interested in the gold-laced polyanthus may like to read the detailed
notes of the old florists' favourites as kept by William Harrison; who
Sam Barlow said was one of 'our best authorities'. The descriptions
are given as they appeared in the *Floricultural Cabinet* for July
1842 and show to what lengths the old specialist growers would go
in determining the qualities of the show polyanthus.

BARKESS'S 'BONNY BESS'. This is an old variety and has perhaps
been one of the most successful competitors ever exhibited. It will
long be grown by the Northumbrian florists as 'The Queen of the
days that are gone'. (*Does this mean that the heyday of the gold-
laced polyanthus had already passed? – Author*). For largeness of
truss I never heard of a variety that could equal 'Bonny Bess'. It is
no unusual thing for a fine circular truss of 15 or 20 pips to be
shown, and these, forming quite a ball of flowers, have a really
handsome and striking appearance. The pips are generally of a
good size, with the exception of a few central ones, the mouth of
the tube is plain, the eye is often tinged with orange, the ground
colour is dark, and the lace is light and beautifully regular. Indeed,
if this variety had been free from the trifling 'foxiness' in the eye
(smudging of the gold into the crimson ground colour) it would
not have been surpassed by any variety in existence, so large are the
trusses and so regular the lacing.

BUCKLEY'S 'CAPTAIN STARKIE'. This is a very notable variety. The
eye is a most beautiful yellow, the tube neatly elevated, the ground
colour very dark at first, but turns red, like many other varieties,
by exposure or age; and the lacing is very regular and correct; but
the indentations between the segments are over deep, this giving
the corolla a very angular appearance. With this solitary flaw it is
still a lovely and desirable variety.

BUCK'S 'GEORGE THE FOURTH'. Another good variety, possessing a
fine yellow eye, with the ground colour of a fine rich crimson. The
lacing is very regular, and the pips uncommonly circular and well
flattened. It is a good trusser, but it has the defect that it is difficult
to get five pips of a uniform size, the first two or three being
generally so much larger than the succeeding ones; notwithstanding
which objection it is a very desirable flower, and no collection
should be without it.

BURNARD'S 'FORMOSA'. This variety was figured in the *Cabinet* some years ago, and on trial it is found to be a strong and vigorous grower, the pips large and uncommonly circular, the eye a fine pure yellow, the tube beautifully elevated, and the ground a rich crimson when the corolla first expands but soon changes to dark brown, nearly approaching to black. It is a noble and attractive flower for the eye of a judge and will no doubt be a winning flower for many years to come, although it has a trifling fault as the lace seems scarcely to reach the eye in the middle of the heart-shaped segments.

CLEGG'S 'LORD CREWE'. This is one of the finest polyanthuses seen so far. As I write, a truss of eight fine full-blown pips stands before me, and I think that such a flower will very rarely be surpassed even by the most experienced cultivator. The pips are very large and regular, and the tube is beautifully elevated above the eye, perhaps disproportionately large, but of a clear strainless yellow; the ground colour very dark, and contrasting well with the purity of the eye, and the lacing neat and uncommonly regular. It is indeed a noble flower; its only fault, that I can see, is the appearance of the pips when they first come out, for they are of rather a pentangular shape, each side of the pentagon being made up of two of the 'heart-shaped segments' of the corolla; but this appearance is gradually modified after the pips have stood for some time, and they then assume a more circular appearance. This variety ought to be in the collection of every competing amateur.

COLLIER'S 'PRINCESS ROYAL'. Another excellent variety; the eye is of a beautiful stainless yellow, the ground colour heavy and very dark, the lace pretty heavy and very regular, and the tube neatly elevated above the level of the eye. It seems a very good trusser, with pips very large and flat, and is a very desirable variety.

COX'S 'PRINCE REGENT'. Another first-rate variety, though perhaps not quite so attractive as many of the foregoing. It possesses a pretty good eye, its ground colour is a darkish brown, and the lace is very regular. The pips are circular, the divisions in the corolla shallow, but the contrast between the colours of the eye and ground is not striking, and the flower has generally rather a dull appearance. It is, however, a very good trusser, with well-flattened pips.

CRAIGY'S 'BERTRAM'. A beautiful variety raised by Mr Craigy of Crawcrook, Newcastle-on-Tyne. The pips are well formed, the eye a very fine yellow, the tube neatly elevated, and the ground colour exceedingly dark. The lacing is light and uncommonly perfect. It

Gold-laced Polyanthus –
Burnard's Formosa (from
an old print dated 1834)

Gold-laced polyanthus
blooms are ideal for floral
decoration in miniature
vases

A fine gold-laced
polyanthus (from a
coloured engraving of 1847)

A modern gold-laced
polyanthus

promises therefore, to be one of the finest varieties in cultivation and when 'come-at-able' will command the admiration of everyone who cultivates it. I have placed it beside Maude's Beauty of England and some of the best varieties noticed last year. I have no hesitation in pronouncing it equal to the best of them.

ECKERSLEY'S 'BLACK AND GOLD'. Another worth-while variety. The tube is neatly elevated, the eye is a very fine yellow, and although it comes occasionally tinged with orange, or 'foxy', to the florists' term, the ground colour a fine dark velvet almost black, and the lacing very correct and neat. It is a good trusser, and well worthy of cultivation by the competing florist. I do not find it in any of the south-country catalogues, but it is plentiful in the north-east, and I think should be in every collection.

ECKERSLEY'S 'JOLLY DRAGOON'. Another good polyanthus, of the red-ground class. The pips are of a good size, the eye a fine yellow, the ground colour a reddish scarlet, and the lace neat. It is well worthy of cultivation by the competing amateur.

FLETCHER'S 'DEFIANCE'. This is another very excellent polyanthus, and is all but a stranger in the north of England. However, I think it will, in future, obtain a place among the very best in cultivation here. The pips are beautifully circular, as the divisions in the corolla between the segments is not so deep as in many other varieties, and for perfect flatness of the pips I think it superior to any variety that I have as yet met with. The tube is very beautifully elevated above the level of the eye; the eye itself is perfectly free from all tinge of orange, and the ground colour a dark brown, but a little inclined to bronze next to the eye; the lace is quite regular and meets the eye perfectly in the middle of each division of the corolla. On comparing it with the far-famed Pearson's 'Alexander' (of which I shall speak presently), I think it is not such a showy and taking flower for the eye of a judge, but it is certainly a much better one, and boasts far finer properties.

MAUDE'S 'BEAUTY OF ENGLAND'. This is another very beautiful polyanthus, but it seems to me so similar to Pearson's 'Alexander', that it would require very exacting judges to distinguish the difference. I have placed them side by side, and must say that the same description will apply to both; but I think the tube of Maude's 'Beauty' is a little elevated and the truss perhaps larger and more regular; and, as with Clegg's 'Prince of Orange', the pips are all of one height and nearly all in bloom together. This, I hope, will give it the advantage over the 'Alexander', for I have only bought it this spring and therefore can only boast of a slight acquaintance with it.

PARK'S 'LORD NELSON'. Considered one of the very best in the north, it will, I think, continue to be a favourite. The flower is somewhat similar to Pearson's 'Alexander', but a stronger and more vigorous grower. The eye is very fine, the ground colour very dark and the lacing extremely regular.

PEARSON'S 'ALEXANDER'. This has long been the leading favourite in the north of England but I think it will now have great difficulty in always carrying off the first prize as it has hitherto done. It is certainly a beautiful flower but far from faultless. I have just now a truss of five fine large pips standing before me and I must say that it is difficult to conceive that anything can be produced more beautiful by the magic wand of nature. The eye is a beautiful yellow, the ground colour exceedingly dark, and the lacing perfectly regular and correct, features which, allied with the fine contrast in the colours, produce a very showy and attractive plant. On looking at it closely, however, its warmest admirers must admit that the divisions in the corolla extend half-way down through the eye, which makes the outsides of the heart-shaped segments very apt to droop and thus spoil the flatness of the pips; and that pretty elevation of the mouth of the tube, which is so great a decorataion to the pips of 'Lord Crewe', Fletcher's 'Defiance', and others, is also wanting in this variety, as the mouth of the tube is quite plain and flattened with the eye. These are all the faults I can see in Pearson's 'Alexander'.

RIDDLE'S 'MINNA TROIL'. A pretty variety of the dark-ground class, raised in 1842 by Mr Riddle, gardener to Mrs Mitford of Mitford Castle. A truss of nine pips was exhibited at the Felton exhibition on the 8th of May (1843), and obtained the seedling prize. The eye is a very fine pure yellow, the mouth of the tube being beautifully elevated above the level of the eye; the ground colour a fine dark velvet and the lacing light or narrow. The lacing was a trifle scarred in two or three places out of the nine pips but this is a trifling fault compared with its many good properties.

STEAD'S 'TELEGRAPH'. A very pretty polyanthus, the ground colour rich darkish scarlet, the lacing regular, and the tube neatly elevated. The truss which I saw consisted of five pips, and was only on a small plant, but they were of a large size and good form. It is a very pretty and estimable variety of the class to which it belongs.

TURNER'S 'EMPEROR BONAPARTE'. Another good polyanthus, the eye of a good yellow, the ground colour dark, and the lace light and neat. As it has only been lately brought into this neighbourhood, I cannot say more than it seems a very good and desirable variety. WILSON'S 'BUCEPHALAS'. A seedling raised by that esteemed and veteran florist, Mr John Wilson of Newcastle, one of the fathers of 'the fancy' on the banks of the 'coaly Tyne'. It is a very good polyanthus, but has the great defect of being rather a shy trusser. It is really difficult to get five good pips expanded at one time. For my part I have grown it for three seasons, and have never succeeded in accomplishing this until this season, and a truss of five full-blown pips now stands before me. The eye and markings are somewhat similar to those of Pearson's 'Alexander', already described, the lacing much about the same, and the divisions in the corolla rather deep. I think the pips are slightly cupped, but yet it is a beautiful and distinct addition to our collections, and does great credit to the fortunate raiser. This variety was raised from seed gathered from 'Alexander', and was in consequence named after the favourite war-horse of that mighty monarch.

These descriptions, which are given in great detail, should provide a valuable guide for what to look for in a new seedling, for it will be on past standards of perfection that new introductions will be judged.

These interesting old polyanthuses bear blooms which have a golden centre, a red or black ground, and gold lacing round the petals. The body or ground colour is generally black, crimson, red or intermediate shades, and there has never been a laced polyanthus with a ground of any other colour, apart from shades of red in varying degrees of intensity.

Though most of the old florists' favourites have long since disappeared, a few may still be found in cottage gardens. In October 1961, in a letter to the author, a Mr Masters of Camber in Sussex told that his family had been growing polyanthuses and primroses is the same garden for more than 160 years, since about the year 1800 and that he had in his collection a polyanthus of maroon-black ground colour and with silver lacing, yet it was believed that all traces of the rare silver-laced varieties had vanished years ago.

Even more recently in an Irish cottage garden, the author was shown plants of the old silver-laced double polyanthus, Silver Annie which has flowers of similar mulberry colouring. The lacing is in no way refined but the bloom is semi-double and bears pollen from which it may be possible to raise double polyanthuses in interesting new colours and with the attractive lacing.

Writing in the 1950 *Year Book* of the Northern Section of the National Primula Society, the late Mr Dan Bamford of Middleton said: 'We are going to have a more difficult job of resuscitation here than with the auriculas, as we have so few parents left . . . I think 'Tiny' is the most refined . . .' This variety is one of the few named gold-laced polyanthuses exhibited in the early years of this century and still obtainable.

In America a serious attempt has been made to revive the gold-laced polyanthus chiefly through the enthusiasm of Mr Peter Klein of Tecoma who, unfortunately, died before achieving his ambition of raising a strain worthy of comparison with the favourites of old.

The story of how the gold-laced polyanthus first came to America is told in a letter from Dr Lester Smith, D.Sc., which appeared in the *Journal of the Royal Horticultural Society* in October 1948. He writes: 'I have had a fascinating account of how the gold-laced polyanthus came to America, in which the writer says, 'Some ten or 15 years ago Mr Briggs (then Secretary of the Northern Section of the National Primula Society) sent a few gold-laced seeds which he had from one of the two main growers there. The grower's gardens had been bombed in the war and his plants blown quite some distance away . . . He started out to gather up what fragments he could find and from that meagre re-beginning these few seeds came to me.' Dr Smith continued: 'It appears that Peter Klein obtained his original stock from Florence Bellis (of Barnhaven Gardens) and practised further selection to improve the strain.' Such was the quality of Peter Klein's strain that the American Primrose Society printed a letter in the 1962 edition of their magazine from Mr Dan Bamford of England in which he said: 'The seedling gold-laced Polyanthus illustrated on the cover of the Fall issue and raised by Peter Klein is the best gold-laced seedling I have seen for over 50 years.' Alas, Peter Klein has passed on and his nursery has been sold. It will thus have to be left to others to carry on the work of reviving the gold-laced polyanthus in America.

Already, interesting results are forthcoming; flowers with almost perfect lacing, conforming in so many ways to the definition of a gold-laced polyanthus as given by the old florists, are now the rule rather than the exception. From this point, amateur growers could take the revival a step further for, unlike the green-edged show auriculas for example, which were the result of mutations (the petals being replaced by leafy structures) and which do not respond to line breeding, the gold-laced polyanthus responds well, while here and there in country cottage gardens, some of the old laced polyanthuses may still survive to form the nucleus of a new collection.

PREPARATION OF THE SOIL

'The soil in which I find the polyanthus to flower best is a strong fresh loam with one-sixth of well-rotted cow's dung, a small portion of sand or gravel intermixed, and about one-fourth of leaf mould,' wrote a grower of old, which is sound common sense today. And it is of interest to recall the advice given by M'Intosh in *The Flower Garden,* in which he says that 'The soil, if we may judge from the places where they grow native, must be tenacious, moist and not too rich.' James Douglas in *Hardy Florist's Flowers* writes : '. . . the polyanthus will succeed in almost any kind of soil but they certainly give the best results when it is of a moderately clayey nature.' Which is so, if additional humus materials are incorporated in the soil in order to open it up, so that bacterial activity may take place and to ensure that the soil is able to retain moisture during summer.

M'Intosh tells us of the method of growing adopted by Revell, the foremost grower of gold-laced polyanthuses of the time (1839). The compost he used consisted of 'light maiden soil, horse dung six weeks old, and leaf mould', the manure being in very limited doses; but so much depends upon the soil and upon the forms of humus to be most readily obtained. M'Intosh tells us that polyanthuses and primroses may be found growing 'in the toughest clay,' which is certainly true. But clay which is shaded and moist and containing plenty of humus, is very different to clay baked dry and hard by the sun, and which is useless for polyanthus growing. A clay soil must be enriched with humus to provide moisture-holding material during summer, and to facilitate winter drainage. Should the soil become waterlogged during winter, the polyanthus roots will die.

A particularly heavy soil, often to be found when making a new garden, should first be treated with caustic (unhydrated) lime.

The action of the lime as it disintegrates serves to break up the clay particles to a considerable degree. As the polyanthus grows best in a soil with a pH value between 6.5 and 7.0, which is only slightly acid in reaction (requiring the same soil conditions as the strawberry), a dressing of lime should be provided to correct any marked tendency to acidity, especially in the soil of a town garden. In early autumn, when the display of summer-flowering plants will be at an end, the beds should be cleared and made ready to take the polyanthus plants. The soil should be enriched with humus, its nature depending upon materials most readily obtainable.

Peat of good quality is excellent, likewise old mushroom-bed compost, which may be obtained by the sackful through advertisements in the gardening papers. After it has grown a crop of mushrooms, the compost will have become well broken up and will be in a suitable condition for working into the soil. Poplar bark fibre is also valuable and readily absorbs and holds moisture in much the same way as peat. Chopped seaweed manure is also an efficient soil conditioner for it will break up a clay soil and at the same time impart valuable trace elements. Seaweed manure, called 'Alginure', which contains sodium alginate, will break up a clay soil and help to bind a sandy soil.

Clearings from ditches and drains also contain valuable humus; and leaf mould, provided that it is true mould and not just dead leaves; hop manure; and shoddy, readily obtainable in the north, will also be valuable. The material should be deeply dug in as the ground is being cleared of all perennial weeds. Where it can be obtained some well-decayed cow or farmyard manure should be incorporated, for this, like the shoddy and the hops, will provide valuable plant food in addition to the humus.

A valuable supply of both humus and plant food may be obtained by composting moistened straw with an activator. Where it can be obtained, incorporate some dry poultry manure to encourage the straw to heat up and make the heap as high as possible.

Where the soil is heavy and the garden low-lying, it will be advisable to raise the bed several inches above the surrounding ground. This will allow excess moisture to drain away during winter. If the ground is low-lying, and winter moisture is apt to be retained, a quantity of weathered boiler ash, gravel or shingle from seashore or riverbank should be incorporated, to provide additional drainage.

Potash, which is so necessary to accentuate the colourings of the flowers of the modern polyanthuses, may be provided in the form of wood or bonfire ash which has been stored dry; or a one ounce per sq yd dressing of sulphate of potash may be provided. This is raked into the surface of the soil during spring, but if a dressing can also be given in autumn, it will help young plants to withstand a severe winter. An autumn dressing is not necessary for established plants.

A light, sandy soil will usually be a hungry soil, plant food being too readily washed away, thus making it necessary to replenish with humus and fertilisers at regular intervals if a good polyanthus display is to be enjoyed. Also, a light sandy soil will be too loose and will dry out too rapidly during periods of drought unless it is well fortified with humus to bind the soil particles.

When growing polyanthuses on a commercial scale on Sedgemoor in Somerset, where the ground was low-lying and the soil was light and sandy, it was necessary to incorporate as much as ten tons of humus to the acre if watering was to be kept within reason during May and June. Even then, vast quantities of water were needed on most days during a dry period to keep the plants from wilting and to enable them to build up strong crowns to bloom in profusion the following season.

In partial shade a light soil, well enriched with humus, should be capable of supporting healthy plant growth even during periods of prolonged dryness. Peat, used hops, shoddy, old mushroom-bed compost and decayed farmyard manure should be used as liberally as possible, incorporating to a depth of at least 18 inches. Where several of these organic manures cannot be readily obtained, use peat or leaf mould and give the beds a dressing with hoof and horn or bone meal at the rate of 2 oz per sq yd, working this in with the humus. Or you may as you would with a clay soil, provide a dressing of Alginure. Apart from a light dressing of sulphate of potash in early spring, to give additional richness of colour, the polyanthus requires no inorganic fertilisers. They only tend to scorch the roots and produce unnatural forcing conditions which the plants will not tolerate.

Plants grown in a well prepared soil, which does not readily dry out in summer and which is given an annual mulch of decayed manure should retain their freshness and vigour for more than just a single year. Again, where grown in partial shade, the plants will retain their vigour for a longer time than they would if growing in a position which is exposed to the direct rays of the sun through most of the day. Regular top dressing of the beds in summer, and syringing the plants during the evening on all unduly warm days, will do much to maintain the plants in a healthy condition for several seasons. The polyanthus, is, after all, a perennial and should be treated as such. But after flowering for two years the plants may have grown so large that they will require dividing. However, if they still appear fresh and have not formed too much woody rootstock (which tends to push up the plant out of the soil, thus depriving the new crown roots of nourishment), they may well be left to bloom for another season before they are lifted and divided. So as to maintain the display, some growers lift half the plants after two seasons, and after replenishing the bed the lifted roots are divided and the offsets are replanted in the ground previously occupied by the plants. They will not produce many blooms the first season after this, but will give an abundance the following year when the original plants should in their turn be removed. Where growing in the same bed as other perennials, these plants may be given the same treatment. There will thus be a continuation of bloom over the years, though every so often it will be advisable to clear the bed of polyanthuses so as to give the soil a rest from this plant for a year or so.

THE TIME TO LIFT AND DIVIDE THE PLANTS

The correct time to lift and divide the polyanthus has long remained a debating point among gardeners and even with specialist growers. While it is now usual to recommend that this must be governed by soil, climate and situation. After it has flowered the polyanthus will continue to grow, and build up a strong plant to bloom the following spring, until the end of August when it begins to die back; and from that time until early spring will enjoy a period of dormancy. During summer, fresh crowns or offsets will be continually forming around the parent plant but they will become more vigorous and form a more active rooting system if they are detached from the older plant. Planted on their own, they have more room in which to develop and more access to nourishment than if left attached to the old plant. Failure to divide frequently will cause the centre portion to lose vigour, the roots being unable to obtain sufficient food and moisture, so that the quality of bloom will deteriorate. Regular division is, therefore, important to maintain vigour; it is also an inexpensive method of increasing the stock.

Exactly when to divide will, however, be governed by soil and climate. To divide immediately after blooming will mean dividing during the usually hot, dry month of June, and however well the ground has been prepared this is never a suitable time to establish new plantings either by offsets, root diversions or seedlings. It will be better to delay dividing the plants until early July, for this is almost always a damp, humid month with heavy dew at night. If the work is done early in the month, the plants will quickly re-establish themselves and will have about ten weeks in which to make new growth before the dormant winter period. But where the soil is light and well drained, the plants may be lifted and divided until almost the year's end, or until the first hard frosts. If bloom is required the following spring, lifting and dividing should be completed by the end of July to enable the plants to become thoroughly established before autumn.

Those plants which are to be grown for cut flowers should be re-planted in prepared ground where they are to bloom; but where required for spring bedding, they should be split up and planted in a shady part of the garden where they will remain until October. It may be that the plants will have occupied a bed for two seasons or more and are ready for removing. This should be done towards the end of May so that the beds may be planted with summer-flowering plants. In this case it will be better to replant into partially shaded ground enriched with humus. If kept watered, the plants should be able to withstand a dry June. If the flowering beds are in shade, the plants may be divided and replanted where they are to bloom the following year, after the soil has been enriched with humus, and they may be interplanted with summer-flowering plants. But wherever possible it is a wise rule to lift and divide during the last six months of the year, July being the most suitable time, and to allow the plants to remain undisturbed during the first six months. Liberties may be taken where the plants are growing on the western side of Britain, where the winter climate is less severe and where a damp, humid atmosphere persists almost the whole year round. In the mild, damp climate of the south-west, dividing may be done at almost any time, though for a satisfactory display either in the open or under glass, July will, as elsewhere, be the best month for the work.

Those who may have a polyanthus (and primrose) border to lift and divide may carry out the work over a period of two years, after which time it will be necessary to begin all over again (rather like painting the Forth Bridge). The work may be done when one's programme and the conditions of soil and climate permit, the plants being lifted and placed in boxes while the ground is cleared and refortified. The plants are then divided and replanted before a start is made on another section. In this way, the work will not become irksome, and there will be little or no loss of colour in the border. In suggesting this systematic process of renewal, Donetta Klaber, writing in the *Journal of the American Primrose Society,* concludes, 'with what pride one looks at the finished bit, dark (well nourished) soil and green and perky plants.'

DIVIDING THE PLANTS

Polyanthus plants should be lifted with care so that the fibrous roots, especially those near the surface, will be in no way damaged. Carefully shake away all surplus soil then, firmly holding the plant, pull apart the various crowns. Miss Frances Perry uses the word 'tease' to describe this parting of the crowns. In this way each crown will come away with its full quota of fibrous roots, and there will be no open wounds as is the case if the plants are cut into sections. M'Intosh has also written that 'by cutting away the slips (offsets) with a knife, there is a tendency to destroy the root', and those who have ever used a knife for root division will recall that the offsets may come apart clearly but entirely without roots. Just 'tease' them apart gently; for every crown, however small, will grow into a flowering plant. A writer in the *Floricultural Cabinet* said : 'I part them by rending them in pieces, as they never do well afterwards if separated with a knife.'

Where the plants have formed large clumps, which they will do if given good cultivation, they should be lifted and divided like any other herbaceous plant, by placing two border forks back to back at the centre of the plant and gently prising apart. The two sections may then be divided as described into numerous offsets and these should be removed to a cool, shaded place without delay and replanted as soon as possible; any pieces of old, decayed rootstock should be destroyed. Any unduly large leaves of the retained plants may be screwed off about three inches above the crown before replanting, in the same way as when lifting and removing the tops of beetroot, for it is not necessary for the plants to have to re-establish these coarse outer leaves. 'I remove all the outer leaves with the exception of one or two of the innermost,' writes a grower of exhibition polyanthuses. The writers of old recommend removing any unduly long tap roots so as to encourage the formation of more vigorous new roots.

Offsets with new and smaller leaves should be replanted without the removal of any foliage, for those young leaves will catch the dew and rains and direct the moisture to the roots, thus enabling the plants to become more quickly established. The offsets should be set well into the ground 'so that the leaves are close upon it; this is required in order that the new roots, which are produced very high up the stem (crown) of the plant, may be able to strike into the soil'. The offsets should be pressed down firmly with the hand, or with the foot where the soil is friable. They must be kept well watered until established.

Small pieces, provided they contain a root, however small, may be grown on but are best planted in beds to themselves, where they may be given that little extra care until they have formed a vigorous new rooting system. With such a plant, as much foliage as possible should be removed so that it will not have to support excess foliage when endeavouring to form new roots. To provide as much help as possible, a shaded position should be selected, and one sheltered from strong winds which would tend to dry out the sparse roots and cause the plant to die back before becoming established.

Though all members of the primrose family may be lifted and divided when in bud or full bloom, this is not advisable, for some bloom will usually be damaged and the plants will become more quickly established when the flower stems are removed. It is thus better to wait until July.

Plants moved during autumn should have almost all the old dead foliage removed before replanting.

EXHIBITING

There is now a welcome revival in the popularity of the gold-laced polyanthus; and as it is primarily a plant for the show bench, we may consider its exhibition qualities first.

Although the gold-laced polyanthus was exhibited more than any other flower during the period 1760-1860 it was not until 1878, five years after the first show was organised by the then National Auricula Society, that a recognised Class was introduced for the plant. This was at the instigation of Sam Barlow of Castleton, but the popularity of the gold-laced polyanthus on the show bench was by then very much on the wane and immediately after Barlow's death, the Class was discontinued. It was not until after the first world war that prominence was given to the ordinary polyanthus on the show bench, from which time its popularity as an exhibition flower has progressed simultaneously with its popularity as a garden plant. Indeed the ordinary polyanthus has, for many years, replaced the old gold-laced form, which was almost always grown in pots, not being considered a suitable flower for garden decoration. This is because the flowers have a tendency to fade slightly where exposed to full sunlight, and have too dark a ground colour for them to be widely used for planting in the shade necessary for them to be at their best. For these reasons they have always been grown as an exhibitor's flower, protected from adverse weather and scorching sun; and the garden is all too often deprived of their great beauty. Yet even a few plants grouped together by the side of a path, in a border or in the alpine garden, will provide so much of interest in the garden in spring time.

A position of partial shade will suit them best, and will be suitable for other polyanthus strains being grown for exhibition. If grown in an orchard, the leaves of the trees will be unfolding as the plants reach their full beauty and will act as a foil for the intense colouring of the blooms. Now, happily, a new generation of lovers of the old gold-laced polyanthus is trying to bring back this plant to its former glory and once again there are classes for the exhibiting of these plants at all the national shows.

METHODS OF THE OLD FLORISTS

As there is now this revival of interest in the culture of the gold-laced polyanthus, the method followed by the recognised champion growers of the day are of interest.

John Revell of Sheffield, in *The Floricultural Cabinet* for September 1834, wrote: 'Those plants I intend for show . . . I plant in August, for if done sooner they are in bloom too soon for the shows . . . In parting the old roots, I cut off all the leaves, then pot them in the above-stated compost (3 barrows of maiden soil: 1 of horse dung six weeks old; 1 of decayed leaf mould) and place them in a shady situation where I let them remain until November at which time I remove them to their winter situation, a pit built of brick and sunk two feet below the level of the surface of the soil, so that when the pots are placed in the pit, the rims are no higher than the surrounding surface; this pit is covered with wooden shutters, instead of glass, in order to secure the plants from the effects of sudden frosts during winter. I suffer them to receive all the gentle showers that fall during February and March.'

He continues: 'When in blow (bloom), I carefully shade them from the sun's rays; for if I was to suffer them to be exposed, the colour of the flower would be damaged, if not totally spoiled. I find that if the plants are placed in perfect darkness for two or three days previous to the show, the colour becomes much darker than if left in the frame.'

'Innovator', whose name hides the identity of a famous grower of his day, had this to say about his cultural methods. '. . . I pot them in 24 or 16 sized pots according to the size of the plants, never placing more than one crown in each pot; if any plant possesses two or more crowns, I part them by rending them in pieces . . . I then cut off all the old leaves with the exception of one or two of the innermost and pot them in the following compost: 2 barrows of good rich loam, one of half fresh horse droppings, and half a barrow of cow dung. In potting, I place a small oyster shell over the hole in the bottom of each pot and upon this a little moss is placed and then it is filled to within 2 inches of the top with the compost which is put in as to form a cone; upon ths cone the plant is placed with the roots spread out equally on all sides. I then cover with the compost until the crown is scarcely visible: after this I water them but I always take care that it does not settle in the heart of the plants as it would rot them.'

He goes on, 'As the plants grow I keep earthing them up with fresh compost for on this depends the whole success of growing them in pots. As soon as the plants are potted, which I always perform about the end of August, I plunge them in saw-dust placed under a north wall or fence and always taking care to shelter them from cold, rains or sleet; here I let them remain until the beginning of December. I then remove them into a shady place and cover them by means of an awning from sun and rain but give them plenty of manure water. As soon as the bloom is over, I turn them with their balls of earth entire, into a bed previously prepared for them, under a north wall. In doing this, I am careful to plant them at least one inch deeper than they were in the pots. I find it best when this is done to tie up the leaves as with lettuce, for a fortnight or so; by which time they will have made fresh roots by every eye under ground (from around the crown of the plant) . . .'

THE POLYANTHUS IN POTS

Not only for exhibition but for display in a light, airy window for a porch, or a cold greenhouse, the polyanthus makes a most attractive pot plant, remaining in bloom for fully a month. The plants require no heat, indeed they will not tolerate any, and apart from an occasional watering they will require no further attention.

The most suitable plants will be unflowered seedlings which were sown in July or August, transplanted in spring, and grown on in outdoor beds in partial shade until ready for lifting and potting the following March. The plants will, by then, have made large clumps and will send up a number of flower stems, coming into bloom several weeks earlier than when flowering in the open. Growing in pots in a cool place will prolong the polyanthus season by several weeks.

The plants should be lifted just as they begin to make new growth, early in March in the north, a fortnight earlier in the south. This will allow the plants time to become established before coming into bloom, though in an article appearing in the *Journal of the Royal Horticultural Society* in January 1956, Mr Allan Langdon, V.M.H., of the famous Bath firm, wrote : 'lifting and potting can be done at any time . . . and I have seen plants lifted with buds showing, and which have made lovely pot plants, showing no signs of distress through having their roots disturbed.' This confirms the observation of John Clare to the effect that the plants may be lifted when in full bloom, the cowslip and primrose behaving in the same way as the polyanthus.

The potting compost should consist of a friable loam, preferably from old pastureland, in which have been incorporated some moist peat or leaf mould and some decayed manure, preferably cow manure. Where this is unobtainable, a pinch of bone meal should be given to each 48-size pot. After the pots have been well crocked, the compost is added, the best method being to fill up the pots to about half-way, over which the roots are spread out. Additional soil is then packed around the roots and made quite firm. The plant is then well watered in.

Throughout their days in the pots, the plants should be shaded whenever the sun's rays become troublesome, and they should be given as much ventilation as is necessary to maintain a buoyant atmosphere. The foliage should be syringed frequently, and an occasional application of diluted liquid manure will bring the flower trusses to perfection. And, as ever, there must be no lack of air and water.

Plants in pots may be taken into any cool room, but so that the stems shall not become 'drawn' it will be advisable to delay their moving until the buds begin to show colour. After flowering, the plants should be removed from the pots, divided, and replanted into a shaded bed outdoors. If the methods suggested by the florists of old are followed, attempts at the culture of polyanthus in pots are likely to be entirely successful.

PREPARING PLANTS FOR EXHIBITION

When preparing plants for exhibition, it may be advisable to lightly disbud the flower trusses as soon as the buds have formed, so that the blooms will not be overcrowded and will be able to open, each one to perfection. Some disbudding will also encourage the individual blooms to attain their maximum size. The centre bud should be removed, for this will generally be smaller than the others and may upset the balance of the truss. 'If you intend to exhibit, you must thin out all superfluous buds,' wrote John Slater, 'those at the centre are the best to be taken away.' Revell never allowed more than seven pips nor less than five (blooms) to remain on a stem, and if any pips were cup-shaped or turned backwards, he would flatten them out with an ivory 'flattener', shaped like a button-hook, as used for auricula bloom. Pips of the gold-laced varieties were dusted with a camel-hair brush to remove dust and give then added lustre. Revell has also said that 'if the plants are placed in perfect darkness for two or three days previous to the show, the ground colour becomes much darker.'

The gold-laced polyanthus, with its smaller bloom, will respond better to this treatment than will the modern large-flowered strains, but it is agreed that all polyanthus bloom destined for exhibition should be given detailed attention. The plants should be sheltered from rain and from the sun's rays as soon as the bloom begins to show colour, for exposure to the direct rays of the sun will take the colour from the bloom as much as if it were growing in excessive shade. Plants growing in pots in a frame or greenhouse should be sheltered from the sun by whitening the inside of the glass, or by fastening brown paper inside the glass on the southerly side. Another method is to insert the pots in rows in the ground so that they are almost touching each other, and to cover with cloches whitened on the inside. By this method the pots will obtain moisture from the ground and will not require so much watering, which is usually necessary for plants growing in pots. It is imperative that the compost should never be allowed to become dry, and the foliage will benefit from a daily syringing with clear water, not only to maintain freshness but also to guard against red spider.

Where only one or two plants are to be exhibited, whether of gold-laced or of other strains, a polythene bag may be placed over the plant and tied to the pot. In this way, the bloom will be protected from rain and soot deposits.

To have the bloom at its best on the day of the show calls for experience and skill in timing. In some seasons the bloom may be too advanced, in others it may be retarded, and both faults are due to inexperience. A more humid atmosphere will help to bring on the bloom and shading may be reduced, but it should be remembered that the polyanthus will resent undue forcing, which will only result in long, weakly stalks and a bloom which will lack colour. To retard the bloom, which may open too soon and will lose some of its quality by show day, a more buoyant atmosphere and more shading should be provided, but here again to shade too long, to deprive the plants of ordinary light, quite apart from sunlight, will only result in a pale-coloured bloom and 'drawn' stems. Though as the old florists discovered, to place the plants in total darkness for 48 hours prior to the show, will greatly enhance the ground colour. Much will depend upon the weather, and from the beginning of April the plants should be observed with care, brought on or retarded as the weather dictates. Too much rain reaching the blooms or excessive sunshine will certainly prevent the gold-laced varieties from being exhibited at their best, but the ordinary polyanthuses are much more able to combat adverse conditions, hence their greater popularity with the modern gardener.

When you take the plants to the exhibition hall, the pots should be quite clean, and it is advisable to fasten the flower stems to a small wooden stick to protect the truss from breakage. It should be remembered that the stems, though strong, will have to support a heavy weight, with possibly a dozen or more blooms open together. The stem should be made secure immediately beneath the truss and again lower down the stem, with ties of wide raffia which will not cut through the stem, should the plant on its journey be subjected to any shaking. The pots should be placed four or six to a wooden box and they should be shaded from strong sunlight. Should any pips (blooms) have become damaged, possibly at the edges, they should be removed, together with the footstalk; and though this may upset the balance of the truss it is better thus in the eyes of the judges than if spoilt by a single damaged bloom.

In most shows, there is a class for cut polyanthus bloom of the ordinary strains, and this will allow the enthusiast considerable liberty in selection and arrangement. Here, not only quality but selection of colours will play a part and with the modern strains, especially those from America, some outstanding new colours may be introduced, though of course quality will come first.

If a dozen blooms are to be exhibited, then at least 20 should be taken to the show, so that the best may be selected on the show bench, and this will allow for any damage to stem or bloom on the journey. The blooms should be fully open, but only just so, if they are to travel well and be exhibited at their best. Cut with as long a stem as can be managed early on the day of the show and place the stems in cold water. After giving a drink for as long as possible, carefully dry the stems before packing into either a wooden or cardboard flower box. Each stem should be placed separately in the box, rolls of good quality tissue paper being placed beneath each flower head to lend support. The stems should also rest on paper rolls to prevent breaking. They are held in position by placing thin canes across the box. When exhibiting in pots, each variety or a particular strain or seedling of an unnamed polyanthus which has been raised from seed by the exhibitor, should be clearly named on the small cards supplied by the show societies. The gold-laced polyanthus is classed with the Show and Alpine auriculas, in that a plant should bear a minimum of five expanded blooms, and this will be confined to a single main stem. No packing is allowed between the footstalks so as to help in the correct placement of the blooms, but cotton-wool placed between the footstalks may be used for conveying the plants to the show. It should be removed, together with the stick to support the stem, as soon as the plant reaches the show bench.

MERITS OF THE GOLD-LACED POLYANTHUS

The merits of a good gold-laced polyanthus as laid down by the old florists have been changed but little since the first of the florists, James Maddock described the qualities of the gold-laced polyanthus in his *Florists' Directory* (1792) which began what may be described as the Golden Age of the gold-laced polyanthus.

As the cult gained in strength, with more and more shows being held throughout the North and Midlands each year, others formed their rules for a meritorious gold-laced polyanthus. The year 1834 saw the publication of George Glenny's *Properties of Flowers,* which eventually became the standard authority on the qualities of the florist's flowers. There was, however, greater need for uniformity of rules according to which the qualities of the gold-laced polyanthus were to be judged; and on 19th March 1834, a sub-committee of the Cambridgeshire Horticulture Society was appointed 'to draw up Rules by which in future, florists' flowers should be adjudged'; and amongst five other signatures was that of Richard Headley of auricula fame. Ten flowers were considered as being worthy of special recognition, and for the polyanthus, they framed the following rules:

'The pips large, flat and round, with small indentures between each division of the limb, dividing the pip into heart-like segments, edged with bright yellow; the edge and the eye ought to be of the same colour; the truss to consist of not less than five full-blown pips, supported on a strong stem, standing well above the foliage.' The truss, it will be noted, should have not less than five opened blooms, but James Douglas in *Hardy Florist's Flowers* suggests the number should be seven. Yet during the heyday of the gold-laced polyanthus as few as three blooms were allowed, so great was the desire to attain perfection. This, however, did not take into consideration the symmetry of the truss; and the natural form of the polyanthus bloom was given little or no consideration.

In a letter which appeared in the *Gardeners' Chronicle* in 1840, Dr Lindley described the properties of a gold-laced polyanthus:

'The pip of the polyanthus should be large and the nearer the outline approaches a circle the better; it should be free from any unevenness, and lie perfectly flat; the edge must be smooth, and the divisions in the corolla, which form it into heart-shaped segments, should reach the eye, but not cut into it. The segments should be well rounded, making the division between them small and shallow. The tube must be of a fine yellow, round and clearly defined, well filled with anthers, and terminating in a narrow ridge, raised slightly above the surface of the eye. The eye should be of a bright rich yellow colour, of a uniform width round the tube. The ground colour must be entire, free from specks or blemishes, of a dark or rich crimson, not paler at the edges, and uniform in every division. The edge should form a narrow and well-defined rim of yellow, perfectly regular, bordering each segment, and passing down the centre of each division to the eye. It is essential that the edge and the eye be of a uniform yellow. These qualities in the pips, and the flower forming a compact truss, standing well above the foliage, on a firm upright stem, will constitute perfection in the Polyanthus.'

Samuel Barlow, the aforementioned authority of the gold-laced polyanthus during the mid-19th century, advocated that the bloom should be between three-quarters and seven eighths of an inch diameter; it should be flat, perfectly circular and smooth; the petals to be without serrations. Each bloom to be composed of five or six petals, the gold edging or lacing being continued down the inside segments of petals and round the outside, though the slight overlapping obscures the lacing down the insides.

The blooms should be thrum- or moss-eyed. One that is pin-eyed, that is, having its anthers near the base of the tube and the stigma protruding from it, will be disqualified by any judge however fine the bloom may otherwise appear. The reason why the pin-eyed bloom came to be so despised was, in the words of one old writer, that 'the flower shows a charm very unpleasant to the eye of the curious florist'. The anthers should curl slightly inwards completely to cover the stigma in the tube. The tube should be perfectly round and placed exactly at the centre of the bloom. It should also not exceed one-third of an inch in diameter. It is important that the lacing be thin, of regular width, and unbroken, while the body or ground colour should not in any way 'run into either the lacing of the centre or eye, which should be perfectly circular and of a clear golden colour'. The ground or body colour should be either black or crimson-red. Sam Barlow called it 'Indian Red', and it should have a velvet-like texture. In the perfect gold-laced bloom, the ground colour should occupy three-quarters of the diameter from the edge of the centre or eye to the edge of the petals, the lacing occupying one quarter. Of the whole bloom, the tube and golden centre should occupy exactly half the diameter. Quite often the centre will be too large with the result that there will be insufficient ground colour. Or again, the ground colouring may occupy too large an area to the exclusion of the golden centre and edging, thus giving the bloom a dull appearance. Nor should there be any difference in colour between the centre and the lacing. If very pale yellow or deep orange colouring, as the centre will sometimes be, this is a fault. Likewise where the ground is of a pale red colouring, a condition known to the old growers as 'foxy', or where it shades out towards the lacing, the bloom will be unlikely to obtain commendation on the show bench. Sometimes the lacing will be found to be too thick and irregular and so will give the bloom a less rich appearance than where there is the correct amount of ground colour. Samuel Barlow has said that 'a first-class gold-laced polyanthus will "fetch" one at a glance by its brilliant appearance,' and how right he was. The perfect bloom has yet to be raised, but what fascination the gold-laced polyanthus holds for its admirers both as an exhibition flower and in the garden!

It may be noted that Dr Lindley suggested that the pip should be large, and Sam Barlow gives a diameter of three-quarters to seven-eighths of an inch. Thus, the blooms were very much smaller than those of the modern strains, which often measure up to two and a half inches across. A letter from Mr M. Warriner which appeared in the 1960 *Year Book* of the Southern Section of the National Auricula and Primula Society has this comment to make on the size of the bloom : 'I have,' writes Mr Warriner, 'the consecutive results of six seasons' breeding in my garden, and from these results I see that the smaller the individual flowers get, the finer the lacing appears to become.' The author, who has spent many years breeding gold-laced polyanthuses, can confirm this. As the blooms become larger, the lacing and the golden centre tends to smudge into the ground colour and the blooms also lose much of their rich colouring.

The Royal Horticultural Society has suggested that ten points should be awarded for the perfect gold-laced polyanthus, to be divided as follows :

	Points
For foliage and stem	1
For truss	2
For centre or eye	3
For lacing	2
For ground or body colour	2
	—
	10
	—

A PRICE LIST OF GOLD-LACED POLYANTHUSES OF 1830

Name	Raiser	£	s	d
Alexander	Pearson		1	0
Bang Europe	Nicholson	1	0	0
Beauty of Iver	Billington		2	6
Competitor	Pearson		7	6
Emperor Bonaparte	Turner		1	6
England	Turner		5	0
Formosa	Burnard		5	0
George IV	Waterhouse		10	6
Invincible	Crawshaw		5	0
Jolly Dragoon	Eckersley		5	6
Lord Crewe	Clegg		2	6
Lord John Russell	Turner		3	6
Lord Nelson	Parks		2	6
Othello	Revell		5	0
Prince Regent	Cox		1	0
Princess Royal	Collier		10	6
True Briton	Cartwright		2	6
Victorian	Hobson		2	6

These were recognised by leading growers as being the best varieties of the time

PREMIER WINNING VARIETIES FOR 1832 at the LEADING SHOWS WERE AS FOLLOWS:

	Firsts	*Total Prizes*
Pearson's Alexander	27	39
Buck's George IV	5	13
Cox's Prince Regent	4	17
Eckersley's Jolly Dragoon	3	6
Waterhouse's George IV	3	3

CHAPTER IV

More Interesting Polyanthuses

Early named varieties – Single polyanthuses – Double polyanthuses –
Miniature polyanthuses – Hose-in-Hose polyanthuses – Jack-in-the-
greens – Pests – Diseases.

Though most of the old gold-laced polyanthuses seem to have
disappeared from gardens, many of the double and hose-in-hose
forms have happily survived and are to be found in cottage gardens
everywhere. They will however, usually have finished flowering by
early summer when the collector of antique plants begins his
travels. A number of them would appear to date from the early
19th century for they carry the influence of the gold-laced polyanthus, the familiar red ground colouring and some degree of lacing
or gold at the centre. Into this category come two of the most
beautiful of all polyanthuses, Fair Maid and Beltany Red whilst
the old 'Eyeless' polyanthus, Bartimeus with its blooms of velvety
crimson is believed to be of the previous century. It may be safely
assumed that the oldest forms had red flowers which first appeared
in the polyanthus towards the middle of the 17th century and it
was not until Miss Jekyll made her famous discovery in 1880 that
the yellow colouring appeared in the polyanthus. Shortly after, the
wonderful Barrowby Gem was discovered in a Scottish garden and
though of vigorous habit it has become extremely scarce and is
now a 'collector's' item, a well grown plant being worth at least a
pound.

Many of the old varieties may be dated by their names. Prince
Albert, with its small crimson blooms marked with a blue candy
stripe down each petal, was introduced at the time of the marriage
of Queen Victoria to Albert, Duke of Saxe-Coburg shortly after
she ascended the throne in 1837. Of later date, came Beamish
Foam and Hunter's Moon, both outstanding plants and which
have now become much sought after by collectors. The latter was
raised from Barrowby Gem and has its powerful almond-like perfume. It is also early to bloom, like its famous parent, the first
buds opening during the milder days of February.

Possibly from crossings with the old double or semi-double red
primroses, several of the old double polyanthuses were raised, one

of the finest being the ancient Scottish Double Red now known as Crimson King. Again, from the deep ruby-red colour of its large blooms, it may be said to have been raised during the 18th century or rather earlier. Later came Derncleugh, also of Scottish introduction. It too, bears double flowers of deep bronzy-red but now the gold edging comes into prominence and so large are the blooms that just one makes a handsome button-hole.

Rex Theodore, also known as King Theodore is equally outstanding and is believed to date from the year 1768 when Theodore I was crowned King of Corsica. The flowers are refined and are of darkest crimson with a conspicuous wire-edge of gold so that it may be likened to a double gold-laced polyanthus. At the turn of the century almost every hardy plant grower listed it at a shilling or so but now, if it can be found anywhere, a plant would be worth at least £5, maybe considerably more.

Not far removed from the red colouring is the purple bloom of Prince Silverwings which 'made its first appearance in a nurseryman's catalogue in 1897 – Queen Victoria's Jubilee year. Its flowers are splashed with white while the petals have the brilliant silver lacing known only in the silver-laced polyanthus of the early 19th century'.

These lovely old plants are distinguished from the primroses by having their blooms held on short footstalks and are clustered at the top of a main stem from four to eight inches in length and though primroses also are borne from a main stem this is so short as to give the flowers the appearance of arising on their longer footstalks directly from the crown of the plant. As there are double forms of both the primrose and polyanthus, so too are there two types of the hose-in-hose and Jack-in-the-Greens, all of them collector's items, plants of old cottage gardens. They have now become rare and expensive but may be found in the more remote parts such as in the cottage garden on the banks of the Shannon where I once saw the lovely Lady Dora, one bloom growing out of another in elegant style and of brilliant golden-yellow with a delicious scent. My plant was a gift but if one could be obtained from a nursery today, it would cost at least £1 and be worth every penny of it.

Because of their long stems, all these old polyanthuses are ideal for cutting and not only do they maintain their freshness in water for a week or more, but will scent a large room with their delicious perfume.

SINGLE POLYANTHUSES

These are plants of the primula family but with the true poly-anthus habit. Some are extremely old, all are interesting and beautiful. They are propagated by root division and where they can be obtained are worthy of inclusion in any collection of old fashioned flowers :

BARROWBY GEM. With 'Beltany Red', this is one of the finest of all spring flowering plants, ideal for window-box or rockery with its sturdy habit. It is the first polyanthus to come into bloom, the first pips opening on mild February days and it remains colourful until June. The blooms may be described as of primrose-yellow colouring, shaded with green and it carries a pleasant almond per-fume.

It is of interest to recall that in her book, *The Scented Garden,* published by the Medici Society in 1931, Miss Eleanor Sinclair Rohde described Barrowby Gem as being a primrose, though nowhere have I seen it other than of polyanthus habit. Yet from her description of its colour, perfume and ability to produce at least a few blooms, throughout the winter, this must be the same plant as that known to the author. Miss Rohde says that it was raised by a Mrs McColl in Scotland and selected from over 200 seedlings. She writes : 'it still preserves something of the ethereal delicacy and charm of the wild primrose,' which it most certainly does.

BARTIMEUS. This is believed to be a polyanthus of the 18th century. It bears a bloom of velvety crimson-black and has no eye, for which reason it is known as the old 'eyeless' polyanthus. In its place is a region of bronzy red. The blooms are not large nor does it form a large truss by modern standards.

BEAMISH FOAM. A delightful primrose of polyanthus habit. The delicate pink star-like blooms are splashed with pale yellow.

BELTANY RED. Its origin is unknown, but it is one of the finest of all garden plants. It forms a stocky, compact plant and bears a large truss of tangerine-red blooms, which have an unusual green centre and an attractive wire-edge of gold. The leaves are vivid green. The plant remains ten weeks in bloom, and two or three planted together can be seen from afar.

FAIR MAID. The author obtained this magnificent variety from Perthshire, so it is well named. The small, but beautifully rounded blooms are freely produced on numerous 15 inch stems, their colour being burnt orange-scarlet with a most striking double centre of gold. The blooms remain fresh in water for fully two weeks.

HUNTER'S MOON. A modern polyanthus and a beauty, for like Barrowby Gem it comes into bloom before all others and carries a fragrance rivalling that of an 'Ena Harkness' rose. Of sturdy habit, the bloom is of a lovely shade of apricot with a chrome yellow centre.

PINK FOAM. Of dainty, dwarf polyanthus habit, its small star-shaped flowers are pale blush-pink.

PRINCE ALBERT. Another old polyanthus, the blooms are small, and borne in clusters rather than in trusses. They are of plum colouring with a blush-blue candy stripe down the edge of each petal. It is of less robust habit than the others.

RASPBERRIES AND CREAM. Of true polyanthus habit, the neat flowers are of an unusual shade of raspberry-red attractively edged with cream. An old favourite of Somerset cottage gardens.

RED ENSIGN. Of polyanthus habit, the large velvet-crimson blooms have a bright golden eye.

TAWNY PORT. An attractive, rare little plant of very dwarf habit and having the darkest or all flowers, with maroon-green foliage and dainty port-wine coloured blooms. Of dwarf polyanthus habit, it comes from the West of Ireland and is very long flowering.

TOPSY. Of dwarf polyanthus habit but of an entirely different colour and formation. The blooms are of a lovely shade of crimson wine-red with an attractive biscuit-bronze centre.

DOUBLE POLYANTHUSES

The old name for these plants was 'Pug-in-a-Pinner'. There are several which bear their flower trusses on long stems and which may be classed as being of the true polyanthus order. Most of them are now difficult to obtain and require a richer soil than other members of the family: a particular requirement is liberal quantities of organic nitrogen, thoroughly decayed farmyard manure being the most suitable source.

BON ACCORD BLUE. This is the only one of the famous Bon Accord double primroses which is of true polyanthus habit. The plants were raised at the beginning of the present century, Bon Accord being the motto of the City of Aberdeen. The blooms of Bon Accord Blue are of the size of a ten pence piece, and are of a lovely shade of amethyst blue.

Mrs McMurtrie, of Kintore, Aberdeenshire, a leading authority on the old double polyanthuses has told of the introduction of some of these old plants. In the *Year Book* of the National Auricula and Primula Society (Southern Section) she writes: 'Between 1915–1918, there were no fewer than 137 double seedlings in the Cocker Bros. nursery. They were started off on this interesting side-line by the late Mr Murray Thomson, of Oamchie, Angus, who himself raised a large number (of doubles) known as the "Downshill" double primroses (and polyanthuses) and he also supplied seed to Mr Stormonth of Kirkbride; Mr. Murdoch of Cluny; and others. Of the Downshill doubles only three have survived – "Downshill Ensign", a bright purple polyanthus with rather ragged narrow-petalled flowers; Ronald, a lilac Juliae hybrid, which blooms profusely, but has single, semi-double and double flowers all of which appear simultaneously on the same plant; the third and best is a fine golden-yellow polyanthus of erect habit which I last saw in Cocker's nursery in 1953, before he sold off all his double primroses. From Murray Thomson's seed at least one fine double (polyanthus) is still grown. This is Maid Marian, a lovely deep blue, which was raised at the Waithman Nurseries, from seed which came from Kirkbride.'

CASTLEDERG. It came from the garden of Mrs Rebecca Scott at Ardmeen, Castlederg, Co. Tyrone and bears large, almost star-shaped blooms of deep sulphur-yellow, splashed with brown and pink. The early blooms open single, later coming semi-double and then fully double.

CHEVITHORNE PINK. Raised by Mrs Spence at Stewartstown, Co. Tyrone, this is one of the best of all the doubles, for it makes a compact but vigorous plant of remarkably easy culture and remains long in bloom. It bears small, beautifully formed flowers of deep orchid-pink and held on short sturdy polyanthus stems. It is an excellent plant for pot culture.

CHEVITHORNE PURPLE. This plant now seems more rare than its pink counterpart but is of similar habit. The blooms are of deep purple-blue, the petals edged with white.

CRIMSON EMPEROR. A very rare old variety but a vigorous grower, the large fully double blooms being of a brightest crimson-red.

CRIMSON KING. This is the same variety as the old Scottish Double Red and it is certainly very old. It is a plant of sturdy constitution and bears large numbers of big, fully double blooms held on short polyanthus stems. The colour of the flowers is deep ruby-red.

CURIOSITY. Also known as Golden Pheasant, this variety was at one time grown in large numbers, but over-propagation to supply the demand has reduced its constitution. The bloom is most interesting, having a deep yellow ground colour, flecked with rose and bronzy markings. The blooms are borne on long polyanthus stems.

DERNCLEUGH. Also called Tortoiseshell. This variety is known to the author only where growing in a small garden in Ireland. The double blooms are of bronzy-crimson, the petals being margined with gold and are borne on polyanthus stems. We are fortunate to have from Mrs McMurtrie, her late husband's description of this handsome plant : 'There is an extraordinary attraction about this plant,' wrote the Rev. McMurtrie, 'so neat in its compact habit and so finished in every detail of its flowers. They are perfectly round and of a good red, flaked on a bright gold ground. The reverse of the petal is dark red with a gold edge, most effective in the crowded heads of fat buds.' Mrs McMurtrie adds : 'I remember well a large bed of Derncleugh in our Manse garden at Skene, covered with crimson and gold as the flowers were opening – a wonderful sight! I have searched in vain for Derncleugh for many years now; it is sad to think that this lovely old plant is now perhaps lost. Both these polyanthus (Derncleugh and Rex Theodore) were old Aberdeenshire plants – not Irish as Mr Murdoch (the Rev. William Murdoch of Cluny, our old friend and neighbour) held. I have been told on good authority that they both originated as natural "sports" in the garden of Sunnyside, Fyvie in Aberdeenshire.'

MRS A. M. WILSON. Raised by the Rev. W. Murdoch it makes a neat plant and bears a profusion of very large flowers which are of a soft raspberry-red.

PRINCE SILVERWINGS. It is a beautiful polyanthus, the purple-lilac blooms being flaked with white and edged with silver. The petals are tinted with orange at the base to form a bloom of great beauty; but though in no way difficult to grow, it is now rare. It sometimes bears semi-double blooms which yield pollen and even single flowers the first year after being divided, and so may be used for hybridising. Mrs Gladys Emerson, of Limavady, N. Ireland, an authority on the old double polyanthuses, has told how this plant 'made its first appearance in a nurseryman's catalogue in 1897 – Queen Victoria's Diamond Jubilee year' and she describes its silver-laced petals as being 'of a bluish purple with gay splashes of bright orange at the base of each'.

RALPH SPOONER. This is possibly the finest double polyanthus ever raised. It bears 20 or more fully double blooms on each stem, arranged in perfect exhibition form and they retain their perfection over a long period. The colour is Jersey-cream and they have a soft, sweet perfume.

REX THEODORE. Also known as King Theodore. It was listed in the catalogues of all the hardy plant growers at the turn of the century, but it is now rarely seen. The bloom is almost crimson-black with the petals edged with gold. This may also have been the double black polyanthus 'edged with white' called Queen Victoria which was popular on the show bench at the beginning of the century. Mr Sacheverell Sitwell, in his delightful book, *Old-Fashioned Flowers* suggests that the plant may have been called after King Theodore of Abyssinia, with whom we fought in 1868, but it is certainly of older date than that. The year 1768, when Theodore I was King of Corsica, is suggested; and Mr Sitwell says that the bloom has 'beyond all question, a lacing or an edging of gold'. From this it would appear that the double form of a polyanthus with gold-lacing appeared at about the same time as the single form.

SILVER ANNIE. A most interesting old double polyanthus now rarely to be seen, though it still exists in Irish gardens and is described by one as being of a 'beautiful mulberry colour laced with silver'. But the lacing, one must admit, is ragged and uneven.

Mrs Gladys Emerson writes: 'I do most certainly believe that this old silver-laced polyanthus was a parent of Prince Silverwings, for from sixteen seedlings (obtained from Prince Silverwings) there were two perfect plants of Silver Annie, whose bloom has a more extensive ground colour of crimson.'

YELLOW DOUBLES. Double polyanthuses of pure yellow colouring are now extremely rare. Mrs McMurtrie writes: 'For a time we had two yellow polyanthuses. The first was raised by the late Mr Smith of Daisy Hill Nurseries, Newry: he named it "Maize Yellow", but referred to it in a letter as "my double golden polyanthus". He sent a plant to my husband who in return sent him a plant of the other yellow; this was found growing in a local garden and resembled the Bon-Accord doubles so closely in its habit (primrose and polyanthus flowers appearing together on the same plant) that it seemed almost certain that it was the variety, Bon-Accord Primrose that was believed lost. It had a large flower of ivory yellow, or deep cream, without a trace of sulphur.' These plants now seem to have disappeared entirely.

MINIATURE POLYANTHUSES

The word 'miniature' is used here to embrace the stalked poly-anthus primroses such as 'Lady Greer and Miss Osborne'.

Producing dozens of tiny flowers on numerous short stems, the miniatures are among the most dainty and lovable plants of the garden. With their small leaves, they make ideal plants for a window-box or for the alpine garden. A year-old plant will have grown several inches across and will be smothered in bloom for weeks on end. The following are named varieties :

KINLOUGH BEAUTY. A beautiful variety of distinct polyanthus habit and bearing numerous small blooms to each stem. The flowers are of an unusual shade of warm salmon-pink with a creamy candy stripe down each petal. It was found in the garden of Mr John-stone in Kinlough, Co. Donegal, a county of many original plants.

LADY GREER. Dainty polyanthus-primrose hybrid and a charming plant for a window-box or trough garden. The tiny yellow blooms are held on eight to nine inch stems above attractively rounded bottle green foliage.

MISS OSBORNE. This dainty primrose which bears tiny sweetly perfumed mauve blooms on short polyanthus stems makes a most attractive companion for Lady Greer to which it is similar in every way excepting colour.

HOSE-IN-HOSE POLYANTHUSES

There are a number of these delightful plants which are of polyanthus habit, the blooms being held on stems about six inches long. They were also known as 'Two-in-Hose' and Gerard illustrated them in his *Historie of Plants* (1592). They may have been so named because at that time the hose worn by men were knitted with a much stronger wool than that used today, and it was the custom for one stocking to be placed in another before being passed to the wearer. Mr James Laver, keeper of Costumes at the Victoria and Albert Museum, London, has described the ancient forms of hose in a letter to the author. He makes special mention of a delightful picture by Gabriel Metsu, the Dutch master born at Antwerp in 1629, the year Parkinson published his *Paradisus*. The picture is known as *A Gentleman and Lady at the Harpsichord*, and clearly shows a typical 'gentleman' of the age with his stockings pulled up to the thighs, with the tops turned down to just below the knees, to give the appearance of one stocking being pulled over another, exactly like the hose-in-hose flowers. The botanical explanation of this delightful effect is that the lower 'bloom' is really a petaloid calyx. There is a variation to the hose-in-hose form where the calyx of the lower flower is striped with green, red or yellow. This has given rise to the name 'Pantaloon' to describe the form, which is unusual rather than pretty.

The hose-in-hose form may be found in both primroses and polyanthuses, the lovely mauve-pink 'Lady Molly' having the true primrose footstalks, while Old Vivid, possibly the brightest flower in the garden, bears its umbels of tiny orange-scarlet blooms, one growing from another, at the end of a nine inch stem in polyanthus fashion. The charming Lady Lettice, may be said to combine the characteristics of both, the blooms appearing on long footstalks which arise from a main stem about two inches long All the hose-in-hose primroses bear the delicate woodland perfume which the native yellow primroses emanate, and which to many is as pleasing as the scent of the violet.

These named varieties are still obtainable :

ASHFORT. It is tall-growing, and bears an umbel of brownish red flowers above pale green foliage.

BRIMSTONE. Of semi-polyanthus habit for its large, clear sulphur-yellow bell-shaped blooms arise from a main stem three inches long. An outstanding variety, remaining long in bloom.

GOLDILOCKS. It bears its deep yellow blooms in umbels on long stems, making it an excellent cut flower.

IRISH SPARKLER. This striking variety is frequently confused with Old Vivid. Its blooms are similarly formed but are of a crimson-red colour without the conspicuous yellow centre. Like most of the hose-in-hose, it makes an excellent cut flower.

LADY DORA. The colour of the small, dainty blooms is brilliant golden-yellow, whilst they possess a powerful perfume.

OLD SPOTTED HOSE. Of full polyanthus habit, the large crimson blooms are borne on sturdy stems; the centre of each petal is quaintly spotted near the edge.

OLD VIVID. This is a most striking 'hose' of polyanthus form; the blooms fit almost completely one inside the other and are of vivid vermilion-scarlet with an equally brilliant orange-yellow centre. Also known as Scottish Sparkler.

JACK-IN-THE-GREENS

Just as there are hose-in-hose polyanthus as well as hose-in-hose primroses, so also are there Jack-in-the-Green forms of both. Here the leafy sepals are so well developed that they overlap the petals; with the result that the corolla is backed or surrounded by a large green ruff or jacket, hence its country name. This greatly enhances the appearance of the bloom and when the flower dies back, the green ruff persists for several weeks. In this form the plants are useful for mixing with ordinary polyanthus blooms for indoor decoration. The polyanthus 'Jacks' are borne on sturdy stems 10-12 inches long, the blooms being large with the ruff in proportion. They are obtainable in shades of red, crimson-brown, rose, yellow and white, the last being the most rare and the most beautiful with its bloom of glistening white backed by a ruff of bottle green. There are also a number of named varieties:

ELDORADO. This is a magnificent plant, the lovely clear golden-yellow bloom backed by a large rich green ruff and held on sturdy 10 inch stems.

SALAMANDER. This old 'Jack' bears the largest bloom of any known polyanthus, measuring more than three inches across and more than four inches if the ruff is taken into account. The colour is brightest crimson-red with a large, clearly defined star-shaped centre.

If the green ruffs are pegged into the ground after the blooms have faded, they will take root, when they may be detached and grown on to form plants to bloom the following spring.

PESTS

BIRDS. If they can be classed as 'pests', birds are by far the most troublesome of all polyanthus foes, as they remove the flower buds as they begin to open, attempting to get at the nectar in the tube. During dry weather, which is frequently experienced at this time of the year in Britain, whole beds may be completely stripped of their flower buds within a few days. House sparrows and bullfinches are the worst culprits and where these are troublesome it will be neces-

Double primrose Marie Crousse, introduced 100 years ago from France

Double primrose – Gerard's Old Double White

Jack-in-the-Green primrose

Hose-in-Hose primrose, variety Brimstone

sary to place black thread across the beds just above the flowering stems. Alternatively small pieces of tin fastened with string to stakes about two feet above ground level, so that they jingle in the wind and so scare the birds away, will prove effective. It should not be thought that a bird or two appearing on the beds will cause little or no damage for they are quite capable of removing both buds and blooms, dropping them around the plants and leaving only the stems and untidy footstalks with nothing to show for twelve months' labour.

Mr Harold Harvey, raiser of the 'Riviera' strain, writes: 'Do put thread over the plants early, for remember, the dear little sparrows have wonderful eyesight and just one peck at a tiny bud means, maybe, a fine head of bloom gone from the plant.' Indeed, sparrows are the worst enemy of the polyanthus grower; but maybe our own plants are rarely troubled by them because we are such great cat lovers!

GREEN FLY. This member of the aphis family will occasionally prove troublesome to the polyanthus. It clusters on the foliage where it punctures the tissue and sucks out the sap, causing the plants to lose vitality. The foilage first turns pale yellow, then becomes limp and less crinkled than normally before finally turning brown. This may be prevented by checking the pest before it obtains a hold. Eradication is an easy matter as the pest does not attack the plant below soil level. The pest may appear from the end of May, shortly after the plants have finished flowering, when they should be sprayed with Lindex solution or dusted with Lindex powder as for the Primula aphis. Take care to ensure that the liquid or dust reaches the crown and the neck of the plant just above soil level, for it is here that the pests congregate. Abol-X is also effective. Use at the strength of a half fluid ounce to a gallon of water for spraying the plants. If used on plants growing under cloches or in frames, the glass should not be replaced until the plants are quite dry.

PRIMULA APHIS. (also known as ROOT APHIS). Where plants are growing in a soil which is either too dry or too wet because excess winter moisture is unable to drain away, the plants will lose vitality and take on a sickly appearance. The first sign will be that the foliage will turn a pale yellowish green colour, far removed from the rich, deep green foliage of the healthy plant. An unhealthy plant will quickly become infested by the Primula aphis, a pest which attacks all members of the family when given an opportunity. The

E

greyish white insects will be found clustering about the neck or crown of the plant, and if the plant is lifted they will also be found on the roots. The aphides will generally appear after the plants have finished flowering, during June, and will continue throughout the summer unless eradicated. They feed on the sap and quickly reduce vigour. Where the attack is heavy the plant will die back completely.

Dry conditions would appear to be the chief cause, so that regular spraying during dry weather, and providing a mulch to maintain soil pressure, will do much to prevent a serious outbreak. To allow the beds to become weed-infested will also encourage the pest, whilst any dead or decaying leaves and flower stems should be regularly removed. Plants which may remain undivided for longer than two years will also begin to lose vitality and be more liable to attack.

Where the pest is observed, the plants should be sprayed with Lindex solution, taking care to reach the crown and neck of the plant. Use half a fluid ounce to two gallons of water. This treatment should be repeated at fortnightly intervals until the trouble is cleared up, or longer should dry weather continue. An alternative method is to dust with Lindex every ten days, taking care to reach the inside of the plant and the neck, where the pests generally congregate. Soaking the soil with Lindex solution around the plants will eradicate the pests below soil level.

If the pest is observed when the plants are being lifted and divided during midsummer, or autumn, they should be washed, including the roots, in a soft soap solution, and again in clean water before replanting. Or use a solution of Tritox which will provide a complete cure for root aphis and may also be used to spray the foliage. This should be done as routine once a month. Where the pests are observed around the neck of a plant, it should be brushed at this point with methylated spirit, before being washed in soap solution and clean water. It will be advisable to treat any particularly valuable varieties or those bearing bloom of unusual colouring, in this way. D.D.T. dust should not be used for members of the primula family.

RED SPIDER. Polyanthus plants which are growing beneath a wall, in a shrubbery or in any position where the soil may tend to dry out frequently, and where the plants may be deprived of moisture on their foliage, will be liable to an attack by red spider. Of this pest Maddock, the famous grower of gold-laced polyanthuses at the beginning of the nineteenth century, said : 'The worst enemy to the polyanthus is a small red or scarlet spider, which in summer spins its web on the underside of the leaves.' Then the polyanthus was almost always cultivated in pots in a greenhouse, and they would therefore be more liable to attack from this pest than where growing outdoors. As a precaution, however, it will be advisable to spray the plants regularly during dry periods, the red spider rarely appearing where the roots and foliage of the plants are kept moist. The secret of growing healthy polyanthus plants is never to allow them to lack moisture during spring and summer when the pest will be most troublesome. During dry periods, the plants should be syringed with clean water, taking care to reach the underside of the foliage where the pests collect.

Where the leaves are to be seen turning brown, first at the edges then all over, red spider may be the cause, although it is scarcely possible to observe the pest with the naked eye. The pests cluster beneath, sucking the sap and undermining the vigour of the plant.

A normal spray will have trouble in penetrating the web or cocoon, so a systemic insecticide should be used. This will quickly be absorbed into the vascular system of the plants and the pests eating the plant will be poisoned and die.

Spraying with Dextrak Derris or Abol Derris solution as routine, using once every month half a fluid ounce dissolved in two gallons of water, will usually prevent a heavy infestation.

SLUGS. These pests can be most troublesome to those plants which occupy a frame or are newly planted out in beds, particularly during a wet season. They may become so troublesome that they could devour a whole bed of seedlings in a night or two and so the plants should be protected as a matter of routine. Immediately the seedlings have been set out, the ground (and plants) should be given a thorough soaking with Slugit, a slug exterminator in liquid form which, unlike the solid forms, is harmful neither to human nor to animal life. The treatment should be repeated every three weeks, and should include tiny seedlings in boxes which are awaiting transplanting, as well as those growing in a frame or in beds. As an additional precaution, the slugs may be removed from the beds or frames at nightfall with the aid of a torch. Everything possible should be done to keep the plants free from attack, otherwise one's labours in crossing and raising new varieties, or where sowing the finest strains, would only end in failure. Nothing is more disappointing than where young plants of great vigour have been raised, only for them to be devoured by slugs.

The pest will also attack the succulent stems of the flowers in spring, severing them near the base, often before the buds have had time to open. Especially are plants growing under cloches liable to attack, for here the stems are particularly succulent and appear when there is little other 'green' about. Plants under cloches should be given special protection from slug attack, by soaking the soil with Slugit before the cloches are put in position early in spring.

American gardeners are recommended to use the powerful Slug-pest manufactured by Regional Chemicals of Seattle and having a 50 per cent metaldehyde content. It is non-injurious to plant life and is applied by sprinkling over the plants and ground.

WEEVILS. The root weevil is often a troublesome pest, the half-inch long, dark grey grubs being found beneath old clumps of polyanthuses, which are generally in need of lifting and dividing. The presence of the larvae in the soil may be noticed by the plant failing to respond to spring conditions, new growth appearing slowly and finding difficulty in becoming established. If the plant is lifted, it will be found that the grubs have devoured many of the fleshy roots and occasionally almost nothing is to be found below soil level. Should the presence of the weevil be confirmed, Gammexane should be dusted over the roots before replanting, whilst the soil should also be given a light application, a quarter ounce per square yard. A too heavy application may cause stunted growth.

WIREWORM. In the old soil of town gardens, or in the newly dug garden, this pest may prove troublesome, attacking the plants below soil level and severing the roots. Should the attack be made before the plants have become well rooted, the plants may die back completely. Indeed, where wireworm is prevalent, serious damage may be done to a newly planted bed of polyanthus.

The old method of treating the ground with Naphthalene was reliable, but at least three weeks should elapse before any planting is done to enable the soil to rid itself of the undesirable fumes. A better method is to fork Lindex dust into the soil while the ground is being prepared, using one ounce per square yard. Or the soil may be given a thorough soaking with Lindex solution prior to planting should the ground already have been prepared. This could be done as a matter of routine before doing any planting.

DISEASES

BROWN ROOT ROT. This trouble is caused by planting in badly drained soil, such as in a heavy soil which has not been opened up by humus or drainage materials, and though the polyanthus enjoys a considerable amount of moisture, stagnant water remaining around the roots during the winter months may cause the fleshy roots to turn brown and decay, this being due to the fungus, *Thielaviopsis basicola*. The leaves turning first pale yellow, then brown, will signify the presence of the disease.

Again, there is no cure once the plant is attacked, but by planting in a well-prepared soil, and treating the ground with Cheshunt Compound as routine, should prevent any serious outbreak.

DOWNY MILDEW. This disease is only occasionally to be found on the polyanthus, where it occurs on the foliage, yellow spots with white mould or down appearing on the underside. As with leaf spot, any affected leaves should be removed and burnt; while spraying the plants with a sulphur spray such as Spersul, at a rate of one level teaspoonful to a gallon of water, will give control.

GREY MOULD (BOTRYTIS). This is Botrytis cinerea which causes grey spots to appear on the flowers and foliage, which become covered in a layer of mycelium-like threads. It may attack the plants growing under cloches or plants which are grown in a greenhouse for hybridising but plants in the open will rarely be troubled. Spraying with Tulisan, one teaspoonful dissolved in a gallon of water, will provide a cure, but as the fungus is able to live on dead leaves, these must be removed and destroyed as they form.

LEAF SPOT. There are various fungus diseases which cause leaf spot on polyanthuses, the most common being *Ramularia primulae*. Where present, the angular spots first appear as a light brown colour, then become darker brown with a yellow margin. On the underside of the leaf, a white powdery mould appears, very much like that of *Ovularia primulana*, which is sometimes to be found on the underside of wild primrose leaves. Another fungus causing leaf spot is *Phyllosticta primulicola*, but where this is present, the white mould on the under-surface of the leaves is replaced by dark brown spots. These fungi are most active in the damper, more humid parts of Britain.

Dusting the plants with flowers of sulphur, especially where growing under glass, will do much to prevent an outbreak, but as the fungus spores will often remain on the old leaves and on other nearby vegetable matter, even through a severe winter, all dead leaves should be removed from the plants as they decay in autumn and burnt immediately. Spraying the plants with Tulisan, using two teaspoonful to a gallon of water, will also give control. The Americans use Du Pont Mangate.

MOSAIC. This is a virus disease, more correctly the Cucumber Mosaic Virus and though yellowing and blotching of the leaves of the polyanthus may denote the presence of red spider or aphis, it may be caused by this virus disease for which there is no known cure. If the plants do not respond to the treatment as advised for red spider and aphis, they should be dug up and burnt, and the ground given a rest period when the remaining plants have finished blooming. Propagation should never be done with a virus-infected plant. The disease may be introduced by aphides, which suck at the sap and so make it possible for the virus to enter the plant. It is therefore most important to keep the plants vigorous and free from aphis throughout their life. A plant attacked by pests will become weakly and lose vitality, and whether the virus is introduced in this way or not, a sickly plant will be more liable to succumb to disease.

RUST. This fungus disease is known by the name of *Puccinia primulae* and occurs in cowslips and polyanthuses but only on the leaves. Brown, rust-like spores form on yellow spots or blotches. Later the spores turn dark brown, then almost black in early autumn when they mature on the leaves. The plants should be cleared of all old leaves as they form and should be sprayed with Tulisan where the first signs of the disease is observed, using a teaspoonful to two gallons of water.

Where polyanthuses are grown well, and nothing is left to chance, disease will rarely make its presence felt, but where an outbreak does occur action should be taken without delay, otherwise a whole bed may become affected very quickly. However, as prevention is always better than cure, routine spraying at the appropriate time will maintain the polyanthuses in a healthy condition.

CHAPTER V
The Primrose

The early writers – Jack-in-the-greens – Hose-in-Hose varieties – Double primroses – Natural 'sports' – Introduction of new hybrids – Soil requirements – Top dressing – Varieties of the double primrose – The single primrose – Its hardiness – Planting – Varieties of the single primrose The Garryarde primroses.

The primrose in its many lovely forms is the collector's plant supreme. It has no equal for it has everything that a good plant should have : interest, beauty, quaintness, in addition to a hardiness and ease of culture. For these reasons almost all the old varieties, those grown in Tudor gardens and those of earlier times, have existed to this day. They are native plants and amongst the easiest of all plants to grow well. One may propagate them by 'teasing' apart the offsets and treading them into the ground with the heel of the shoe. All they require is a friable soil, plenty of moisture in summer and partial shade. Hence, they do well in cottage gardens as they have since earliest times, where, in a humus-laden soil, sheltered by nearby plants or in the dappled shade of an orchard, they are so often to be found. Though of such easy culture, they are becoming more rare with each year, chiefly for two reasons. One is the demand by collectors which has greatly reduced stocks of the finest varieties. Another is that they are rarely given the conditions they require to flourish and multiply, the result being that in town gardens open to the sunlight and growing in a soil fortified only by artificial manures which contain little or no humus, they struggle for a few years and then die back, often proving difficult to replace. For this reason many of the old double primroses which once grew like cabbages in those gardens with a humus-laden soil and which could be purchased for a few pence a root, now cost several pounds. One example is the lovely Marie Crousse, raised in France possibly by the firm of Crousse (of paeony fame) towards the middle of the 19th century. Until quite recent times it was included in the catalogues of most hardy plant nurseries and could be obtained for a shilling or so a plant. Today, its price varies between 50p and £1.00 if it can be obtained at all for it becomes more difficult to find each year. Gerard's Double White could, until recently be purchased for a couple of shillings or so from most cottage gardens; now it will cost at least 25p and the price continues to increase each year. Quaker's Bonnet is another, which since the end of the 1960's has greatly increased in price and it will continue to do so. Yet even at present day prices they are a valuable investment for those who can provide them with the conditions they require.

Not least amongst the many desirable qualities of the primrose is its earliness to bloom. Indeed, the plant takes its name from primaverola, a diminutive of prima vera, first flower of springtime. From this, the obvious development was primerole which later became 'primerose' which in Elizabethan times was a plant held in so great esteem as to give its name to the language as used to denote excellence.

'She is the pride and primrose of the rest,' wrote Spenser and in *Daphnidia*, the husband lamenting the loss of his young wife says :

> Mine was the primrose in the lowly shade !
> Oh ! that so fair a flower so soon should fade.

In the *Miller's Tale*, Chaucer describes a lady of quality :

> Her shoos were laced on hir-legges hyghe,
> Sche was a primerole, a piggesneyghe
> For any lord have lying in his bedde,
> Or yet for any goodde yoman to wedde.

Shakespeare used the modern spelling in his frequent use of the word as in the touching scene in *Cymbeline* when Arviragus, bearing home the supposed dead body of Imogen says :

> With fairest flowers,
> Whilst summer lasts, and I live here Fidele,
> I'll sweeten thy sad grave; thou shalt not lack
> The flower that's like thy face, pale primrose. Nor,
> The azur'd harebell, like thy veins.

It was during the reigns of the Tudors that primroses first came to be grown for the beauty and interest of their flowers, for by then many variations of the yellow wild primrose had become known. Tabernaemontanus, writing in the year 1500, described the double yellow primrose which may be still found in various parts of Britain. Variations of the primrose *Primula acaulis* or *P. vulgaris*, are extremely numerous and quite apart from the lovely double forms, there are the dainty Hose-in-Hose forms and the Jack-in-the-greens, which originally must have been found growing in the wild in all parts of Britain. By Elizabethan times, these lovely primroses were planted in the dainty knot gardens of both manor house and cottage, for besides being of extremely perennial habit, the compact form of the plants made them ideal for this type of gardening.

Though the different forms of the white and yellow primrose must have been well known to cottage gardeners since earliest times, they had not been mentioned in any detail until the works of Gerard and Parkinson appeared during the last years of the sixteenth century and the beginning of the seventeenth century. John Gerard was a native of Nantwich but moved to London at an early age. Though he was not a gardener by profession he looked after Lord Burleigh's garden in the Strand and eventually had a famous garden of his own in Holborn, In his *Herbal*, he described and illustrated the double white primrose, (*alba plena*) and also a number of the interesting forms, especially the Jack-in-the-Greens.

JACK-IN-THE-GREENS

Here, the blooms are single and are backed by a ruff-like arrangement composed of tiny replicas of the primrose leaf, which provides a pleasant contrast to the clear colourings of the blooms. They were widely planted during the sixteenth century, the arrangement of the leaves behind the blooms greatly appealing to the Tudors, as could well be imagined. The plants later became known as Jack-in-the-Pulpits.

An interesting form of the Jack-in-the-Green is the Jack-a-napes-on-Horseback. This is the Franticke or Foolish primrose (or cowslip) described so well by Parkinson in his *Paradisus* of 1629. It is a plant of polyanthus form and in Parkinson's words, 'it is called Foolish because it beareth at the top of the stalk a tuft of small, long, green leaves with some yellow leaves, as it were pieces of flowers broken and standing amongst the green leaves'. It is illustrated in Parkinson's *Paradisus*, the leaves being further apart and not held in close circular formation as for the Jack-in-the-Green. It should be said that the striping of the leaves is of the same colouring as the bloom.

Gerard's Jack-a-napes has a larger flower which sits on a saucer of the same colour, striped with green. It possibly takes its name from a striped coat which was fashionable during the seventeenth century. In his diary dated 5th July, 1660, Samuel Pepys writes, 'This morning my brother Jon brought me my Jackanapes coat . . .' Of the Franticke or Jack-a-napes-on-Horseback, the leaves are more jagged. A book of early Stuart times described the flower as being 'all green and jagged', whilst Gerard says that it is so named by the women, 'the flowers being wrinkled and curled after a most strange manner', though I have yet to understand where 'the Horseback' part comes in. Most of the old 'Jacks' have been rediscovered in Ireland, where the mild, moist climate is so suited to primrose culture and where many gardens have been undisturbed for centuries.

Yet another form is the Gally Gaskin. This is a single bloom which has a swollen, distorted calyx and is now rarely to be found. It has also a frilled ruff beneath the bloom. A picture attributed to Henri Coiffier de Ruse in the National Gallery, aptly illustrates this form, a frilled ruff appearing beneath the knees of the gentlemen which appear large, like the swollen calyx of the Gally Gaskin.

HOSE-IN-HOSE VARIETIES

ABERDEEN YELLOW. A very old variety bearing small clear yellow blooms, with the duplex clearly defined.

CANARY BIRD. It is very early flowering, its bright, pure canary-yellow blooms being borne with great freedom.

CASTLE HOWARD. A lovely hose of true primrose habit, discovered in the grounds of the famous Yorkshire house bearing that name. The blooms are of true primrose-yellow colour.

ERIN'S GEM. It bears a most interesting and dainty cream-coloured flower, the lower one having an attractive bright green stripe

FLORA'S GARLAND. This is a lovely old hose-in-hose, bearing well-defined flowers of deep pink.

IRISH MOLLY. A hose of great charm and of true primrose form, bearing a profusion of large flowers which are a soft shade of mauve-pink. Also known as Lady Molly.

LADY LETTICE. In his interesting book, *Old Fashioned Flowers*, Mr Sacheverell Sitwell so rightly says that this plant should be in every garden. Planted along a path, its fairy-like flowers provide a delightful effect. It comes early into bloom in March and continues until the end of May, bearing masses of apricot-yellow flowers which are tinged with salmon-pink. Sadly, it is now almost extinct.

WANDA HOSE. This is the hose-in-hose form of the ever-popular Juliae primrose, Wanda. It has the same habit, the bright purple-red bloom being borne on short stems.

DOUBLE PRIMROSES

'Our garden double primrose, of all the rest is of the greatest beauty', wrote Gerard in 1597, and he makes special mention of the Double White. Thirty years later, Parkinson gave a full description of double primroses and said that the leaves were larger than those of the single primrose, 'because it groweth in gardens'. In other words, the double primroses were then popular garden plants. Parkinson describes the flowers as being 'very thick and double and of the same sweet scent with them (as the common single primrose)'. Indeed, the double primroses are amongst the most beautiful and interesting plants of the garden, and though they are considered by modern gardeners to be difficult to grow, the fact that Gerard's 'Double White' and the 'Double Sulphur' primrose of Tabernaemontanus (1500) are still with us and remain of vigorous constitution must surely do much to refute that charge.

The earliest writers repeatedly mention the ease with which the plants were grown. Philip Miller, Curator of the Chelsea Physic Garden about the year 1720, wrote in his *Gardener's Dictionary* (1731), 'they will grow in almost any earth provided that they have a shady situation', and John Rea in his *Flora* published in 1665 said, 'were it (the double primrose) not so common in every country-woman's garden, it would be more respected, for it is a sweet and dainty double flower . . .' Thus, through the years, the garden writers seem to have taken it for granted that those who grow the double primrose, and this would appear to be most gardeners, found it amongst the easiest of all plants to manage. Why, then have these quite charming plants become little more than 'collector's pieces' with present-day gardeners? The town garden with its acid and inert soil, due to continual deposits of soot and sulphur and complete lack of humus has now taken the place of the country cottage garden, where the soil was continually being revitalised with humus-forming manures. These took the form of night-soil, decayed farmyard manure, sheep and poultry droppings, decayed leaves, supplying not only humus but food in the form of nitrogen, which the double primrose loves so well and without which the plants will not survive for long.

Though the double primrose will grow well in a town garden, given the right conditions, it has survived only in the cottage garden where, during recent years, a number of varieties have been rediscovered which were thought to have been long extinct. The author discovered the wonderful double primrose of the early 19th century, Rose du Barri, growing in a Wiltshire cottage garden near Salisbury. The owner, a man of advancing years, said it had been the only variety grown here, and both his father and grandfather had cherished the plants before him.

In a cottage garden on the West Coast of Ireland was discovered a superb double yellow primrose, the blooms being almost the colour of a Gold Flake cigarette packet, and it is in Ireland that so many of the quaint and rare double primroses are to be found. They do still exist, and it would be a rash person indeed who stated that any particular variety was extinct, for under the conditions they enjoy, these delightful plants may be found in the most out of the way places, thriving where they were thought to have disappeared long ago. But the almost complete extinction of the double primrose during more recent years has been due to factors other than lack of suitable soil conditions. The interest taken in the gold-laced polyanthus during the latter half of the 19th century, its place in turn being taken by Miss Jekyll's new Munstead Strain, almost sounded the death-knell of the double primrose, and its slow propagating powers in comparison with other garden plants, which may be raised in their millions from seed, has of more recent years forced the double primrose into the background, high overhead costs now making it essential for the nurseryman to raise large numbers of plants as quickly and as inexpensively as possible.

The vogue for more formal bedding, also brought about a lack of interest in our native plants, but this does not entirely account for so many varieties becoming almost extinct between two World Wars. It is said that towards end of last century, those wonderful doubles, Rex Theodore and Madame Pompadour, were grown by the acre by specialist nursery growers who sold them for a few pence a root, yet today, of all varieties they are the most difficult to obtain and the most difficult to rear.

Writing in the 1952 *Year Book* of the National Auricula and Primula Society, Dr J. N. Smith said, 'Once I had six plants (of Madame Pompadour) growing beside some gooseberry bushes. The sunlight filtered through the branches, the plants increased in size, they were apparently healthy. They lived through a winter in the North or England, and when spring came they increased more. They were within a month of flowering – then something happened. The temperature rose or the wind changed and all six quietly wilted and petered in unison'. But not all double primroses are so temperamental, indeed most of these old favourites which have been recently rediscovered will prove vigorous given the correct cultural conditions; those they enjoyed before the rapid increase of the urban population.

NATURAL 'SPORTS'

The most vigorous of the double primroses are those plants which bear bloom similar in colour to our native single primrose, those bearing a yellow, cream or white bloom, and which must be natural 'sports' which have appeared quite by accident. Indeed it may be possible to find double primroses bearing bloom of the same colours growing amongst colonies of single primroses in various parts of Britain. They may be found in a particular wood in Dorset and in various parts of Ireland where industry and the motor car has not yet despoiled the countryside. Double primroses having been found growing wild at Great Everden, near Cambridge, and in *Country Life* of 27th June, 1957, appeared a photograph of a double white primrose growing in a wood in Kent.

As long ago as 1879, Richard Dean, in an article in the *Gardener's Chronicle*, mentioned that 'the white, lilac and yellow double primroses are much grown around London for market purposes, planted out in beds between currant and gooseberry bushes and underneath the boughs of apple, pear and plum trees'. He goes on to say, 'hundreds of these plants are purchased (sold) every spring and planted out in an unskilled manner in improper soil, where they soon die'. With the rise in population in the towns to which there was a continual drift from the countryside, it would appear that most of the double primrose plants found their way into the hands of the monied town gardeners, who not only gave the plants very limited time with their culture but little by way of plant food. As the increase of heavy industry gathered strength and with the disappearance of the horse, the townsman's garden has continued to receive little humus and plant food, and gradually the more difficult double primroses have found it impossible to survive, whereas the more robust *P. juliae* hybrids, the single primroses, are better able to adapt themselves to town conditions.

To confirm my contention that the natural 'sports' have retained most vigour, it may be remembered that Richard Dean made special mention of the white, lilac and yellow doubles, these being Gerard's Double White (*alba plena*), the Double Sulphur (yellow), mentioned by Tabernaemontanus in 1500, and the double lilac which we know best by its old name of Quaker's Bonnet which is believed to be a natural 'sport' of one of the oldest double primroses we know, and it is significant that they remain the most vigorous and easiest to grow. Plants of the intermediate shades of cream and greenish-white, both rediscovered growing wild during recent years, are also showing this extreme vigour. Few of the hybrid doubles have survived for long, and of the dozen or so named varieties raised in Scotland by Mr Murray Thomson at the beginning of the century, and described by him as possessing 'extreme vigour', only one, Downshill Ensign, is known to have survived to this day though others may be hiding in some Scottish garden.

INTRODUCTION OF NEW HYBRIDS

It has been suggested that carelessness in propagation whereby this was carried out to an excessive degree, led to the disappearance of many of these hybrid doubles and this may be so. The introduction of the hardy and vigorous *P. juliae* in 1900 seems to have encouraged several breeders to try their hand at raising double primroses, for besides Mr Murray Thomson, the Cocker Brothers in Aberdeen took up the work at the very same time and, like Murray Thomson, used *P. juliae* to give additional vigour, though it is known that both used the single 'Wilson's Blue' as a seed bearer, crossed with the pollen of the double purple, Arthur du Moulin, one of the very few doubles to produce pollen with any degree of freedom. This variety, of semi-polyanthus habit, was raised in Belgium, and first appeared in this country towards the end of the 19th century, which coincided with the appearance of Wilson's

Single Blue and of *P. juliae*. It would, therefore, seem that the many varieties raised at this time perished either through excessive propagation, or through the townsman's lack of knowledge in their culture, for from all accounts the plants possessed extreme vigour, and indeed those which have been handed down during the past 50 years are extremely robust, e.g. Bon Accord Gem and Downshill Ensign.

Until the hybridising of the Cocker Brothers and Murray Thomson at the turn of the century, there were few if any named double primroses for those that appeared previously were natural 'sports', closely resembling either the white or yellow primroses. Dingy, Cream and Burgundy were amongst the names used to describe the blooms, and certain of these descriptive names are used today for plants which bear bloom of similar colouring. They may, in fact, be the same plants. The number of double primroses grown in our gardens must have been extremely limited, and it is a pity that the introduction of several wonderful named varieties 50 years ago coincided with the loss of interest in the less formal plants when geraniums and calceolarias were grown to follow the stiffly flowered hyacinth and tulip. This, however, does not mean that the new double primroses were completely neglected. There was a demand for them for spring bedding, and to meet this one must come to the conclusion that nurserymen propagated all too vigorously plants which are naturally slow to increase, the result being loss of constitution, to be followed by lack of interest, as would be expected amongst gardeners. Nurserymen ceased to stock them until by the late 1940's, following the destruction of many old favourites with the war-time necessity for increasing home food production, double primroses had almost ceased to exist, to which end they were aided between the two world wars by adverse soil conditions of town gardens and a lack of understanding of their requirements. It should also be remembered that until the ending of the First World War, double primroses had generally been grown commercially in orchards where the plants appreciated the partial shade given by the trees when in full leaf. Modern ideas of orchard maintenance, which for economic reasons began to be put into practice during the 1920's, made for little or no underplanting and so the double primrose was relegated to the nursery beds, where often conditions were probably against its survival.

Perhaps it may be said that the natural 'sports' which have been grown since earliest times and which have continued down the years to be grown where they were always to be found, namely in country house and cottage gardens, have received the culture they required. Those hybrid doubles, raised by artificial means, would have been grown mostly in town gardens where soil conditions would be vastly different, resulting in the loss of the plants before they ever became fully established. By the late 1930's double primroses, except for the white, yellow and mauve varieties, had certainly become a rarity to be found only in a few farm and cottage gardens situated away from the towns. It is perhaps not without significance that whenever an old double primrose, believed to be extinct, has been re-discovered this has always been in a country garden in some remote part, town gardens yielding nothing in this respect.

It is also interesting to recall that almost all the artificial hybridising of double primroses was carried out in the North-East of Scotland, first by Murray Thomson and the Cocker Brothers, later by the Rev. W. Murdoch, the Rev. McMurtie and William Chalmers, all working in the same district, and who must have passed on their knowledge to each other. Alas, these enthusiasts are no longer with us.

Those gardeners who are showing a new interest in these quaint and lively plants are mostly those who knew of the plants 30 or more years ago, before they became almost extinct. In letters to the author they recall their love for these plants when growing in gardens of childhood days and regret the fact that they are now rarely to be seen.

For those starting a collection of double primroses, it should be said that certain varieties are easier to cultivate than others. Into this category come the natural 'sports' and others of ancient origin. These lovely primroses possess the vigour of the *juliae* hybrids; in other words, they may be expected to flourish where soil conditions are not entirely in their favour though they should not be neglected if they are to be seen to advantage and are to be long lived :

alba plena	Cloth of Gold
Arthur du Moulin	Crimson King
Bon Accord Blue	Downshill Ensign
Bon Accord Gem	Marie Crousse
Bon Accord Purple	Out Pat
Bon Accord Rose (Old Rose)	Quaker's Bonnet
Chevithorne Pink	Tyrian Purple

SOIL REQUIREMENTS

To grow double primroses successfully, a soil containing humus and ample supplies of plant food, a yearly mulch and regular division are necessary to their culture. Like most double-flowering plants they thrive on good fare and seem to use up supplies of food in the soil more quickly than the single varieties. In addition, the plants do enjoy partial shade, which seems more necessary to them than it does for the *juliae* primroses, though care must be taken to plant away from mature trees which would deprive the plants of moisture. Beneath young orchard or ornamental trees will suit the plants well, or select a bed with a northerly aspect. The more vigorous varieties, however, may be grown in full sun provided the soil is enriched with humus.

Artificial manures should not be used for double primroses, though specially prepared compost to be made where manure supplies are limited will prove valuable. Straw or dry bracken may be made into compost which will supply both humus and plant food. It should be first saturated and an activator must then be sprinkled over the material before it is made up into a pile to heat up. Poultry manure, which has been kept dry, and used with the activator will not only help the material to heat and decompose more rapidly but will provide valuable plant food in the form of nitrogen. This is the most important food in the diet of the double primrose without which the plants will never make headway and the more 'difficult' varieties will die back completely. The old garden writers describing double primroses made special mention of the need to provide them with a rich soil. Philip Miller said, 'They delight in a strong soil,' and William Hanbury, Rector of Church Langton in Leicestershire, said, 'A shady border, as rich as possible.' John Hill, who was knighted by the King of Sweden for his great work, *The Vegetable Kingdom* of 25 volumes, put the requirements of the double primrose in a nutshell : 'Part the roots at autumn and plant them in fresh pasture ground, enriched by a little wold-pile earth (leaf mould) and cow-dung.' Almost a century later (1838), M'Intosh wrote that 'the plants grow and flower luxuriously in a mixture of rich loam and leaf mould'. Thus, all the old writers said almost the same thing, it being necessary to provide a little shade, humus, some plant food and frequent division.

Mr H. G. Moore of Dorchester, an authority on the double

primrose, writing in the 1936 *Year Book* of the National Auricula and Primula Society, said that to grow them successfully they must have, '(a) a naturally rich soil of a retentive nature, (b) moisture, (c) partial shade, (d) division of roots not later than every second year'. He added 'and possible removal to a new site for more plant food, unless an application (mulch) of suitable manure is made'. This he added not without reason for he had previously written, 'I well know that plants left to themselves soon succumb, either through soil exhaustion or ravages of pests.' The latter reason, I feel, is not nearly so important as soil exhaustion for all primroses remain reasonably free from pest and disease, through my experience of plants grown continuously in the same bed is that, however well they have originally been provided with plant food, they do tend to lack vigour and the leaves will sometimes turn yellow due, one would imagine, to some form of virus disease. But how does one account for the robustness of Rose du Barri, growing in that Wiltshire cottage garden for almost a century and those vigorous plants of Madame Pompadour seen in Ireland where, I was told, they had been growing for almost the same length of time?

Double primroses are gross feeders, and whatever the texture of the soil it should be made friable and be well fortified with plant food before any planting is done. Quantities of leaf mould or peat should be incorporated into any soil which is of a clay nature and also where it is light and sandy, for the first consideration is for it to be retentive of moisture. But neither peat nor leaf mould will provide the plants with food, and the soil of a town garden especially will require very much more food than where planting into fresh pastureland, or in an orchard where the ground may not have been worked for many years and which will, as a result, have stored up valuable nutrition.

Most of the early writers suggest a clay soil for double primroses, one retentive of moisture, but if a clay soil is not provided with humus it will dry out too rapidly in summer and will become waterlogged in winter thereby causing conditions under which the plants would perish. First provide the right conditions and then the plant food.

There is no denying that well decayed farmyard or cow manure is the fare most enjoyed by the double primrose. Where it can be obtained and in this respect the countryman is more fortunate than the townsman, it should be used as liberally as possible, digging it well into the soil before planting. Old mushroom-bed compost, obtainable through mail order, and artificially-composted straw are both rich in nitrogen and will prove almost as valuable as farmyard manure. What is more, each of these foods will considerably augment the humus content of the soil, though being more expensive and not so readily obtainable they should be used in addition to either peat or leaf mould and not as an alternative. Other forms of nitrogen of an organic nature and which will also provide valuable humus are chopped seaweed, for those living close to the sea; shoddy, for gardens of the industrial towns of the North; and hop manure, readily available almost anywhere. Each of these materials is clean to handle and inexpensive to obtain. They are also readily worked into the soil. The countryman will also find the haulm of peas and beans a valuable source of nitrogen if dried and chopped so that it may more easily be dug into the soil. Also, material from the garden compost heap may also be used, in fact anything which will provide both humus and plant food.

Double primroses will also appreciate some potash which will help to build up a hardy plant and which will accentuate the colour of the blooms. It will also prevent much of the looseness of petal which is apparent with a number of varieties where potash is lacking. Potash is best given in the form of wood ash which has been stored dry to prevent the potash content from being washed away. The wood ash should be raked into the soil just prior to planting.

With the rapid increase in town gardens for which vast sums of money are spent each year on their beautifying, it is obvious that here double primroses have to overcome soil conditions very different from those of the country garden where the continual falling of leaves, liberal applications of farmyard manure and material from the garden compost heap all play their part in providing an everlasting supply of both humus and plant food. In earlier times, the use of night-soil on the garden also contributed to the supply of plant food. I have also used the clearings from ditches to great effect on light, sandy soil, and this material is a source of humus widely used in the country to this day. The town garden must make use of humus-forming materials in the same way as the countryman from earliest times, and without a liberal supply of food double primroses should be left to those who have a better opportunity of growing them well. Lime is used to dress new pasture land to release the supplies of food in the soil and lime should also be used to correct any unduly acid tendency of a town garden soil. Primroses and polyanthuses grow best where the pH value of the soil is around 7.0 or only very slightly acid. If excessively acid, give a heavier dressing with lime, or if the reaction is too alkaline work in additional peat.

In addition to enriching the soil with supplies of food in the humus form, double primroses will also benefit from the addition of various organic foods of slow-acting properties. Dried blood, fish waste and bone meal will each prove beneficial, especially where planting in a town garden, or where the plants are of necessity, to be given only the minimum of attention. These fertilisers will release their food values over a period as will those humus-forming organics, each of which will provide the plants with the essential nitrogen, without which they will never make healthy growth.

TOP DRESSING

However well the soil will have been prepared, the secret of the cottage gardener's success with double primroses lies in top dressing the plants. In the cottage garden, often enclosed by trees, this process continues almost uninterrupted, for besides a continued supply of leaf mould, clearings from the hen house or cow shed, vegetable refuse and in some cases night-soil, are thrown over the ground to provide an unending supply of humus. This top dressing is vital for the double primrose plants tend to force themselves out of the ground from the old rootstock even more so than the *juliae* hybrids. The result is that if not continually top dressed, the new roots will be unable to find food and moisture and in consequence the plants will perish. Even if supplies of plant food persisted in the soil from planting time they would play little part in the continuing vigour of the plant if not in contact with the new roots. Double primroses are gross feeders and quite apart from the need to bring the newly formed roots into contact with the soil, the plants will require additional supplies of food each year where they are being left undisturbed.

Without a yearly mulch or top dressing, the new crowns will not make headway and a mulch should be given immediately after flowering in early June, so that the new crowns will receive nourishment from this time. A top dressing will also help to maintain the moisture content of the soil during summer and suppress annual weeds. If the top dressing is given at this time, the new crowns will have formed their new rooting system by the end of summer when they may be divided or left until March, to be divided just before they come into bloom. The plants may be left for two years without dividing, but this is advisable only where they are given a top dressing each year. Even where the plant is not to be divided, the crowns will continue to push themselves out of the soil and to form new roots above soil level. For them to remain robust and healthy, these roots should be helped in every possible way until the old rootstock is discarded and the crowns separated and replanted into freshly prepared beds. The process is continuous and top dressings should be given at least once each year, for it must be remembered that the double primroses may be propagated only vegetatively and for this reason must be helped so that stock may be increased as quickly as possible.

The leisure gardener or those who might find top-dressing materials difficult to obtain will find that the plants will obtain some assistance in forming new roots if soil is drawn up around the crowns after flowering has ended. But wherever possible, a top dressing should be used to augment the rapidly diminishing supplies of food and humus in the soil, for double primroses are gross feeders. An excellent compost may be made by using fresh pasture loam of a fibrous nature and preferably one which is slightly greasy to the touch, together with some peat or leaf mould and very well decayed manure, cow manure being preferable. The materials should be used in equal quantities and should be passed through a sieve (riddle) to remove any undesirable vegetative matter and stones before being thoroughly mixed together. The compost should be pressed around the crowns with the fingers, using it in as friable a condition as possible. As soon as the new roots come into contact with the top dressing they will grow away rapidly if the plants are kept comfortably moist. The supply of plant food will be utilised by the vigorous new roots, the leaves quickly taking on a rich, velvety green appearance.

VARIETIES OF THE DOUBLE PRIMROSE

ARTHUR DE SMIT. Now rare but it is one of the loveliest of the doubles, and was raised in Germany. The blooms, borne on single footstalks, being of rich purple edged with yellow.

ARTHUR DU MOULIN. It goes by many names and is believed to have been introduced from Ireland towards the end of the 19th century, for de Moleyns is the family name of Lord Vertry. It is also known as Dumoulin and des Moulens. It is the most important double, being the first to bloom and being the only variety to yield pollen in quantity, with the exception of the semi-double blooms of Prince Silverwings. The flowers are of beautiful formation and are of deepest violet, borne on short stems.

BON ACCORDS. More than a dozen double primroses were raised at the Cocker Brothers' nurseries near Aberdeen during the first years of this century, and all, with but one or two exceptions (Bon Accord Salmon and Yellow) are still in cultivation and show no signs of losing their original vigour. Almost all the blooms are similar; having the flat rosette-like appearance of Red Paddy, being neat and symmetrical. They are of easy culture and flourish under average conditions, and for one wishing to start a collection of double primroses, the dozen Bon Accords still in cultivation would give satisfaction. Bon Accord is the motto of the City of Aberdeen. They are 'bunch' primroses, a number of the flowers being borne on footstalks after the manner of the native primrose, whilst others on the same plant appear from a short polyanthus stem.

BON ACCORD BEAUTY. The blooms are large and of deep purple-blue, the petals being edged with white and spotted with white towards the edges.

BON ACCORD BLUE. The largest of all the Bon Accords, the blooms are of a lovely shade of rich blue borne on decidedly polyanthus stems. Though now scarce it is one of the easiest to manage.

BON ACCORD BRIGHTNESS. Believed to be extinct, this must surely be the variety now called 'Crathes Crimson', for it answers the description in every aspect.

BON ACCORD CERISE. The petals are flat and perfectly rounded, forming a near button-like rosette of a lovely shade of clear cerise-pink, the bloom being sweetly perfumed. Of strong constitution.

BON ACCORD ELEGANS. Outstanding amongst the Bon Accords but is the most difficult to grow well, requiring a rich diet. The attractive orchid-pink flowers are edged and flecked with white.

BON ACCORD GEM. The blooms are of bright rosy-red, shaded with mauve and are produced with freedom. The attractively waved petals accentuate the beauty of the blooms. The easiest and most vigorous in this section.

BON ACCORD JEWEL. A magnificent variety but is now rarely to be found. The large deep purple flowers are shaded with crimson on the reverse side.

BON ACCORD LAVENDER. The blooms are large with attractively waved petals and are of a lovely shade of purest lavender with a golden centre.

BON ACCORD LILAC. Of easy culture, the blooms are flat and are of a pleasing shade of lilac-mauve, the petals being marked with yellow at the base.

BON ACCORD PURITY. This must surely be one of the lovelist of all double primroses. The blooms, which are large and full petalled, are of a lovely shade of creamy-white tinged with green, providing a most attractive appearance where growing in partial shade. The blooms, with their frilled petals, are held on sturdy footstalks so that they are held above the bright green foliage.

BON ACCORD PURPLE. The blooms are large and borne on polyanthus stems and are of a glorious shade of burgundy-purple flushed with crimson on the reverse side.

BON ACCORD ROSE. This variety of robust constitution and of semi-polyanthus habit was sent to me as 'Old Rose', yet I can find no trace of such a variety in any gardening literature, whilst Bon Accord Rose is said to be extinct. My belief, however, that it is Bon Accord Rose is because of the dainty, rounded bloom which is rather flat like most of the Bon Accords and has the same conspicuous orange markings at the base of each petal. The habit, too, is the same as the Bon Accords. The colour is deep old rose.

BURGUNDY. The plants in my garden bear a large well-shaped bloom of deep burgundy-red, flecked with white. This is an old variety which retains its original name but is tending to lose vigour unless well grown.

BUXTON'S BLUE. It bears bloom of pure turquoise-blue and is a plant of vigorous habit, though is now rarely to be found. It is a 'sport' from the single blue primrose, found in a garden at Bettws-y-Coed at the beginning of the century.

CASTLEDERG. A chance seedling discovered by Mrs Scott of Castlederg, Co. Tyrone, the large star-shaped blooms being of deep sulphur-yellow, splashed with pink and brown. The early blooms may open single, but it is quite lovely and is a plant of vigorous habit.

CHEVITHORNE PINK. Raised by Mrs Spence at Stewartstown, Co. Tyrone, it makes a compact plant and is of easy culture. It remains long in bloom and bears small, beautifully formed flowers of a lovely shade of orchid-pink held on short polyanthus stems.

CHEVITHORNE PURPLE. This plant now seems much more rare than its pink counterpart but is of similar habit. The blooms are of deep purple-blue, the petals being edged with white.

CLOTH OF GOLD. A magnificent variety, of robust constitution and is extremely free flowering. It is thought to be a 'sport' from the 'Double Sulphur', for it possesses the same habit, having large pale green leaves. The bloom is bright yellow but is of not so deep a colour as Carter's 'Cloth of Gold' which is now extinct.

CRATHES CRIMSON. This lovely variety is said to have been found in the grounds of Crathes Castle in Scotland, though from the familiar shape of the blooms it could be Bon Accord Brightness, thought to be extinct. The round, neat flowers are of bright purple-crimson and possess a sweet perfume.

CRIMSON EMPEROR. It possesses a rather stronger constitution than Crimson King, whilst the bloom has a slightly more purple tint. It is, however, said to be the same variety which may reveal variations of colour and vigour where growing in different gardens.

CURIOSITY. Also known as Golden Pheasant, this variety was at one time grown in large numbers, but over-propagation to supply the demand has reduced its vigour. The bloom is most interesting, the deep yellow ground colour being flecked with rose and bronzy markings. The blooms are borne on dwarf polyanthus stems.

DOUBLE CREAM. Now rare, it is a plant of robust habit and bears fully double blooms of a lovely shade of Jersey cream.

DOUBLE GREEN (a). This is not really a true double for it is caused by the sepals of the flower being developed as foliage leaves, a condition known as 'phyllody'. It is to be found occasionally among a batch of primroses in any part of the British Isles, but seems to be more prevalent in Ireland. For some unknown reason it is often called the Exeter primrose. In appearance it is unique and interesting rather than beautiful.

DOUBLE GREEN (b). There is also a true double green as mentioned by Parkinson, which was thought to be extinct; it has recently been found again in a Dorset garden, whilst plants may be obtained from Ireland.

DOUBLE SULPHUR. It is pleasing to know that this interesting primrose, mentioned by Tabernaemontanus in 1500, still exists and still retains its original name. Forming large sage-green leaves, it is similar in every respect to Cloth of Gold, but the bloom is a shade paler.

DOUBLE WHITE. Gerard's Double White and a plant of true primrose habit, the fully double blooms being of paper white and held on long, single footstalks making them ideal for posy bunches, for which purpose the plants should be grown under cloches, otherwise they may be washed into the soil by heavy rains. It is a plant of vigorous habit and of easy culture and is most free flowering.

DOUBLE YELLOW. Obviously 'sports' from the wild primrose must abound in various forms and especially with yellow flowering varieties. Giant Yellow, Giantess Yellow, Early Yellow and Late Yellow are all forms which at some time or other have been described in the garden Press. That in my garden, which is quite distinct from both the Double Sulphur and Cloth of Gold, bears a large, bright yellow bloom, the base of the petals being shaded with orange.

DOWNSHILL ENSIGN. It was raised with a number of others by Mr Murray Thomson early this century. The then recently introduced *P. juliae* seems to have had some influence in their raising for each of the dozen or more varieties bear bloom of various shades of blue and purple. The variety 'Bluebird', now lost but which received an Award of Merit in 1930, appears to have been the best for its blooms were more than one inch across and were of a lovely shade of lavender-blue. Ensign is the last of the double primroses to bloom, its rather shaggy blooms being of bright violet-blue and held on very long footstalks from a short polyanthus stem. The foliage is smooth and of brilliant green.

FRENCH GREY. The earlier writers named this variety 'Dingy', and the name fits the description well, the blooms being of a dirty white shade or French white or grey as it is called. The blooms are borne with freedom on long footstalks whilst the plant is of easy culture.

MADAME POMPADOUR. This lovely variety, so difficult to grow, bears a large double bloom of deep velvety crimson on single footstalks. The texture of its bloom is unique, hence it is always in demand at more than one guinea a root. It originated in France about 150 years ago and is also known as Pompadour and Crimson Velvet.

MARIE CROUSSE. I could not disagree more with Mr Sacheverell Sitwell when he describes this variety as being 'not worthy of outstanding merit', for in my opinion it is everything a good garden plant should be. It it a strong, easy grower, increasing rapidly, and bears a large, densely double bloom on short, sturdy polyanthus stems. The blooms are of a lovely shade of Parma-violet, splashed and edged with white, and they carry a delicious perfume.

The description given in *The Garden* for April 1882, shortly after the plant had received the Award of Merit from the Royal Horticultural Society, describes it well : 'the blooms are one inch across and perfectly double, the petals forming a compact rosette . . .'

OUR PAT. It was found amongst a batch of *P. juliae* at the Daisy Hill Nurseries, Newry, and was named after the owner's daughter. It is unusual in that the olive-green foliage is veined with crimson-bronze. The small sapphire-blue flowers are borne in profusion on long footstalks. The plant is of vigorous habit and is of easy culture and is one of the last of the doubles to bloom, thus extending the season.

QUAKER'S BONNET. A very old variety probably a 'sport' from *P. rubra*. The bloom is the most beautifully formed of all the doubles, making a rosette of perfect symmetry and being of purest lilac-mauve. It blooms with as great a freedom as Double White and is a plant of sturdy constitution. Also, *Lilacina plena*.

RED PADDY. It is the *Sanguinea plena* and *Rubra plena* of old Irish gardens and a charming variety. It is a strong grower and bears large numbers of small, symmetrical rose-red blooms which have a salmon-pink flush and an attractive edge of silver. The blooms are flat and dainty and possess a sweet perfume.

ROSE DU BARRI. Without doubt this is one of the two or three loveliest of all double primroses. It is now extremely rare and seems to have been grown in one or two gardens for so long that it now resents moving to any other place. Mr Sacheverell Sitwell states that 'it is probably of early Victorian origin' and I should not think this to be far wrong from what I have been told of those plants growing in a particular Wiltshire garden. The blooms are big and cabbage-like and are of a glorious shade of purest pink, flushed with orange – like 'Picture' rose.

TYRIAN PURPLE. One of the best of all primroses, indeed it is one of the best plants in the garden. The blooms are the size of a 10p piece and held on sturdy primrose footstalks. The colour of the bloom is bright purple, flushed with crimson, whilst the foliage is brilliant green. It makes a large plant of robust constitution. It is said to have originated in Cornwall.

THE SINGLE PRIMROSE

Besides the double primroses and those of quaint form, the single *P. juliae* hybrids and varieties of *P. acaulis* possess outstanding beauty and many have become collectors plants of antique value. One of the most beautiful of the singles is Miss Massey, a variety of the Common primrose, raised towards the end of the 19th century. Until 1950, at a nursery situated on the outskirts of Manchester, it grew in large beds covering an acre and the plants cost sixpence each. Here some short distance from the smoke laden atmosphere of the city, Miss Massey flourished as nowhere else but in 1950, the nursery was purchased for building purposes and if the variety is still obtainable, plants will cost at least £1. Miss Massey is an outstanding variety, bearing large bright ruby red flowers of thick velvet-like texture. It was used in the breeding of the equally fine Julius Caesar, its crimson flowers covered in a grape-like 'bloom' and which has become almost as rare, though it is still obtainable from several growers in Ireland.

Of greater antiquity is the single white, Harbinger so prized because of its earliness to bloom and which has also become extremely rare. The exquisitely lovely Dorothy with its beautifully frilled petals has also become almost extinct though it is a plant of the strongest constitution, likewise Sir Bedivere with its star-shaped blooms of chocolate-brown and bright green foliage. Each of these lovely primroses has outstanding beauty and will amply reward those who search for them. They must not be allowed to become extinct.

P. juliae from which many of the single primroses are descended was introduced into Britain from the Caucasus in 1900, and with its hardiness and freedom from disease, its free flowering qualities and compact habit, it must be one of the most important plant introductions of all time. For some years it remained in comparative obscurity growing in the gardens of St John's College, Oxford, the original home of many of our most popular plants. Then, soon after the ending of the First World War, it received the attention of several enthusiastic hybridists who were to cross it with our native primrose, also with the oxlip and cowslip. Later it was crossed with the polyanthus, until today we have 200 or more garden plants containing *P. juliae* 'blood', though only a small number retain the true *juliae* form. All these lovely plants, which differ but slightly in their form and habit, are ideal plants for the modern labour-saving garden, and indeed *P. juliae* may truly be said to be a plant of the 20th century. The *juliae* hybrids are now known as Juliana hybrids, though the origin and application of this name calls for some explanation, unknown to the author, and there seems little point in its use in preference to the more correct term of *juliae* hybrids.

The *P. juliae* hybrids, in almost all instances, possess the same healthy glossy foliage as the parent plant, whilst the leaves are of a deep green colour and are neat and compactly formed, being more so than those of *P. acaulis,* which are larger, more upright and considerably more crinkled. It is, however, in many cases difficult to differentiate between those plants of polyanthus form and those of the true primrose habit, and whilst there are plants which are truly representative of both forms others may be classed somewhere between the two and may be called semi-polyanthus in habit.

ITS HARDINESS

Though the primrose is a native of the Northern hemisphere, from North America to Siberia, it is remarkable how well the plants will tolerate extremes of climate. Through my articles on the primrose in the Gardening Press and my previous books on the subject many letters continue to arrive from all parts of the world requesting plants, and it is surprising how well they adapt themselves to their new homes with only a little help, in S. Africa, Australia and other warm places. In the more temperate climate of New Zealand they grow well, giving no trouble at all, whilst in Europe, particularly the cool, mountainous regions, they are to be found in their full beauty. In the U.S.A. they grow well in the Eastern Seaboard States where the plants receive the cool, moist conditions they appreciate so much, but even in California they are widely grown. Across Canada, from British Columbia to New Brunswick, primroses thrive in the cold winter climate, and even from Uranium City in Alaska, a letter from an Irish immigrant describes his primroses, which he took out with him, as being perfectly happy growing under near arctic conditions.

The ability of the native British primrose to withstand such extremes of climate is well illustrated in a letter which appeared in the *Journal of the Royal Horticultural Society* in 1952. Dr D. G.

Barton, writing from British Coumbia, says, 'Kamlopps, in British Columbia, is situated in what is known as the "Dry Belt", the rainfall averaging only 8 inches each year. The soil, for the most part very sandy, overlies strata of rock or boulders. I was amazed to find that polyanthus and *Primula acaulis* grow to perfection. Some of the best blooms came from the gardens where plants grow in full sun with no shade at any time.' To quote Mr Barton again : 'During the winter of 1949-50 the thermometer dropped to 40° below zero, with only a scant covering of snow. I saw many varieties of bloom the following spring and they were very fine indeed. Even the lengths of stems were excellent.' What other plants would be able to stand up to 70° of frost without any protection, and five months later temperatures reaching 100°F, and bloom to perfection year after year?

Though well able to tolerate such extremes of temperature, there is no denying that the primrose is happiest in a cool, temperate, moist climate for which reason the British Isles can claim to be its real home. Even in Britain, the plants grow better close to the sea and down the Western side of England and Ireland where they enjoy the warm, moist west winds better than the cold, dry winds of the east. In parts of Ireland and in the South-West of England (the West Country) the plants will make at least twice as much growth in a season as they will in the drier parts, whilst the plants will come into bloom at least a month earlier. In the South-West, primroses may be gathered from mid-February until the end of April, whilst near the North-East of England and in Scotland, the plant will not begin to bloom until the first days of April, with but one or two exceptions, and will continue in bloom until the end of May. Here, in a late spring, 'Lady Lettice' and the long flowering 'Barrowby Gem' will often be found in bloom until the middle of June.

Primroses growing in a moist climate take on a quality of bloom not to be found where the plants are growing in a cold, dry climate. Moisture not only accentuates the colour of the bloom, but also its size and length of stem, whilst the foliage takes on a rich bright green appearance. Where abundant moisture is not supplied naturally, then the plants should be given as much help as possible by providing the soil with ample supplies of humus and with artificial watering during periods of drought which, especially in the North, are often experienced in May, when the primrose will still be in full bloom.

It is one of the characteristics of the primrose that the plants may be moved whilst in bud and bloom without harming the bloom in any way. It is one of the very few plants to withstand transplanting at almost any time of the year, and only during a period of dryness or when the ground is troubled by frost, should this be avoided. In his poem, Cowslips and Primroses, John Clare makes mention of this quality:

> The cottager when coming home from plough
> Brings home a cowslip root in flower to set
> Thus ere the Christmas goes the spring is met . . .

The ability of the primrose to tolerate being moved when in bloom lies in its extremely fibrous rooting system. Although its main roots, like those of all members of the family, are fleshy, numbers of small fibrous roots grow from the main roots and to which the soil will adhere unless it be dry and dusty when the plants should never be lifted. If planted without undue delay, there will be no loss of bloom if the plants have begun to open their buds, whilst even the fully opened blooms will not resent the change of position if the plants are watered in.

From John Clare's poem it would appear that the time of year played its part in moving the roots when in bud and bloom, for this must have been towards the end of February or early March when the cool, moist conditions ensure that the plants quickly become established in their new quarters. The leaf structure of the plant also contributes greatly to its ease in transplanting; and indeed plays a large part in maintaining the health of the plant during periods of drought.

All members of the primrose family have been endowed by nature with large wrinkled leaves. This wrinkling is due to the veins of the leaves being deeply set to form grooves or channels down which the smallest drop of dew can trickle down to the roots of the plant. Again this is helped on its way to the roots by the formation of the leaves around the crown of the plant at ground level, thus moisture has no escape when once it falls on the surface of the leaf and is directed to the roots of the plant by the shortest possible way. The fleshy roots, too, enable the plants to store up the maximum amount of moisture, whilst the masses of fibrous roots search far and wide for moisture and nourishment. All of which enables the primrose to survive under almost all conditions to be found in the average British garden, though being lovers of moisture, primroses grow best where they can obtain their moisture requirements throughout the year. 'Their crimpled, curdled leaves' do however permit the plants to receive valuable moisture during the nights of late spring and early summer when the plants are building up their constitution for next season's flowering, and which is so often a time of year when dry conditions prevail.

Nor must the ability of the primrose to resist attacks by pest and disease be overlooked, for in this respect it is one of the healthiest of all plants, rarely troubled in any way when given the conditions it desires.

PLANTING

Being so fibrous rooted, the primrose hybrids may be planted at almost any time except when the ground is frozen or during a period of drought. It is said that immediately after flowering is the best time to do so but this means during May or June which is generally a dry period, hot sunshine accompanying warm drying winds. Moreover, there would seem to be little point in planting primroses in beds at a time of the year when the plants may be expected to make no contribution to the summer display.

Where the soil is light and the climate dry, between October and early March seems the best time to plant, preference being given to the late autumn months so that the plants will receive ample supplies of moisture during winter to enable them to become fully established before the spring which is usually a dry period of the year. Also, where primroses are being used to carpet a bed of bulbs or for inter-planting with other spring-flowering plants then autumn, when the beds are being planted afresh following the summer display, will be the most suitable time to plant.

As a general rule, the best time to transplant primroses is in autumn and during the early weeks of winter where the soil is light. Early spring is the most suitable time where the soil is of a heavy nature though here again, with the ability of the primrose to survive being moved when in full bloom, planting may be done throughout the spring months when conditions are right. By planting in autumn, the plants will have time to become firmly established before the frosts which may lift them out of the ground. Where this occurs, the plants should be trodden back as soon as the frost has left the soil.

The plants must be set well into the ground, spreading out the roots with a trowel. The primrose (and polyanthus) is one of the few plants which cannot be planted too deeply, for it is from the crown of the plant that the new roots are produced and if not set well into the ground, these roots will fail to come into contact with the soil and will play no part in the health of the plant. The plants should be made quite firm, and where the soil is friable it is advisable to tread in the plants. They will come to no harm even if the leaves are crushed. Where planting into heavy soil all that should be done will be to press the plants firmly in with the fingers. Should dry conditions prevail at planting time, give the plants a thorough soaking after planting.

The time of year when the plants first begin to bloom is decided by situation. A primrose, growing in Cornwall will bloom before the end of February, possibly earlier if growing along the sheltered banks of the Helford River, whilst a plant growing in North-Eastern England will not have attained its full beauty until mid-April and even later if the spring is unduly cold. Position will also play a part in determining the flowering period, for where planted in a pocket which attracts the sun the plants will bloom 10-14 days earlier than those growing on a northerly slope in the same garden. Also some varieties will naturally bloom as much as a month earlier than others, though possibly growing alongside each other. This will enable the flowering season to be greatly extended, for when those which come first into bloom, e.g. *Altaica grandiflora* and 'Mauve Queen', have finished flowering, others will be coming into bloom. The lovely 'Felicity' and 'Afterglow' come late into bloom, continuing the season until the end of May in a northerly garden. The flowering times are given for plants growing in central England. Further north or south they will bloom 10-15 days later or earlier as position and climatic conditions dictate.

VARIETIES OF THE SINGLE PRIMROSE

(1) In bloom mid-March   (3) In bloom early April
(2) In bloom late March   (4) In bloom mid-April

AFTERGLOW (3). Originating near Drake's old home at Buckland in Devon, this is a superb new primrose, of rich rust-orange colour with a distinct eye.

English tulip Sir Joseph
Paxton (flamed bizarre)

Old English tulip Sam
Barlow (flamed bizarre)

English tulip Scarnell's Bijou (feathered rose). From a coloured engraving
of 1850

ALTAICA, GRANDIFLORA (1). An old variety from the Caucasus, it is early to bloom, the flowers being of pure mauve-pink and most prolific.

ALTAICA, RUFFLES (1). This is a form of *Altaica grandiflora,* bearing a bloom of the same colour, held above pale green leaves. The petals are attractively frilled.

ANITA (2). A startling primrose with its navy-blue flowers, suffused with crimson and held above the foliage, almost like a cineraria. It is ideal for window boxes and is very long flowering.

APPLEBLOSSOM (1). Of this beautiful old primrose, Mr Sitwell says, 'it has the appearance of a bud of apple blossom opening in the sun'. The fully opened bloom is of appleblossom pink.

AVALON (1). Enjoys shade, and when first seen by the writer was thought to be a bed of 'Princess of Wales' violets, with which it is almost identical in its violet-blue colouring. A lovely primrose, remaining in bloom for a very long period and is most prolific.

BELLE DES JARDINES (3). A lovely old variety, the bloom being of an attractive shade of clear rosy-red.

BELVEDERE (3). This grand old primrose bears blooms of a true lilac colour, and which are of immense size.

BETTY GREEN (1). A Dutch variety having vivid claret-red blooms of medium size, very freely produced, and attractive rich apple-green foliage.

BLUE HORIZON (3). Found in a Kentish garden and introduced by Six Hills Nursery Ltd., Stevenage, and what a gem it is! The blooms are clear sky-blue, freely produced. In habit it is like Wanda, from which it is a 'sport', and it flowers for ever.

BLUE RIBAND (1). Possibly the best blue primrose of Juliae habit. It was raised in Scotland by Mr George Murray of *Chrysanthemum maximum* fame, and as would be imagined, it possesses a hardy and vigorous constitution. The leaves are deep green, the blooms being of mid-blue with red shading at the centre.

BRIDGET (4). Rich mauve-pink with large yellow eye. Very late and of very dwarf habit. An uncommon primrose and one of the last to bloom.

BUCKLAND BELLE (3). A Champernowne introduction, and a superb primrose of deep violet-blue flushed with crimson and of extremely strong constitution. It has a large pale yellow eye.

BUNTY (2). Lovely deep-blue with large flowers freely produced over a long period. Has a deep yellow eye.

CECILY MORDAUNT (4). A most attractive hybrid, having deep green leaves, its violet-blue flowers being shaded with crimson at the centre.

CHARLES BLOOM (3). A superb variety, of semi-polyanthus habit and of sturdy constitution. The blooms are of a rich velvet crimson-purple with deep orange eye and are freely produced.

CHERRY (2). Its name amply describes the colour of its blooms, daintily borne on such dwarf polyanthus stems that it could not truly be classed as a polyanthus. It forms a plant of compact habit.

COTTAGE MAID (3). A lovely old variety bearing bloom of deep lilac-pink with a wide candy stripe down each petal.

CRADDOCK WHITE (3). It has deep green leaves, the veins being of bronze, its white blooms with their yellow centre providing a striking contrast to the foliage. The flowers possess a strong fragrance.

CRIMSON CUSHION (2). It has the same compact form and circular leaves as Purple Cushion, its bright blood-red blooms which are free of all purple colouring, being held on short crimson stems.

CRIMSON GLORY (2). It seems to have much *P. acaulis* 'blood' and bears a huge pure crimson-red bloom above extremely crinkled pale green foliage.

CRIMSON QUEEN (3). Extremely hardy, the large magenta-red blooms are held above glossy pale green foliage.

CRISPII (2). A lovely primrose, covering itself with a mass of mauve-pink blooms. Of *P. acaulis* habit.

DAVID GREEN (1). The dark burgundy-red blooms are very free and against the vivid emerald-green foliage, with the evening sun behind, it makes a plant of outstanding beauty. A bloom with almost complete lack of eye.

DINAH (2). A gem from Holland, remaining eight weeks in bloom. The dainty blooms are like real velvet, burgundy-crimson in colour, and have a unique olive-green eye. In bloom again in late autumn when it is more colourful than any primrose.

DOROTHY (2). A rare pale lemon-yellow of excellent habit and having a long flowering season. Very strong grower. Has delightful frilled petals, and flowers again in autumn. A really lovely primrose.

E. R. JANES (2). An older variety, but a beauty. An ideal rockery primrose, for when in bloom it shows almost no foliage – just a mass of salmon-pink blooms, flushed orange, slightly scented and held in clusters to the sun. It flowers again in late autumn and may remain in bloom over winter in a sheltered garden.

F. ASHBY (2). An amazing little primrose, its bronze foliage, red stems and deep crimson blooms give it an almost black appearance. It is a plant of most dainty, compact habit.

FLENE (1). Similar in colour and texture to Miss Massey, but the velvet-crimson blooms are of a unique shape.

FRUHLINGZAUBER (1). Deep royal purple, the large flat blooms are held well above the foliage. The best true purple. A magnificent primrose of strong constitution and very free flowering. Increases rapidly.

GEM OF ROSES (2). An old *P. acualis* hybrid and a beauty, the large rose-pink blooms having a large yellow eye which is surrounded with white.

GLORIA (2). One of the first *juliae* hybrids, it covers itself with a mass of glowing crimson-scarlet blooms which have attractive white markings on the inside edge of the petals.

GROENKEN'S GLORY (3). A Dutch variety of compact habit. The blooms are a bright mauve-pink with a unique green eye. One of the most attractive of all.

HARBINGER (1). A very old variety which comes early into bloom and is now very rare. It bears a large white bloom with a yellow centre above *P. acaulis*-like foliage. Has not such a strong constitution as the *P. juliae* whites.

HENLEIGH BEAUTY (3). Raised in Devon, the dainty blooms are of a light pinkish-red colour with a golden centre.

ICOMBE HYBRID (3). A plant of vigorous habit with apple-green foliage and bearing a large bloom of rosy-mauve with a white eye.

IRIS MAINWARING (2). Delicate pure pale blue, flushed pink. The foliage is deep green and the whole is of very compact habit. One of the best primroses and an excellent rockery plant.

JEWELL (3). A very free flowering crimson-purple, ideal for the rockery. A little gem amongst primroses.

JILL (2). An unusual little primrose rather like Tawny Port as to daintiness of habit; and the mauve blooms are quite flat in form with an unusual greenish-white centre.

JOAN SCHOFIELD (1). A superb variety, one of the best half-dozen primroses in cultivation. Its huge blooms are wine-red, flushed vermilion, and have a large yellow star-shaped eye. The earliest of all primulas to bloom, and it flowers for weeks.

JOHN ASHWORTH (3). A grand variety of compact habit, bearing dark mahogany-red blooms held above deep green foliage.

JOHN HAMMOND (3). A distinct large cherry-red bloom with large orange centre. A rare variety, and the colour is quite unique.

JULIAE (2). The most dwarf of all. The small dainty blooms are of a deep purple-blue flushed crimson. An ideal rock primrose.

JULIAE ALBA (3). Similar in habit to the better-known *juliae*. A primrose well worth growing. The bloom is purest white and the constitution robust though dainty of habit.

JULIUS CAESAR (1). A fine primrose, raised by Miss Wynn of Avoca, Co. Wicklow. It has Miss Massey for a parent, hence its large bright claret-red bloom accentuated by the dark bronze foliage. One of the first to bloom.

KEITH (3). Another very rare variety having frilly petals, and being of very dwarf habit. The colour is a delicate pale yellow, the blooms being tiny, like those of Lady Greer.

KINGFISHER (3). Of dwarf, compact habit, the blooms are of rich sapphire blue with a yellow and red centre, and are held on 1 inch stems.

LILAC BUNTY (1). This is the lovely rose-lilac form of the better known Blue Bunty. The plant possesses a stronger constitution.

LILAC TIME (3). A charming little variety, the pale lilac-rose coloured blooms being borne from a small polyanthus stem giving it a most dainty appearance.

LINGWOOD BEAUTY (3). A late variety, having bright cerise-crimson flowers with deep orange eye and bright green foliage.

LIZZIE GREEN (2). A unique new primrose having small star-like brick-red flowers, but unfortunately blooms for only a short period.

LUCINDA GREEN (1). Like all the 'Greens' it is early to bloom, the flowers being of deep mauve with a candy stripe down each petal.

MADGE (3). A charming primrose of very dwarf polyanthus habit and bearing a large bloom of phlox pink with an attractive silver sheen. The best *Juliae* of its colour.

MARTIN ARGLES (2). A lovely novelty having bloom of deep claret-purple with a bright orange and crimson centre. A most colourful primrose.

MAUREEN GENDERS (4). An outstanding primrose. The blooms are deep mahogany-crimson edge white, with a large pale yellow star-like centre. Free flowering and late, being at its best early in May.

MAUVE QUEEN (1). Very early indeed and excellent for bunching, the pure lilac-mauve blooms are held well above the foliage. Ideal for edging and window boxes.

MIRANDA (1). Early to bloom, its flowers are of a rich purple-crimson, held above the deep green foliage.

MISS MASSEY (1). A lovely old variety now almost extinct. The habit is dwarf and the blooms are of a rich bright ruby-red with the leaves a bright cucumber green. Mentioned by Walter Wright in *Popular Garden Flowers,* published 1911.

MORTON HYBRID (4). Of very dwarf habit, the brilliant red blooms have a very large clear yellow centre. Very showy, but of not too easy culture.

MRS FRANK NEAVE (3). A long flowering, magenta-crimson variety, bearing a small dainty bloom with attractive bottle-green foliage.

MRS MACGILLAVRY (2). Produces masses of rich violet-mauve flowers in March. Of sturdy constitution, a grand primrose.

MRS PIRRIE (3). Of Scottish origin, this is a fine rock plant of dwarf habit; the rich mauve bloom is freely produced.

PAM (2). Dainty crimson-purple, very free flowering over a long period. An ideal rock primula, having the smallest of all blooms.

PAULINE (3). A magnificent primrose enjoying a stiff soil and bearing a very large bloom of intense terra-cotta orange, shaded with yellow.

PERLE VON BOTTROP (1). This is one of the finest plants of the garden, being a *Juliae* hybrid of German origin. The blooms are of vivid claret-purple, held well above the glossy dark green leaves and being of true primrose habit.

PRIMAVERA (3). Possibly the most striking variety. The flowers are of a brilliant orange-scarlet-crimson with no trace of mauve or magenta. The large orange eye makes it shine like a beacon.

PRINCE ALBERT (3). An old polyanthus-primrose, the blooms being borne in clusters rather than in trusses. The bloom is of a crimson-plum colour, with a blush-blue candy stripe down the edge of each petal. Not of so robust habit as the others.

PURPLE BEAUTY (3). A lovely primrose, having flowers of rich crimson, flushed mauve, and attractive pale geen foliage.

PURPLE CUSHION (3). Rich claret and navy, like a super Wanda but not so tolerant of the sun. The foliage is unique, like that of a violet plant with stems of the leaves a brilliant red.

PURPLE SPLENDOUR (2). A lovely variety having large frilled crimson purple blooms with distinct pale yellow eye and pale green foliage.

QUEEN OF THE WHITES (2). An excellent variety, it bears a profusion of large clear white flowers above bright green foliage.

RED CARPET (1). Raised by Dr Douglas Smith. The plants are covered with a mass of tiny flowers of a most vivid scarlet-red shade.

RED STAR (2). Of true primrose habit, the blooms are large and of a brilliant cardinal red colour with a large bright yellow eye.

REINE DES VIOLETTES (2). Its semi-polyanthus habit is hardly distinguishable; the deep violet blooms have a large yellow centre.

RIVERSLEA (3). A very dwarf primrose and most uncommon, having large dark mauve flowers held well above the cushion-like foliage.

ROMEO (2). A superb variety, bearing huge vivid parma-violet blooms, flat like a pansy. Very prolific, early, and a strong grower. One of the best primroses in cultivation. Lovely when used as a carpet for yellow tulips.

ROSY MORN (1). An old *P. acaulis* hybrid, bearing blooms of purple-pink with a large yellow centre.

RUBIN (1). A magnificent variety, the bronzy-green leaves having red stems. The blooms are small and are of a lovely shade of pinkish wine-red with an orange eye.

SINGLE GREEN (2). Very rare indeed, but so interesting that one plant should be in every collection. The 'bloom' is of leaf construction rather than petals.

SIR BEDIVERE (3). This is a beautiful primrose having long, crinkled leaves of bright cucumber green and bearing eyeless chocolate-red star-shaped flowers.

SNOW CUSHION (2). A Dutch introduction of extremely neat habit, it has bright pale green leaves and bears tiny blooms of purest white on 1 inch stems.

SNOW-WHITE (1). A lovely new white recently introduced from the Continent. It makes a plant of cushion-like foliage and bears its bloom on short footstalks.

SUNSET GLOW (3). It makes a compact plant of cushion-like habit and on short stems bears flat blooms of purest orange-scarlet. Should be grown in partial shade to prevent fading of the bloom.

SWEET LAVENDER (2). An old favourite, the flowers which are of pure lavender being flushed with pink. Possibly extinct.

THE SULTAN (2). This is a large *Juliae* hybrid bearing bloom of a rich brown shade. From the garden of that great primrose grower, William Goddard of British Columbia.

TINY TIM (3). Like an orange-red 'Pam' and possibly has even smaller blooms. A perfect rockery primula.

TRIZONE (3). Found in a Devon garden; a most unusual variety having a dark red ring round the eye, with outer rings of purple and blue.

VERONICA (4). A lovely variety of true *Juliae* habit. The flowers are steel-blue with a deep orange centre and are freely produced. Of most unusual colouring.

WANDA (2). This variety started the vogue of the *Juliae* primroses. One of the earliest to bloom and latest to finsh, and the claret-red flowers thrive in full sun. Does well anywhere.

WANDA'S RIVAL (2). Of true Wanda type but having flowers of a rich rosy-mauve colour. A grand primrose for edging. New and easy to manage.

WENDY (2). Very pale pink, flushed mauve. A large bloom with frilled petals. Easy to propagate and very long flowering indeed, it is a plant of *P. acaulis* habit, with pale green foliage.

WISLEY CRIMSON (2). A new primrose discovered in the grounds of the Royal Horticultural Society at Wisley. The large purple-red blooms are held above bronzy-green foliage.

THE GARRYARDE PRIMROSES

Raised in the village in Ireland bearing their name, the Garryarde primroses are plants of *P. juliae* habit, characterised by the rich reddish-bronze colouring of their leaves. They are hardy and free flowering and are perhaps the loveliest of all the single primroses. Several are of distinct polyanthus form, a number have semi-polyanthus habit, whilst others possess the true *juliae* primrose habit. They come into bloom later than the other single varieties.

BUCKLAND VARIETY (3). Of polyanthus habit, this variety was raised near Drake's old home in Devon and bears a bloom of pure rich velvety cream, as many as a dozen open together on a crimson polyanthus stem.

CANTERBURY (3). This is a superb variety of polyanthus form, its blooms being of a rich cream colour, attractively shaded with apricot-pink. The leaves are bronzy-green.

ENCHANTRESS (2). It is a most beautiful variety with bronzy-green leaves and bearing a creamy bloom, heavily veined and flushed with rose-pink. It is deliciously scented.

ENID (4). Similar in habit and freedom of flowering to its sister 'Guinevere', but with blooms of a much deeper pink, though not necessarily more beautiful.

GUINEVERE (3). A magnificent primrose having deep bronze foliage and large pink blooms held in clusters above the foliage.

HILLHOUSE PINK (3). Similar in habit and the colour of its foliage to Guinevere, it bears a pale pink bloom with a distinct orange eye.

HILLHOUSE RED (3). It has deep bronze-red foliage and bears flowers of burgundy-crimson over a long period.

THE GRAIL (3). A rare variety bearing blooms of attractive Elizabethan brick-red colour, with a large yellow eye.

VICTORY (4). Another of this much-sought-after race from Ireland, with cucumber green leaves and bearing attractive peony-purple blooms.

CHAPTER VI

The Double Hyacinth

The first double hyacinths – Indoor culture – Propagation – Varieties of
the double hyacinth.

It was not until 1830 that the English florists took up the cultivation of the double hyacinth which is now, happily, almost a century and a half later, returning to favour. The first double was
raised in Holland early in the 18th century by Peter Voerheim. It
was named Mary but was soon lost to cultivation. Shortly after
came Voerheim's, King of Great Britain which Henry Phillip's in
his *Flora Historica* (1829) said was the oldest double still in cultivation and it could be obtained until the end of the century. When
first introduced, a single bulb cost upwards of £100 but as much as
£200 was often obtained for an important new double hyacinth
and £10 was the price of a newly established favourite.

Writing in the *Flora Historica,* Phillips, a friend of John Constable, the painter who frequently stayed at his home in Brighton,
said that 'the criterion of a fine double hyacinth of the time consists of its stem being strong, tall and erect, garnished with
numerous large bells each supported by a short and strong footstalk, in a horizontal position so that the whole may have a compact pyramidal form with the uppermost flower erect. The flowers
should be large and perfectly double, that is, well filled with broad
bold petals, appearing rather convex than flat and hollow. The
flowers should occupy about one-half the length of the stem . . .
strong bright colours are in greater request, and make a higher
price than those that are pale. Under bad treatment, good hyacinths will degenerate within two or three years; but in Holland
they have been preserved perfect for almost a century'.

Such was the interest in the double hyacinth in Holland during
the early years of the 18th century that by 1725, Philip Miller said
that there grew more than two thousand varieties many of which
were remarkable in their colourings. Though Henry Phillips has
said that those bearing flowers of rich bright colours were most
in demand, the Dutch growers favoured those which were shaded
inside with a contrasting colour, i.e. the inner petals were of
different colouring from those of the outside which were pointed and

169

reflexed. In his *Scottish Gardener's Directory* (1754), James Justice, who introduced the pineapple into Scotland, wrote of the double white variety Assemblage de Beaute, 'its stem is not very high but is adorned with bells, some of which are broader than an English crown piece, erect and well-reflexed, displaying a large heart (centre rosette), charmingly mixed with violet, scarlet and carnation colours . . . it preserves its fine colours until it fades . . .'

The rosette centre for which the double hyacinth was famed is beautifully depicted in a hand-coloured plate by Mons F. Seligman which appears in Trew's *Plantea Selectae* of 1750. It is one of the most beautifully illuminated botanical works of the time, indeed of all time and the finest floral artists of the day were commissioned to provide the plates. The hyacinth is Gloria Mundi which bore a bloom of soft violet-mauve, the pointed outer petals being gracefully rolled back to reveal the rosette-like centre, a characteristic which is nothing like so prominent in the double hyacinth of today.

One reason for the popularity of the hyacinth was derived from Madame de Pompadour's decision that the French Court should adopt it as one of the 'fashionable' flowers for indoor decoration during winter and spring for the plants could be forced into bloom at a time of year when there were few other flowers about, whilst they would scent a large apartment with their sweet balsamic perfume. Soon they came to be imported in large numbers into Britain when they were grown in glass jars or in pewter or porcelain hyacinth bowls containing only water. They were thus clean to manage and almost trouble free. After flowering, the bulbs were thrown away for growers believed that they were of no further use.

INDOOR CULTURE

The method of growing indoors was to use a top size bulb and to set them with the base of the bulb just above the water. Use rain water if possible and do not allow the roots which form at the base of the bulb to lose contact with the water through its evaporation.

Early in September, introduce the bulbs to the container and allow them to remain in a cool, dark place for two months, until they have formed a strong rooting system and have begun to sprout. When the shoots are about 2 inches high, remove them to a light airy room, comfortably heated when they will come into bloom for

Christmas or shortly afterwards. Or plant the bulbs in pots or bowls containing a mixture of fibrous loam, peat and sand in equal parts. Allow sufficient room between each bulb for the fingers to press the compost around the bulb which should have the neck exposed just above the level of the soil. Place in a dark cupboard or cellar and keep the compost comfortably moist. When removed to a heated room, the plants will require copious amounts of moisture as hyacinths are heavy drinkers. It is for this reason that they are grown almost entirely in the low lying siltland soils of the Zuider Zee where the same varieties have been preserved for centuries without any loss of vigour.

Another method of growing hyacinths indoors is to plant them in pots filled with moss. The method was first put forward at a meeting of the West London Gardeners' Association held in 1841 when Mr Henry Bowers, head gardener at Haleham, near Chertsey described his methods. He would plant early in October three sound bulbs to a size 32 pot (32 to the cast) at the bottom of which was placed an oyster shell. Then the pot was filled with fresh green moss made as compact as possible and into it the bulbs were pressed so that their noses were just below the rim of the pot and covered with a thin layer of moss.

The pots were then placed outdoors in a plunge bed and covered with a six inch layer of boiler ash or old tan and here they remained until the first batch were taken indoors early December and placed in a temperature of 60°–65°F. They would then come into bloom for Christmas. Mr Bowers has told that he watered the bulbs daily, with rain water heated to the temperature of the room or greenhouse.

Growing in sphagnum moss has proved an excellent method of hyacinth culture in town flats for no soil is necessary and if there is no garden to provide a plunge bed, the pots may be placed in a cool dark cupboard until rooting has taken place. The plants when in bloom, are light to handle and may be used in fancy baskets suspended from a wall or ceiling and of such a depth that the pots will be concealed.

After the bulbs have finished flowering indoors, remove the flowering spike and place the bulbs beneath the greenhouse bench or in the garage on shelves until the foliage has died back. When the foliage has turned brown, it should be removed and the bulbs stored in boxes of dry sand or peat until such time as they are planted outside in prepared beds in October. They should not be allowed to bloom the first year after flowering indoors, the flower spike being removed as soon as it appears in spring.

Double hyacinths could be grown in Britain as a specialist crop in those parts where the soil is of a silty loam and where the ground is low lying yet the moisture does not become stagnant and sour about the bulbs. These are the conditions under which the Dutch raise their hyacinths by the million, in a sandy loam which is flooded every so often by the sea or by water overflowing from dykes and ditches.

In Holland, the soil is of a considerable depth. Hogg tells of a friend who when on a visit to a famous bulb grower was shown how it was possible to push down one's arm almost up to the shoulder into a recently prepared hyacinth bed. The same person reports, in an interview with the grower that well decayed cow manure was used in quantity for hyacinths, dug into the soil to a depth of about 12 inches below the planting depth of the bulbs whilst the top 'spit' was given a dressing with leaf mould or peat and fresh soil each year.

PROPAGATION

To propagate hyacinths, top size bulbs should be obtained and several cuts made across the base with a sharp knife to a depth of about half an inch. This is done just before the bulbs are planted 6 inches apart in prepared beds early in October. In spring, remove the flower spike and during dry weather keep the bulbs well supplied with moisture. The energy of the bulbs will then be concentrated on the formation of bulbils which will form from the base where the cuts were made, six or more being produced at the base of each bulb.

As soon as the foliage of the mother bulb begins to die back in summer, the bulbs are carefully lifted and placed in trays on the greenhouse or potting shed bench when the tiny bulblets are detached and re-planted at once in prepared ground, setting them 4-5 inches apart in shallow drills, like peas. They should be planted on a layer of sand and covered with a sprinkling of peat before the soil is raked over them.

As the offsets or bulblets will occupy the ground for eighteen months before lifting they should be covered with decayed leaves or bracken in December to protect them from hard frost, the covering being removed in March when the soil between the rows should be hoed. The growers of old fixed hoops over the beds to which they tied canvas. Around the beds in spring should be erected hurdles to protect the plants from cold winds as they begin to grow. Or surround the beds with wire netting against which are tied sacks or hessian canvas. It is important that the young foliage does not become browned by the winds.

From early summer, water the plants with dilute liquid manure once each week and whenever the weather is dry, give copious amounts of water, actually flooding the ground for if the soil is sandy, the moisture will quickly drain away. When the foliage has died down completely, towards the end of summer, lift the bulbs and place on trays in an airy room to dry. Then remove the foliage and when quite dry, clean the bulbs and replant into beds of freshly prepared soil. Early the following summer the bulbs will form a flower spike and this should be removed to enable the bulbs to utilise all their energy into making a large healthy bulb. They should be grown on during summer and the lifting and re-planting repeated for another year when the bulbs will have attained a size of 18–20 cm. This is the size required for indoor cultivation; for outdoor flowering, a 16 cm bulb may be used. M'Intosh said that 'a good hyacinth bulb, such as is most likely to flower best should be solid and conical; those of flat shape being apt to break into offsets and at best produce very inferior flowers'. It was his opinion and that of the growers of the time, that a five year old bulb produced the finest flowers. 'In Holland', wrote M'Intosh, 'individual bulbs have been known to produce blossoms more than a dozen times (years) and never have been observed to die of old age'. And Hogg, in his *Treatise* said, 'I hold it the extreme of folly in anyone who has a garden, to cast away the roots which have flowered in glasses, much less those in pots; the thousands that are suffered to perish in this way every year in London is astonishing; one year's accumulation of these cast-away bulbs would produce an ample stock for an experimental florist to commence with.'

For the bulbs to remain healthy and vigorous, M'Intosh has told that the Dutch growers 'taught by experience that hyacinths throw out a considerable quantity of poisonous matter from the roots', avoid their planting in the same ground for more than two successive years and where growing as a specialist crop, this is a wise precaution.

Though most of those varieties held in greatest esteem by the growers of the early 19th century have long since perished, there are a number of handsome double hyacinths available to present day growers and the cult of this flower may begin again. It is the earliest of the florist's flowers to come into bloom, those being grown in a warm room indoors being in bloom for Christmas or the early new year. Then come primroses and polyanthuses, auriculas, the old tulips, pinks and carnations and lastly the pompone dahlias and chrysanthemums which will continue the display until once again, the double hyacinths come into bloom. The old florists grew them all in pots and so had something of interest and beauty to enjoy all the year round.

VARIETIES OF THE DOUBLE HYACINTH

BEN NEVIS. Of more compact habit than the single whites, it bears a thick, handsome spike with ideal exhibition placement of its brilliant snow-white florets which have a wax-like appearance.

CHESTNUT FLOWER. A variety of charm, bearing a broad handsome truss around which are arranged neat florets of a lovely shade of apple-blossom pink.

ECLIPSE. A 'sport' from Jan Bos and bearing large florets of similar brilliant red colouring and early flowering.

GENERAL KÖHLER. One of the finest of all doubles for bedding, making a broad spike of pyramidal habit and remaining long in bloom. The colour is of a most unusual and exquisite shade of soft lavender-blue.

MADAME HAUBENSAK. The very double blooms are of a beautiful shade of soft shell-pink as many as 90-100 bells appearing on a well developed stem.

MADAME SOPHIE. A 'sport' from L'Innocence, bearing a huge spike made up of large florets of purest white.

SCARLET PERFECTION. A 'sport' of Madame du Barri, bearing a large symmetrical spike of deep crimson-red, the florets gracefully arranged around the sturdy stem.

VICTORY DAY. A 'sport' of La Victoire, bearing large double florets of deep blood-red. Plant it with Ben Nevis for the striking contrast of its colour.

These double hyacinths can be obtained for about 12½p each which compares favourably with prices asked by the 19th century

florist for named varieties of which there were many, amongst the
most popular being :

Variety	Colour	s	d
Augustus Rex	Red	3	0
Bouquet Constant	Blue	7	0
Catherene la Victorieuse	Red	7	0
Comtesse d'Hollande	White	5	0
Diana of Ephesus	White	2	0
Duchesse de Parme	Red	1	6
Elise	White	5	0
Helicon	Blue	7	0
Henri Quatre	Red	7	0
Josephine	Red	7	6
Kaiser Alexander	Blue	7	6
La Belle Gabrielle	White	7	6
L'Importante	Blue	7	6
Madame St. Simon	White	1	0
Napoleon Bonaparte	Blue	5	0
Noire Veritable	Blue	5	0
Prins van Waterloo	White	6	0
Rouge Pourpre et Noir	Red	5	0
Temple of Apollo	White	5	0
Vekours Rouge	Red	5	0
Venus	White	2	6

CHAPTER VII

The Ranunculus

Its garden qualities – Its introduction – Culture – Famous growers
– Growing from seed.

Of the florist's flowers, the Persian king-cup is that which has
passed into the most complete obscurity. Today, it is to be found in
few gardens yet it is a plant of such easy culture. It gives a display
of great brilliance in the garden whilst it is long lasting as a cut
flower and does not drop its petals. Of neat habit, it is exactly right
for the small modern garden and as in former days, it may be
grown in pots or boxes on a terrace or verandah or in the enclosed
courtyard of a town house. 'The Persian king-cup is a florists' flower
which blows (blooms) in May and June,' wrote M'Intosh, 'succeeding the tulip and exhibiting endless varieties. The ranunculus
excells most flowers in the symmetry of its shape and in the brilliancy and variety of its colours. A bed of choice flowers presents
one of the most attractive objects which nature exhibits in her
gayest mood. Every shade of violet, purple and black is seen
mingled with snow-white and golden yellow whilst some are striped
like the carnation, edged like the picotée or mottled, marbled and
spotted in the most innumerable diversities.'

Writing in 1829, Henry Phillips said that 'the English have raised
more varieties of the ranunculus than any peoples' and said that
the flower was held in high esteem from the middle of the 18th
century. It remained so for about a hundred years.

In 1792, Maddock told of his growing more than 800 varieties
and Mason's catalogue of 1820 lists at least 400 kinds. It was
Maddock's opinion that there were more varieties of this flower
than of any other for he observed that the seed in no instance,
ever produced two flowers exactly alike. The best named varieties
are propagated by division of the tubers, a somewhat laborious task
for modern gardeners to perform but a collection of named varieties
of outstanding beauty could be raised from seed and the best
perpetuated by dividing the tubers.

For brilliance of colour, no other flower is its equal. The poet
Thomson wrote of

  . . . Auriculas, enrich'd
  With shining meal o'er all their velvet leaves;
  And full Ranunculus, of glowing red.

Thomson's plant was *R. sanguineus,* a native of North Africa which was used to impart the brilliant scarlet colour of its flowers to other strains. It was named as a separate species by Philip Miller and was a parent of the Persian strain.

ITS INTRODUCTION

The Ranunculus gives its name to the family of plants which includes the native buttercup and anemone, the clematis and marsh marigold, all plants which grow naturally in damp places and it takes its name from rana, a frog. The so-called Asiatic ranunculus, to be found growing naturally in Persia and Afghanistan and around the shores of the Black Sea was first cultivated in Turkey by the Vizier, Cara Mustapha who brought it to the attention of the Sultan. So great an impression did the beauty of the flowers make on him that he had his emissaries search the area for further species. Several reached France during the reign of Louis IX (mid-13th century), brought back by him when returning from the crusades and they grew in the garden of his mother, Blanche of Castille. Perhaps their culture was not properly understood and they quickly died out for there is no mention of the plant reaching England until the end of the 16th century, Gerard in his *Herbal* (1597) being the first to mention it, saying that 'my Lord and Master, the Rt Hon. the Lord Treasurer had plants sent to him (from Constantinople) whilst others arrived from Syria . . . for our gardens, where they flourished as in their own country'. It is believed that it was the Red Ranunculus, *R. sanguineus* that Gerard mentions and he would almost certainly have received tubers from the Lord Treasurer to plant in his own garden in Holborn. But it was left to the Dutch growers to take up the culture of the plant on a commercial scale and so great was its popularity on the Continent that by the beginning of the 18th century it was being imported into England by the million and in 1720 there appeared the first description of its culture. This was given in *The Complete Florist*, a work written by Henri van Osten, a Dutch gardener of Leyden. Of the ranunculus, he begins by saying that, 'the flower is admired for its beautiful and lively colours which dazzle the sight when the sun shines down upon them'.

Writing in 1731 Philip Miller said that the blooms were so large and of such rich colours 'as to vie with the carnation itself'. In France, it was the Turban ranunculus that was most prized, the Golden Turban or Turban Doré with its scarlet flowers, spotted with gold. Soon, each form was interbred by hybridisation and each country came to be noted for its own particular strain. There were the Scottish and Dutch strains, French and Persian strains whilst the flowers were being continually improved upon, with the markings of every conceivable form and colour. As Maddock said, 'no two flowers were exactly alike'. It had reached its peak of popularity by about 1845 and five years later, Glenny said that it had become 'a neglected flower' for the ranunculus demanded care in its cultivation which an industrial age no longer permitted. It was one of the first of the florist's flowers to die out yet some idea as to the popularity of the flower during the time when it reached its peak may be gathered from a letter which appeared in the *Gardener's Chronicle* of 1844, the writer saying that each year he grew 'from 20 to 30 large beds, planted at various seasons (for succession): but the best time to plant to secure a good bloom is the first week in March'.

Perhaps today with a shorter working week, there will be time to take up the culture of this interesting flower again for in addition to the brilliance of its colours, the ranunculus blooms early in summer, when the tulip is beginning to fade, a time when the garden is usually devoid of blossom whilst waiting for the summer bedding plants to come into bloom.

CULTURE

The criterion of a good show ranunculus was that 'it should have a strong stem, from 8-12 inches tall and that it should bear a flower of at least 2 inches diameter, well filled with concave petals that diminish in size as they approach the centre. The bloom should be of hemispherical form: its component petals imbricated in such a manner as neither to be too close and compact, nor too widely separated but have rather more of a perpendicular than horizontal direction, to display their colours with best effect. The petals should be broad and free from fringe or indentures at the edges, whilst the beauty of their colouring consists in their being dark, clear, rich and brilliant; either of one colour throughout, or otherwise diversified, on white, ash, pale yellow gold, or fire-coloured ground, either in regular stripes or spots, or marble-mottled'.

The natural situation where the common wild ranunculus flourishes, is where the soil is a light but rich loam, low lying and moist but where excessive winter moisture may drain away. It requires a soil that is cool and moist during the heat of summer and yet the surface, by its sandy nature, should not be liable to 'pan', thus cutting off the supply of air to the roots. M'Intosh said that the soil should be 'stronger and more loamy than for tulips and hyacinths'.

James Hamilton of Almondbury, Yorkshire, writing in *The Florist's Magazine* (1845) describes the preparation of his ranunculus beds. 'The first week in February I have the soil dug out to a depth of 2 feet. At the bottom, I place 6 inches of rich turfy loam, chopped into small pieces. In the preceding autumn, I had soil of similar quality mixed with cow manure and collected this through winter until I had sufficient to fill up the excavation for a bed 24 yards long. The heap was turned several times previous to filling in the bed in late February. The compost is rich, light and cooling with the cow manure which, being distributed throughout the soil, combines to form a compost in which I have not failed a single season since 1830, to grow and bloom the ranunculus unequalled by any others I have seen.'

The writer concludes his treatise on ranunculus growing by saying that the surface of the bed was made even, and fresh sandy loam 'from the bank of a hedge' was spread over it to a depth of 3 inches. 'In this, I plant the tubers in rows, 6 inches apart and 2 inches deep. Upon taking up the tubers, I find the fibres abound right to the bottom of the bed.'

'The foundation of all good culture,' wrote the Rev. Tyso 'is in the adaptation of the compost to the natural habitat of the plant. Experience teaches us that the ranunculus delights in a rich hazel-like loam, like the top spit of a pasture, which is tenacious but not clayey.' This he wrote in a treatise of 28 pages published in 1847 and entitled *The Ranunculus, how to grow it; or Practical Instruction in the Cultivation of this favourite Florist's flower, being the result of many years' experience.* It was published by Jackson and Walford of St. Paul's Churchyard and cost a shilling.

All the old florists insisted that the soil should be prepared to a depth of at least 2 feet, incorporating plenty of decayed manure, used hops, old mushroom bed compost, clearings from ditches and any other humus-forming materials, together with a liberal quantity of coarse sand or grit. And if growing in pots in which the plants will bloom, a compost of similar quality should be made up. To grow all the florist's flowers well, a humus-laden compost containing plenty of decayed manure must be prepared. This is the secret of success.

The ranunculus also requires an open, sunny situation, yet one protected from prevailing winds. In the south, the first plantings may be made early in March; in the north, at the month end, preferably under cloches and further plantings may be made at monthly intervals until the end of May when the first plantings made in the south will be coming into bloom. In the very mildest parts and where the soil is of a light sandy nature, a planting of the tubers may be made about mid-October when they will bloom the following April but winter protection may be necessary, covering with bracken or frame lights. Plant claw downwards, placing the tubers on a layer of peat. As soon as the leaves appear, hoe between the rows and water copiously in dry weather. To conserve moisture, the old growers would place moss between the rows. Today, peat is equally efficient and is more readily obtainable.

By planting in pots or boxes in August and September, and introducing them to a slightly warm greenhouse in batches at monthly intervals, bloom may be enjoyed throughout the latter weeks of winter and early spring. The pots should be stood in a closed frame, or in deep boxes covered with glass from planting time until moved indoors. Ranunculuses are not completely hardy and must be protected from frost whether growing in pots or in the open ground.

After flowering, remove the dead blooms and allow the foliage to die back completely. Then when the soil is dry, lift the tubers with care so as not to damage the claws and place them in shallow boxes or trays to dry off before covering them with peat and placing in a frost free room until required for use again.

Many tubers will form offsets which are readily detached at this time and grown on in spring. Should offsets be few, the tubers may be divided with a sharp knife. From the crown will be noticed several small protuberances and as when dividing a begonia tuber, each piece must contain an eye from which the plant will grow. It is not usual to divide the tubers into more than two pieces.

FAMOUS GROWERS

Perhaps the most famous of the ranunculus growers of the early 19th century were Waterson and Lightbody of Selkirk, and the Rev. Joseph Tyso of Wallingford in Berkshire who issued an annual catalogue listing his own introductions, the proceeds from which he gave to worthy causes. In 1833 he published a *Catalogue of choice Ranunculuses (selected from about 800 varieties) and of select Tulips, Dahlias, Pelargoniums and Carnations, grown and sold by the Rev. Joseph Tyso of Wallingford.* The *Floricultural Cabinet* tells us that the catalogue was a one folio sheet, folded as a letter, for distribution 'gratis' and it says 'that the catalogue is admirable, very descriptive and easy of reference, and to the Florist is highly valuable. We should be glad to see it become the standard catalogue'.

The author stated that the collection had taken him 25 years to build up and amongst his finest varieties were Leonora and Reform for both of which he refused the sum of £20. Later, his eldest son took up the culture of his father's ranunculuses and at the Chiswick Show, held on 13th June, 1846 won the Large Silver medal with 24 varieties, mostly of his fathers raising. These included :

Alexis. Yellow ground with brown spots.

Attractor. White ground with a thick purple edge.

Creon. Pure lemon ground with coffee coloured edge.

Delectus. Deep yellow ground with red wire edge.

Gozan. Buff ground with scarlet edge.

Lydia. Yellow ground, mottled with scarlet.

Victor. A dark plum coloured self.

Prices varied from 5s each to £5 a hundred in the catalogue of the Rev. Tyso & Son.

In the *Floricultural Cabinet* of the same year (1847) appears a descriptive list of the best named varieties sent out by George Lightbody of Falkirk. Amongst these he listed :

Arnot Lyle. Clear white ground with rose edge.

Colonel Dennie. Yellow ground with red edge.

Commander Napier. Straw ground with crimson edge.

Gen. Robertson. Cream ground, spotted with crimson.

Larne. Purple mottling on a pure white ground.

Nereus. Pale rosey-pink spots on a pure white ground. This flower is described as of 'extraordinary size . . . one of the finest ever raised'.

Prince Albert. Straw ground with chocolate edge.

Richard Dixon. Clear white ground and purple edge. 'A large massive flower, newly raised.'

Zebrina. Clear white spotted with rose-pink.

Other famous varieties of the time included :

Aust's Nonsuch. White ground with wire edge of purple.

Biddal's Duke of Wellington. Yellow ground, delicately edged crimson.

Costar's Coronation. Buff ground, mottled with pink.

Costar's Tippoo Sahib. Dark red self.

Giles' Eliza. Fine straw self. A super variety!

Kilgour's Queen Victoria. White, with a wire edge of purple.

Lightbody's Rob Roy. Cream ground with crimson edge.

Lightbody's William Penn. White, with a distinct purple edge.

Tyso's Flaminius. Yellow ground, spotted with crimson. One of the best of its class.

Tyso's Laureate. Pure pale yellow self.

Waterson's Epirus. Lemon ground, spotted with red.

Waterson's Robbie Burns. White with a pale purple edge.

A delightful idea of the times was to print the raiser's name with each variety for upon the quality of the plant, the raiser's reputation either increased or was damaged and in consequence, few poor varieties ever saw the light of day. M'Intosh has said that if from several thousand seedlings, the raiser could select just one variety worthy of carrying his name, he would be well satisfied. In the *Flower Garden*, M'Intosh lists nearly 450 varieties, Lightbody's Rob Roy being priced at 3s; Tyso's Lydia 1s; Waterson's Robbie Burns 6s; Lightbody's Sir Water Scott 4s; Biddal's Duke of Wellington 2s 6d; Groom's Marquis of Sligo 5s; Tyso's Midas 10s; Lightbody's Alexander 15s.

GROWING FROM SEED

Modern strains cost about £1 per 100 tubers and are considerably cheaper if purchased by the thousand. From them, a number may be selected which will form the nucleus of a collection of named varieties, for the ranunculus is one of the easiest of plants to hybridise and raise from seed. Modern strains are double or semi-double flowered and are grouped into Persian, French, Turban and Paeony flowered. The Persian type is distinguished by the beautiful symmetry of the blooms and should be used for the raising of new varieties in preference to others. It is however, less hardy than the Turban with its larger, coarser flowers. The Paeony-flowered strain bears large double blooms, usually in shades of rose-pink, whilst in the French strain, the flowers are both double and semi-double and in this strain yellow and orange shades predominate. The Rev. Tyso has given detailed instructions for raising new varieties. Those bearing semi-double blooms which will set seed readily are selected as the seed bearing parent and he has given a list of those most frequently used by the florists of old. In Edged varieties, Grand Monarque and Venus were often used and in spotted, Lord Cochrane and Princess of Wales. The blooms should have their centre and anthers exposed and only the best show varieties should be selected.

To transfer the pollen, use a camel-hair brush to dust each bloom and this should be done between 10 a.m. and 3 p.m. on dry sunny days, repeating the crossing twice daily until the blooms begin to die. Then tie each stem to a cane to prevent them from breaking. A greater degree of control may be obtained by growing in pots under glass. As the seed pods swell, water sparingly and when they have become quite brown, gather and dry in a shaded airy room. It was the opinion of Mr Sweet, a famous grower of the early 1800's that to obtain best results, those varieties showing the greatest colour contrast should be pollinated with each other.

If seed is sown under glass in gentle heat in February in boxes 6 inches deep, it will germinate within six weeks. Early in May, after hardening, plunge the boxes to the rim into the open ground. Towards the end of July, the foliage will begin to die back, then lift the boxes, place in a greenhouse or shed and dry off the tubers, before lifting from the soil. Keep them in boxes of peat until time to plant them out in spring when they will bloom in summer. The best may then be selected for future propagation by division of the tubers and in this way a stock of named varieties built up.

CHAPTER VIII

The Tulip

Its introduction – Tulip vocabulary – Properties of a first-class tulip –
Exhibiting tulips – Their culture – Varieties of the florists' tulip.

Like the hyacinth and ranunculus, the oriental tulip is native of
the Near East. The first reference to the plant was made by Auger
Busbec, Ferdinand I's ambassador to Turkey, in a letter written to
the Sultan in 1554. In this he says that 'he had seen some unusual
flowers growing in a garden near Constantinople'. He writes, 'As
we were passing through the district (Adrionople) an abundance of
flowers was everywhere offered us – Narcissus, Hyacinths and those
which the Turks call "tulipam". ' The name is derived from tulband
(or turban), the Turkish name for the Persian dulband, meaning an
eastern head-dress which the flower resembles both in form and
colour. Busbec is believed to have sent either seed or bulbs back to
Austria and Germany and five years later, Conrad Gesner, the
German botanist wrote of having seen the flower in bloom in the
garden of John Harwart on Augsburg 'sprung from a seed (or
bulb?) which had come from Constantinople . . . It was flowering
with a single beautiful red flower, large, like a lily, formed of eight
petals and it had a very soft sweet and subtle scent'.

In 1561, Matthiolus published his *History of Plants* in which
appeared the first illustration of a tulip. But it was not until 1578
that the plant reached England. Richard Hakluyt, writing in 1582
said, 'within these four years there have been brought into England
from Vienna, diverse kinds of flowers called tulipas and those and
others procured a little before from Constantinople by an excellent
man called Carolus Clusius'. The first tulip to be introduced was
Gesner's 'Red Scented' which was later named *T. gesneriana* in
honour of the German botanist. For its scent, the flowers were in
great demand by the French aristocracy for evening wear. This
tulip, discovered by Ferdinand's ambassador may have been a
variety of *T. suaveolens* which is prominent in S.E. Europe, around
the Sea of Azov and in Persia. It also bears scented flowers and is
early to bloom. Both *T. suaveolens* and *T. gesneriana* are now
naturally distributed across S. Europe. From these species was
evolved the dwarf early flowering tulips known as the 'Duc van

184

Thols' which for almost two centuries have been forced in their thousands to flower in small bowls as Christmas time. They too, are scented and grow to a similar height of about 4 inches.

The double tulip first appeared in 1581 in Vienna and was recorded by Clusius. It is almost certain to have reached the Austrian capital by way of Constantinople for the Turks were excellent gardeners and may have been experimenting with tulips for some considerable time before Busbec sent the first bulbs to Europe.

The first illustration of the famous 'striped' or 'broken' tulips appeared in the *Hortus Floridus* of Crispian de Pas, a celebrated Engraver and by the time of the publication of his Paradisus (1629), Parkinson mentions 140 kinds for by then the tulip was being widely grown in England. Parkinson must have known of the most famous variety of the time, Semper Augustus, which Nicholas Wassenauer, writing in 1623, said 'had been sold for thousands of florins'. It was thought that there were only 12 bulbs in existence, each being worth this sum. John Rea in his *Flora* of 1676 describes it as 'hitherto being of much esteem; it hath a flower not very large but well veined and striped with deep crimson and pale yellow, the bottom dark violet purple'.

This tulip brought about the 'tulip mania' in France and Holland and in 1636, a single bulb sold for more than 5,000 florins (about

Fig. 5. Semper Augustus

185

£375) and another for 4,600 florins, together with 'a carriage and horses'. The petals were long, narrow and pointed, like those of *T. gesneriana,* resembling the modern 'water lily' tulips, though the flower was smaller.

The speculation in tulips as in all other things where the price has been artificially run to great heights, ended early in the following year when everyone thought about selling at the same time for no apparent reason other than prices were considered excessive. Within days, their value had tumbled, losing fortunes for many speculators. The tulip mania may be compared to the South Sea Bubble of 1717.

The speculation lasted for only three years but the interest in the plant continued and in 1690, the introduction of the first Parrot tulip with its brilliant colours and lascinated petals brought about a new interest so much so that *The Tatler* for 31st August, 1710 made ridicule of the owner of a tulip bed of quite small dimensions who said that he valued the ground at 'more than the best 200 acres of land in all England'. As the florists' clubs took up the culture of the tulip so did prices continue to remain excessive for the finest varieties. In Maddock's catalogue of 1792 several of the 665 varieties offered were priced at 5 guineas or more each and by 1827, the celebrated Fanny Kemble made £100 for its raiser Mr William Clark of Croydon, this sum being paid to his executors by one Thomas Davey, who purchased this outstanding variety when aged 75. Shortly after, Davey (raiser of the famous Trafalgar) himself passed away and the bulb, together with its two offsets were sold by his widow to Mr John Goldham of Pentonville for 70 guineas. It was a Bybloemen, handsomely feathered with markings of dark 'in memoriam' purple. In the Supplement to his treatise on the cultivation of florists' flowers, Hogg said 'it is considered the first flower of its class and is the best that has ever been produced in England'. Writing in 1823, Hogg has told that 'a moderate collection of choice tulips could not be purchased for a sum less than £1,000'. There were highly expensive varieties in most catalogues and in Groom's list for 1832, the variety Parmegian was priced at £50 and Shakespeare at 20 guineas. As so many qualities went to make up the perfect show bloom and so few varieties possessed all of them, it was only to be expected that those which in the eyes of the florists were of the highest quality, commanded the highest prices. In 1836, the *Floricultural Cabinet* reported that 'a new tulip Citadel of Amsterdam had been purchased by an amateur for

£650'. As with all antiques, the 'cream' always comes to the top and is in greatest demand.

As late as 1854, several varieties in Groom's catalogue were priced at 100 guineas each. These included Duchess of Cambridge and Miss Seymour, whilst many others were listed at 10 guineas and upwards. Yet the following year every one of Groom's quarter of a million bulbs were sold by auction, as they stood in the rows, at very low prices indeed, due said James Douglas 'to the system of bedding-out tender plants in summer, rapidly increasing in popularity . . . and with it, in the same ratio, the taste for the tulip and other florist's flowers declined'.

The old growers made their beds about 5 feet wide with paths all round so that it was possible to inspect every variety with the greatest care and at the prices paid, each bloom was given the most detailed inspection. It often took several hours to come to a decision as to whether a particular variety was worth the asking price. Moore alludes to the tulip beds of the time in his poem Lalah Rookh :

> What triumph crowds the rich Divan today
> With turban'd heads of every hue and race,
> Bowing before that veil'd and awful face,
> Like tulip beds of different shape and dyes,
> Bending beneath th' invisible west wind's sighs.

In the beds, each was arranged in its appropriate height, the tallest being planted at the centre, the shortest at the outside and they were termed first, second, third and fourth row flowers which fact was usually given with the description of each variety in the catalogues for failure to state the exact position for planting caused much unpleasantness between buyer and seller when the bulbs came into bloom.

TULIP VOCABULARY

Each flower (variety) was divided into one of three classes known as Bizarres, Bybloemens and Roses. These terms took the place of Marillon, Agate, Marquetrine and Jaspée originally used in France to describe the forms of striping and the colours and which were first set out in La Floriste Françoise of 1654 and remained in use for a century or more. The new terms were first given in *The Dutch Florist* of 1763 and have been recognised until the present time.

The 'breaking' or striping of tulips is unknown with any other flower and is due to a virus which also attacks lilies but not in the same way. When a seedling flowers for the first time, it is self coloured and the offsets continue to bear a similar flower maybe for many years until suddenly, a bloom will appear in which the colour has disappeared except for some stippling or striping. When once this has taken place, the bloom (variety) continues to appear in this form, also its offsets during the entire life of the variety. Once 'broken', it remains 'broken' and the original form is known as a 'breeder'. Not all bulbs of a variety will 'break' so that with some varieties, both 'breeders' and 'broken' flowers exist and may be seen growing together. One example is Sir Joseph Paxton raised by Willison of Hull and which 'broke' in 1845, at the height of the tulip vogue and which may still be obtained in both its original and 'broken' forms. It is of interest that seedlings raised from 'broken' forms appear as 'breeders' just as they do when obtained from a 'breeder' and it is only at a later date that the 'breaking' occurs. An offset, still attached to its parent, a 'breeder' may bear a 'broken' bloom so that the two may be seen growing alongside each other. The modern tulip grower maintains his stock in a high degree of health and 'broken' blooms are rare but those which survive have a considerable historic and aesthetic interest and at least a dozen varieties may still be obtained to form the nucleus of a valuable collection.

The earliest known instance of 'breaking' took place at the beginning of the 17th century, one of the first being Zomerschoon, a Cottage tulip of 1620 which is still obtainable at 25p a bulb and it is in the Cottage tulips that 'breaking' is most common. That there were so many different varieties of 'broken' tulips during the heyday of the florists' flowers was because each 'broke' in a different way, so that not only were they grouped into three distinct classes but each class was sub-divided into 'feathered' and 'flamed', a fine flamed bizarre being the acme of perfection, the most prized of all tulips. Again, in each variety, the ground colour must be either pure white or clear yellow and any 'foxing' told against it. 'I consider nothing detracts so much from the beauties than a tinged bottom', wrote John Slater.

The beauty of the 'broken' tulips was in their intensity of colour and the contrast between the streaking and the pure ground colour contributed to this. When a variety 'broke', the colouring took on a greater depth. Pink or crimson turned to vivid scarlet and pale lilac became deep purple-black. It was as if the concentration of the colouring into a smaller area had brought about this greater intensity. Thus the old tulips have a beauty which those who have not yet seen, cannot imagine. 'There is surely nothing in creation so lovely, so varied, and so magnificent as a fine collection of tulips' wrote William Harrison in 1843. 'There is so much to wonder at and admire; so much contrast from the pale lilac to the dark purple – from the delicate feather to the heavy flame – from the pretty pillar, to the finest pencilling, all is beauty.'

To fully understand about the old tulips, a description of the terms may help :

BAGUETTE. A French word for strong growing tulips bearing large flowers.

BASE. This is the bottom of the inside of the flower. In the florists' tulip it should be either pure white or clear yellow. William Harrison, secretary of the Felton Florists' Society in Northumberland, said 'foul-bottomed flowers are not tolerated at all as show flowers; and I cannot help thinking that the time is now come when all florists will agree in admitting that a pure bottom is the true substratum on which to build the superstructure of a fine tulip. Without it, a tulip is not fit for exhibition, is not worth cultivating and much less is it worthy of a price'. Purity of base also meant that the filaments must also be of the same colour, white in the roses and bybloemens; brilliant yellow in the bizarres. The base too, should be well and clearly defined, to about one-third of the way along the petals.

BEAM. The term for the broad band or ray of colour at the centre of each petal. 'By a beam,' wrote John Slater, tulip fancier of Lower Broughton, Manchester, 'I do not mean that a straight line up the centre of a petal is a beam . . . They want pencilling branching out from this beam right up to the feathering, the more the better, if sufficient of the ground colour is shown. The branching or flaming should begin at the bottom of the petal and continue right up, the feathering as in a feathered flower.' A flower with a well feathered beam is known as 'flamed'.

BEARD. This is the term used when the feathering runs more thickly down the centre of the petals.

BIZARRE. A florists' tulip which has a yellow base (as against white).

It may be a 'breeder' or it may be striped ('broken') and flamed. William Harrison wrote : 'If I wished to elevate any individual tulip to the championship of all England, I would say frankly and fearlessly, it must be Dickson's Duke of Devonshire. I had the pleasure of seeing it growing in the valuable collection of Thomas Bromfield at Warren Mills and it far exceeded anything I ever saw. It is a strong growing middle row bizarre, finely feathered and flamed with darkest brown, approaching black, on a brilliant yellow ground. The cup measured 4 inches in diameter.' Another famous flamed bizarre was Davey's Trafalgar which was the parent of the equally fine, Sir Joseph Paxton; and Sam Barlow, still obtainable and which perpetuates the name of the best and most respected of all florists. He was also one of the last.

BREEDER. A self-coloured tulip which always remains so.

BROKEN. The term used when the pigment or colouring matter is broken or split into stripes. It is also known as 'rectified'. The condition is caused by virus introduction which slightly weakens the plant, causing the bloom to come smaller and the stem shorter. The stem foliage is also mottled or striped though this may be difficult to determine without experience.

BYBLOEMEN. A Dutch word originally denoting 'the next bloom'; next in size to the Baguettes. With the English florists, it later came to mean those flowers with purple markings over a white almost transparent base, e.g. the feathered Miss Fanny Kemble.

DRAGON. The old name for Parrot tulips on account of their monstrous formation.

DUKES. Parkinson's name for the single Duc van Thol tulips which are still in cultivation.

ENGLISH. The name given to the old 'broken' tulips many (but not all) of which were raised in England. Amongst the first of the tulip florists were Maddock, Clark, Holmes, Groom, Lawrence and Willison, followed by Hogg, Slater, Barlow, Tom Storer of Derby; Headley of Cambridge and George Lightbody of Falkirk. Of William Clark of Croydon, Hogg said he was 'a scientific and experienced florist and has the best breeders in the kingdom. He raised from seed of Louis XVI, Charbonniere Noir, Trafalgar, etc., all with finely shaped cups and clear bottoms'.

FEATHERED. The term used to define one of two variations which takes place when a tulip 'breaks'. When the colouring is confined to the edges of the petals, the flower is 'feathered'. 'In estimating the value of a feathered tulip,' wrote William Harrison, 'the feathering must start at the bottom of each petal and go completely round the top, without a break to divide the colouring in any one place.' The colour should be heavy along the top and beautifully pencilled downwards to about a quarter the length of the petals. Amongst Harrison's selection of outstanding feathered bybloemens are Ambassador, Black Baquet, Constant, Transparent Noir. Others were Violet Alexander, Sir Edward Knatchbull, and the celebrated Parmegian.

In an article published in the *Floricultural Cabinet* of March 1840, John Slater said 'the northern florists require a feathered flower to be beautifully pencilled all round the petal, without the least break in the feathering; any mark or blotch, except the feathering would be considered a fault'. In this way the northern tulip fanciers set so high a standard that southern growers found difficult to equal. Commenting on Mr Slater's formulations, the editor of the magazine said 'they are the best practical observations on the tulip we ever saw'.

FLAMED. A tulip was classed as flamed when the bloom or colour runs up the centre of each petal and branches out to the feathering, so admirably described by John Slater (see Beam). The feathering at the edges should also conform to the highest standards. 'The flamed bizarres,' wrote William Harrison 'are very splendid and one of the finest I ever saw was a bloom of Lawrence's Bolivar. It was regularly feathered on every petal, and the flaming uniform and perfect. And those who have seen Strong's Titian, Lawrence's Shakespeare and Tyso's Polydora grown to perfection, will not readily forget them.'

Of flamed bybloemens, Incomparable la Panache, Alexander Magnus, La Belle Violet, Lawrence's Friend, Violet Alexander and Victoria Regina were considered amongst the finest for the show bench.

FOUL. A tulip is said to be foul when the ground colour is flushed with the colour of the feathering.

MARQUETRINE. The name used in the 17th century for a 'sort of tulip that excels all others' in that it was multi-coloured, possibly like the so-called 'green' tulips of today.

PARROT. A 'broken' tulip with irregular petal edges, in cultivation since 1665. They are not florist's tulips but 'sports' from bybloemen breeders.

Early Parrot tulips are depicted in a water colour drawing about 1700 and now in Teyler's Museum, Haarlem. The artist is Herman

Henstenburg and though an amateur painter, it is a work of tremendous vigour and beauty.

PLATED. When the featherings on the petal edges have run together, making the edging too wide.

QUARTER. A tulip is said to 'quarter' when the petals of the opened bloom become too wide apart. This was considered a serious defect when exhibiting tulips.

ROSE. The third important classified form of tulip, together with the bizarre and bybloemen. The famous Semper Augustus was a 'rose' and at a later date, the equally famous Triomphe Royale which like its famous predecessor had pointed petals but a glistening pure white base with red markings.

PROPERTIES OF A FIRST CLASS TULIP

The earliest definition of 'the properties of a good Tulip, according to the characteristics of the best florists of the present age' were given in Philip Miller's *Gardener's Dictionary* of 1732:

i. It should have a tall, straight stem.

ii. The flower should consist of six leaves (petals), three within and three without; the former larger than the latter.

iii. Their bottom should be in proportion to the top; and the upper part should be rounded off and not terminate in a point.

iv. The leaves (petals) when open, should neither turn inward nor bend outward but rather stand erect, and the flower should be of middle size, neither over large nor too small.

v. The stripes should be small and regular, arising quite from the bottom of the flower, for if there are any remains of the former self-coloured bottom, the flower will be in danger of losing its stripes. When a flower has all these properties it is esteemed a good one.

A hundred years later, John Slater in *The Floricultural Cabinet* sets out the properties of a good tulip as required by the florists of the time:

i. The stem should not rise to less than 30-36 inches upwards from the surface of the bed; it should be strong and elastic so as to shew (note the spelling) the flower to best advantage which a short weak stem cannot do. But a flower must not be discarded because

English tulip Tyso's Polydora (feathered bizarre). From a coloured
engraving of 1843

Old English pink,
Chaucer's Sops-in-Wine.
Note: this is mentioned in
Chaucer and may have never
before been photographed

Old English pink, Unique

it does not reach the prescribed height, as there are many fine varieties which do not come up to this standard.

ii. The cup should be in proportion to the stem; that is, a tall stem should support a large flower and vice versa, so as to appear neither too light nor too heavy.

iii. The flower should consist of six thick and fleshy petals which should run out from the centre, at first a little horizontally and then turn upwards, forming almost a perfect cup with a round bottom, rather wider at the top; the three exterior petals should be larger than the three interior ones, and broader at the base.

The opinion that the exterior should be larger than the interior has been copied by all who have attempted to describe a fine tulip, but in my opinion, a flower whose petals are equal in size and form will, when expanded, present the most admirable form and make the nearest approach to that perfection which all florists imagine but few witness.

iv. The top of each petal should be broad and well rounded and perfectly level; the parts of fructification as the stamens and anthers, should be strong and bold and the filaments free from tinge or stain, which qualities add much to the appearance of a fine tulip when open.

v. The ground colour of the flower at the bottom of cup in a bizarre, ought to be bright yellow; in a bybloemen or rose, perfectly white and transparent. In a feathered flower, the feathering should be broad and regular and go right round the edge of the petal and not to break out at the end and show the ground colour. It should terminate in fine broken points towards the centre of the petals, elegantly pencilled. The centre of each petal should be free from any stripe, spot, stain or tinge of any kind. The feathering of a fine Bienfail Incomparable is not excelled as a feathered stage flower. (To the Southern florists, the cup was of greater importance than the feathering; to the Northern florists, the feathering came first though the cup was also considered of great importance.)

A flamed flower must have a beam right up the centre of each petal as near the colour of the feathered edge as possible, commencing nearly at the bottom of the petal and reaching up to the feathering at the top of the petal; but not to break through it; the feathering at the edges the same as in a feathered flower. The Albion and Rose Unique may be considered good flamed tulips.

The darkest colours in the bizarres rank first, brown second; scarlet third. In bybloemens, black first, dark purple second; light purple third. In roses, bright scarlet first; crimson or cherry second. Colours of greatest contrast were in greatest demand by the florists.

EXHIBITING TULIPS

When presenting the flowers on the show bench, these were displayed in what was known as a 'pan' consisting of 12 blooms, two feathered and two flamed flowers of each colour. There were to be no two similar and the overall appearance of the presentation was the degree of contrast between the flowers. Each bloom was placed with its stem through a small hole made into a wooden board, arranged in four rows of three, the stems being placed in tubes of water, enclosed within the box and obscured from view. The box and display board were painted green.

'*An Account of the different Flower Shews*' gives 16 shows for tulips as being held in 1826 and each had the same six classes for single blooms in roses, bybloemens and bizarres, feathered and flamed in each. The flowers were displayed singly, in glass containers.

To display 12 blooms of outstanding quality called for a considerable degree of skill in growing only the best varieties and in large numbers. It was often necessary to shade the plants as the blooms opened so that they would be in exactly the right condition on show day. If a bybloemen was creamy-bottomed upon opening, it would take several days to bleach in the sun when the bloom would perhaps be too open on show day. Those with pure bottoms usually reached their best two days after opening. Slater said that the flowers of many of the southern growers had cream bottoms as a result of using King of Siam in their breeding programme.

James Maddock in his *Florist's Directory* (1792) said that 'the ground colour of the flower at the bottom of the cup should be clear white or yellow; and the various richly coloured stripes which are the principal ornament of a fine tulip should be regular, bold and distinct as the margin, terminating in fine, broken points, elegantly feathered or pencilled'. The colouring was that of the breeder but in greater depth.

In 1840, George Glenny in his *Properties of Flowers* laid down 12 points that constituted a top class tulip and gave prominence to the shape of the bloom; its quartering (which was prohibited) and the even disposition of the markings, especially the beam. No flower measured up to all 12 points but a number came very near to doing so e.g. Miss Fanny Kemble and Charbonnier Noir.

To have the blooms in the peak of condition at the time of judging on show day presented many problems. May is normally one of the most fickle months of the year. One day the temperature may be 70° in the shade and next day, an icy cold wind with snow showers may prevail. If the weather was warm, the florists would provide shade for their tulips by surrounding the beds with canvas; if cold then the bloom would be cut and taken indoors to be placed near the kitchen range which shone with constant black-leading. There, with their stems in water and near the fire, they could be coaxed into exactly the right condition so that by the morrow, they would be sufficiently open to allow for the small circles of cardboard or wood to be placed in the flower to enable it to keep its shape whilst being taken to the show. For days before, the fanciers would often stay up all night, to prevent their blooms from being stolen and to protect them from adverse weather.

Before the mill took over from the handloom, the florist working at home, was able to watch his tulips, day and night as the buds began to open. Early in April, canvas sheeting or garden lights would be erected over the beds about 4 feet above the ground to protect the blooms from hail and rain. Whenever the sun shone from a cloudless sky, the 'umbrella' protection be removed and with one eye on his loom and the other on the sky, the florist would be ready to replace the covering with the minimum of delay.

When no longer able to work at home, it was impossible to grow the tulips in the manner show standards demanded and rather than that there be any decline in the quality for which the old florists were famed, it was considered better to grow them no longer. At the end of the 19th century, the last of the old tulip shows was held at the Swan Inn at Butley, in Cheshire, and the last of the tulip fanciers were Sam Barlow of Chadderton and the Rev. Francis Horner who were growing, exhibiting and judging until the end of the century.

Yet in spite of every care and precaution in their culture, a variety which had produced a first class exhibition flower for several years may for no apparent reason 'lose face'. The feathering may come wrong or the cup may be far from pure but as J. W. Bentley in *The English Tulip* said, 'it is the bewitching combination of anticipation, disappointment and unexpected delights which made tulip growing so fascinating'.

COLLECTING ANTIQUE PLANTS

THEIR CULTURE

Owing to its inconsistency in its markings, the florists' tulip was always one of the more difficult flowers to manage and the fanciers believed that over-feeding and a too rich soil was one of the main causes of a cup becoming marked with the colouring of the feathering. At the same time, as the 'breaking' was caused by a virus which brought about a weakening of the plant's constitution, it required as much help as possible to attain the desired height and for the cup to be as large as exhibition standards required. It was therefore necessary to strike a balance in their culture, a happy medium between the two extremes.

James Douglas has described his own method of preparing his tulip beds, trenching them to a depth of almost 2 feet and incorporating large quantities of decayed cow manure in the lower 18 inches. Into the top 6 inches, was incorporated decayed turf loam, which had been stored for 12 months. The beds were prepared early in September and were left for two months to settle down before planting. Hogg said that he followed the advice given him by a tulip fancier and made up his beds as follows:

> One half rich yellow loam
> One quarter leaf mould
> One eighth two year old manure
> One eighth sea sand

In the *Floricultural Cabinet* for April, 1834 one grower wrote, 'the standard soil should be a strong, rich yellow loam' and the manure composed of 'equal proportions of horse and cow dung, laid up in a heap for at least 18 months, turned once a month and formed into a substance as fine as mould. Then use at the rate of one-third to two-thirds of loam'. He added: 'This I find to be highly beneficial in producing fine full green foliage, a strong upright stem, and a vigorous and perfect bloom.'

The tulip beds were known as 'boxes' for they were surrounded with planks of wood inserted into the ground and raised about 9 inches above the surface, two planks each 9 inches wide being fastened together. Each bed was made 4-5 feet wide and to any length. Growers would erect paling around the tulip beds, painted green to give a neat and ornamental appearance but the palings were also valuable to give protection from cold winds.

196

The usual time for planting, near London, according to the *Florists' Calendar* was Lord Mayor's Day, 9th November, and that the distance between the rows was to be 9 inches and from bulb to bulb in the row, 7 inches; the depth 4 inches. The first days of November, depending upon the weather was the usual planting time, the tulip being the last of the bulbs to be planted.

Each variety was planted in the row according to its height. Thus, the taller growing kinds were planted at the middle of the bed with the most dwarf at the outside. In this way each bloom could be seen to advantage and carefully inspected when walking round the bed if a sale was being made.

Again, each class was planted together e.g. flamed bizarres; roses; etc. and great care was taken when the bulbs were lifted to grade them into the various heights and classes.

When the plants began to form their buds, it was usual to pass lengths of green twine along the rows, looping it just below the buds to prevent breakage whilst above the blooms as they opened, 'dunce cap' protectors would be fixed, held just above the flowers on a thin cane. The twine prevented the bloom from rubbing against the cane.

To plant, the growers used a blunt-ended dibber or trowel with a mark on the handle to denote the requisite depth which was about 4 inches, covering the bulbs with 3 inches of soil. Before placing the bulb in the hole, a small amount of sharp sand or peat should be placed at the bottom and on which the base will rest. The hole should be made large enough to permit the base to be in contact with the soil. Give no water at any time and protect the blooms from adverse weather when the buds begin to show colour. After flowering, remove the heads of all those not used for exhibition so that the new bulbs, the offsets can build up to good flowering size. They will be helped in this by feeding during early summer with dilute manure water which should be given once each week until the foliage begins to die back in July. The bulbs should then be carefully lifted and dried on trays in an airy room, at the same time detaching the offsets for growing on. Each variety should then be placed in a small open paper bag on which the name is clearly written.

VARIETIES OF THE FLORISTS' TULIP
(Those marked * are still in cultivation)

ADONIS. One of Richard Headley's raising, it is a bybloemen with a smooth, well formed cup though with rather thin petals. The feathering is deep purple. Barlow described it as being better when flamed than when feathered.

ANNIE MCGREGOR*. It 'broke' first to Martin of Whalley in 1848 and for years was the leading exhibitor's flamed rose. The flower is of good size with crimson markings on a pure white ground. Though dwarf it is a good 'doer' and increases well.

BRITOMART. A strong grower, it makes a large cup and is beautifully feathered with dark purple on a clear white ground. Raised by Hall.

CECIL DOLLING. One of Hall's finest, it is tall growing with a large cup though the petals are rather narrow. A bybloemen with flaming of richest purple.

CYRANO. Raised by George Hall, it was a seedling from Sam Barlow and Joseph Paxton. Of medium height, it makes a large flower with heavy feathering of almost black on a deep yellow ground. A magnificent bizarre when grown well.

DR HARDY*. One of Tom Storer's finest varieties which broke in 1862 and was named after the eminent tulip fancier of Warrington. Of medium height, it has stout petals and a short medium sized cup that stands to the last. A bizarre, flamed with dark brown over a brilliant yellow base.

DUCHESS OF SUNDERLAND. Raised by Walker of Hammersmith about 1830, it is of dwarf habit with somewhat pointed petals. A flamed bybloemen, the flaming is of bright plum-purple on a clear white ground. 'A charming flower,' wrote Barlow 'unsurpassed in purity'.

DUKE OF HAMILTON. One of Slater's finest being a second row flamed bizarre which ranked high as a show variety. It 'broke' in 1843 from the breeder. The cup is good, better than Polyphemus, being shorter; the bottom pure; the ground colour being deepest yellow, the feathering almost black.

EMILY. It was originally raised from seed by William Clark of Croydon and 'broke' when in the possession of Mr Hogg. A fine bybloemen of beautiful form and with a pure white cup, it is feathered with deep violet.

GEORGE EDWARD*. Raised by Schofield, it is tall growing and forms a fine cup of great substance, and flamed with deep purple on a clear white ground.

GEORGE HAYWARD*. Raised by Lawrence of Hampton, it 'broke' in 1853 and is a bizarre, flamed with plum-red on a brilliant yellow ground. Tall growing, it forms a large globular cup though the petals are rather narrow.

GOLDFINGER*. It may still be found but is now rare. It was raised by Hepworth and is a bizarre of great brilliance, the medium-sized bloom having flaming of brightest orange-scarlet over a deep yellow ground.

INDUSTRY. Raised by William Lee of Hammersmith, it was one of the finest roses in cultivation, a winner at the National Tulip Show (1848) when it was the best feathered in any class, the markings being of brilliant carmine on a clear white ground.

LADY SEFTON. Introduced by Martin of Whalley, Barlow said it was second only to Annie McGregor in its class and was 'unique in its way' being a rose, flamed with bright carmine-scarlet on a clear white ground.

LORD CAVENDISH*. Raised in 1869 by Hardwick of Wakefield, it was an outstanding bizarre and is still to be obtained for it was exhibited at Chelsea as recently as 1939. Making a beautiful globular bloom, it is handsomely flamed on a clear yellow ground.

LORD STANLEY*. Raised by Storer, it is obtainable as a breeder, being of rich chestnut-red with a clear yellow base and from which a flamed bizarre was obtained in 1860. The flaming is mahogany-red on a golden ground.

MABEL*. A sister seedling to Annie McGregor and equally fine, being taller growing with a slightly longer cup. A flamed rose, the colouring is deep cherry red on a pure white ground.

MASTERPIECE. Raised by Slater of Manchester, it is a flamed bizarre of great beauty with black feathering on a rich yellow ground.

MISS FANNY KEMBLE. It was illustrated in *The Floricultural Cabinet* for October 1833, drawn and painted from life by Mr. E. D. Smith when it was 'in an advanced stage of blooming'. In the same publication it was described by Joseph Harrison : 'Out of respect for the well known veteran florist Mr Davey of Chelsea, now in his 75th year, and in whose breast the fancy for tulips is as predominant as ever, who gave last autumn one hundred sovereigns to the executors of the late Mr Clark to entitle him to the possession of that loveliest of all tulips, Miss Fanny Kemble, I feel bound to attempt a short description of the flower which was the pride and boast of its late owner, and which excited the envy and admiration of all those amateurs who went to view it. This 'precious gem', a bybloemen was raised from one of Clark's breeders and 'broke' three years ago. It has produced two offsets since and is adapted to the second or third row in the bed. The stem is firm; the foliage full and broad, of a lively green; the cup large and of the finest form; the white pure and wholly free from stain; the pencilling on the petals is beautifully marked with black or dark purple, the feathering uniform and elegant. It preserves its shape to the last, the outer leaves not sinking from the inner. In a word it is considered the first flower of its class and the best that has ever been produced in England. Being now in the possession of Mr Davey, it may be viewed when in bloom at his garden, in the King's Road, Chelsea'!

MRS COLLIER. Introduced by Thomas Collier of Bedford Leigh, it was for long the best feathered rose with heavy pencilling of bright cherry-red.

NANCY GIBSON. Raised by Hepworth of Wakefield, Barlow describes it as the finest feathered rose ever seen. The feathering was brilliant scarlet on a pure white ground.

POLYDORA. A handsome third-row bizarre purchased by Rev. Tyso of Wallingford in 1839 from the collection of William Walker of Hammersmith. It had a large full cup with handsome petals and a rich yellow ground colour, the petals being margined with deep feathering of chestnut-brown.

QUEEN OF MAY*. A feathered bybloemen of beauty, the feathering being of purple-black on a clear white ground whilst the bloom is of ideal show quality in size and shape.

ROSE UNIQUE. A second row flamed rose, highly esteemed for its excellent markings and whilst the cup is inclined to be long, the colours are rich.

ROYAL SOVEREIGN. Introduced by Strong of Hammersmith in 1840, it was for years the finest flamed bizarre with crimson markings on a lemon ground.

ROYAL STANDARD*. It was known in 1750 and is a particularly fine form of Silver Standard, being a flamed bizarre with pencilling of scarlet on a clear golden ground.

SABLE REX. A fourth row flamed bybloemen, colour almost black; the cup good. A fine bed and stage flower, said to have 'broken' from a breeder in the possession of Roger Farrand, Esq. of Manchester.

SAM BARLOW*. One of Storer's finest, raised from his own Dr Hardy and possessing all the qualities of a top class bizarre, for years the best of its class. Flamed with crimson-red on a clear yellow ground, it is early and has a large cup which opens well though the petals are somewhat thin.

SAN JOSE. A third row flamed bizarre of good form with thick fleshy petals, bottom pure, colours rich yellow and brown. It is early and is when 'caught', one of the finest flamed bizarres in cultivation.

SEVENTY-ONE. Raised by Buckley, it is a second row flamed bybloemen and a good stage flower with a clear bottom and dark purple flaming on a yellow ground.

SHAKESPEARE. Raised by Mr Lawrence, keeper of the Red Lion Inn of Hampton, Middlesex, it is a third row flamed bizarre; the cup rather long, the bottom pure, the ground colour rich with the feathering and flaming almost black. An early variety, it is a first rate stage flower.

SILVER STANDARD*. Said to have been introduced in 1637, it is possibly the oldest known of the striped tulips with a handsome cup, feathered and flamed rose-red on a white ground.

SIR E. KNATCHBULL. A second row feathered bybloemen with a good cup, pure bottom and 'broken' from one of Mr Clark's celebrated breeders.

SIR JOSEPH PAXTON*. It first 'broke' in 1848 at the nursery of Willison of Hull. It is tall growing and late flowering with a rather long cup. Sometimes feathered, it is usually exhibited as a flamed bizarre, being marked with chocolate-brown on a pale yellow ground.

TALISMAN. Dr Hardy's finest, it 'broke' about 1860, and grows tall and opens late. Like Paxton it appears both in the feathered and flamed classes, the pencilling being almost black on a clear white ground. 'Best as a flamed flower,' wrote Barlow, 'the finest in existence.'

TRIOMPHE ROYALE. A second row flamed rose, the cup rather long, the bottom pure, slightly pointed at the tips but in every way a top show variety, with the beam regularly branched out to the edge.

VIOLET IMPERIAL. A second row flamed bybloemen with a good cup and pure bottom, the flaming being of darkest purple.

WALWORTH. Introduced in 1790 by Maddock of Walworth, it is late into bloom and is a fourth row feathered rose with a good cup, creamy bottom and good markings. The ground colour takes several days to bleach.

The descriptions are taken from the florists' magazines of the time, when each variety was achieving considerable popularity on the show bench. The following are very old tulips, still obtainable but which cannot be classed as true florists' varieties, though possessing both beauty and interest :

BACCHUS. Introduced in 1780, it grows 2 feet tall and has egg-shaped flowers of deepest purple covered in a grape-like 'bloom'.

BLUE CELESTE. A rare double late tulip introduced in 1850 and producing large full flowers of a unique shade of soft purple-blue.

GRACE DARLING. Like Keiserskroon it is a single early of similar height and bears orange-scarlet flowers olive green at the base.

JOOST VAN DER VANDEL. A single early growing 16 inch tall and bearing elegantly pointed flowers of brilliant cerise-red, stippled with white.

KEISERSKROON. It was introduced before 1750 since when it has remained the world's most widely planted tulip. Growing 16 inches tall, it is an ideal bedding variety, bearing single blooms of vivid scarlet with a deep contrasting edge of golden-yellow.

ZOMERSCHOON. It appeared in 1620, a 'broken' cottage tulip, its large handsome blooms being beautifully marked with salmon-rose on a white ground. Growing 2 feet tall, it is one of the most attractive of tulips.

Still flourishing is the Wakefield and North of England Tulip Society, founded in 1836. They held their early shows in the Brunswick Hotel near Wakefield market, where members met at six-weekly intervals throughout the year. One of the most respected members was George Hardwick, raiser of the famous bizarre, Lord Frederick Cavendish, which still appears on the show bench, and amongst past Presidents was Sir Daniel Hall whose monograph, *The Book of the Tulip* remains the classic work on the flower.

CHAPTER IX

The Pink

Its introduction – The laced pink – The Paisley pinks – Culture of the
pink – 14th century pinks – 15th century pinks – 16th century pinks –
17th century pinks – 18th century pinks – 19th century pinks – 20th
century pinks – Modern laced pinks.

Native of the north temperate regions, the pink is able to tolerate
extreme cold but it does not enjoy excessive wet. The Athenians
held the plant in so great esteem that they named it Di-anthos,
Flower of Jove, awarding it the highest honour. It was the chief
flower used to make garlands and coronets, hence its early English
name of 'coronation' from which the name carnation is a derivative.

It was the opinion of Canon Ellacombe, the Victorian authority
on the history of plants, that *Dianthus caryophyllus,* a native of
southern Europe, reached England with the Norman invasion, possibly attached to stones imported from northern France (Caen) by
the Conqueror for the erection of castles and houses of worship.
Canon Ellacombe reported having seen it in bloom in 1874, on the
walls of the Conqueror's Castle of Falaise (where he was born) and
in England it is to be seen to this day, growing on the walls of
the castles of Dover and Rochester in Kent, both built by the
Normans, and on the walls of Fountains Abbey in Yorkshire where
it blooms early in July. Indeed, several of the writers of old believed
its country name of 'Gillyflower' to be derived from 'Julyflower'.
Herrick was of this opinion :

> A lovely July flower
> That one rude wind or ruffling shower
> Will force from hence and in an hour. . . .

Sir Francis Bacon also wrote that 'in July come gillyflowers of all
varieties . . .' from which it would appear that the reference was
to double pinks or carnations (which Gerard called the Great
Double Carnation) rather than to single pinks for he suggests
growing the pink for earlier flowering. In his essay 'Of Gardens' he
wrote that in May and June 'come pinks of all sorts especially
the blush pink', with possibly in mind *D. plumarius,* parent of the

hybrid pinks or *D. caesius,* a native plant, both of which bloom early and were known to gardeners of the time.

With the scent of the flowers resembling the perfume of the clove, it was called by the French 'giroflier' which name accompanied the plant to England with the Norman invasion. Whether it was *D. caryophyllus* or *P. plumarius* to which Chaucer alluded in the *Prologue to the Canterbury Tales* (begun in 1387) is uncertain but all those plants bearing clove-scented flowers were at the time much in demand to flavour wine (and ale) possibly a French custom and pinks, known as sops-in-wine, were to be found until the end of the sixteenth century, growing in tavern gardens everywhere :

> And many a clove gilofre,
> And notemuge to put in ale,
> Whether it be moiste or stale . . .

Chaucer's spelling of the word differs but little from the early French whilst the poet Shelton, wrote of 'The Gelofer amyable'. By Shakespeare's time, it had become 'gillovor' or 'gillyflower', the word being used for all clove-scented flowers, such as the Queen's Gillyflower (*Hesperis matronalis*) and the Stock Gillyflower.

D. caryophyllus takes its botanical name meaning 'nut-leaved' from the name of the Clove tree, *Caryophyllus aromaticus,* not because its grass-like leaves have any resemblance to those of the clove tree but because the clove scent of the flowers resembled the fragrance of the fruits of that tree.

By Tudor times, there would appear to be two groups of dianthus, those with single flowers, known as the pinks and descended from *D. plumarius* and those bearing double (or semi-double) flowers, offspring of *D. caryophyllus,* both species reaching England at possibly the same time with the Norman invasion or shortly afterwards.

In the *New Herbal* of 1578, Lyte distinguished between the two forms by his use of the word 'coronations' and of 'the small feathered gillofers, known as Pynkes, Soppes-in-Wine and small Honesties'. Writing at the same time, the poet Spenser separates the two in his lines from *The Shepherd's Calendar* :

> Bring hither the pincke and purple cullambine,
> With Gilleflowres;
> Bring Coronations and Sops-in-Wine,
> Worn of paramours

Spenser here also differentiates between the pink, the carnation and sops-in-wine which may be a distinctive form of the dianthus (possibly a small semi-double pink) for it is doubtful whether the earlier reference to 'the Pinke and Purple Cullambine' really meant Columbines of pink and purple colouring as the word 'pink' signifying the particular colour was not introduced into the English language until late in the eighteenth century. Before that, the colour we now call 'pink' was always described as 'flesh' or 'blush' or even 'carnation' as in Byron's line :

Carnation'd like a sleeping infant's cheek.

The earliest carnations (or semi-double pinks) bore flowers of flesh colour which may be described as deep 'pink' and alluded to in Shakespeare's *Henry V* when in Mistress Quickly's house in Eastcheap, the Boy says ' . . . and (he) said they were devils incarnate'. To which Mistress Quickly replies : "A could never abide carnation; 'twas a colour he (the dead Falstaff) never liked.'

But to the Elizabethan poet Shenstone, both the colour and the perfume of the carnation was most agreeable :

Let yon admired carnation own,
Not all was meant for raiment, or for food
Not all for needful use alone;
There, while the seeds of future blossoms dwell,
'Tis colour'd for the sight, perfumed to please the smell.

The Roman historian Pliny has told of how the clove-scented pink was discovered in Spain during the reign of the Emperor Augustus when it received considerable attention in Rome to flavour wine. The plant had been found in that part of Spain bordering the Bay of Biscay, then inhabited by the warlike Cantabri after whom the plant was originally named. As late as the mid-sixteenth century, Dr William Turner, a close friend of Bishops Latimer and Ridley and himself Dean of Wells, called the pink the *Cantabrica gelouer* in his *New Herball*, the first part of which was dedicated to Queen Elizabeth.

John Tradescant reported that on several islands in the Mediterranean he found the clove-scented pink 'growing naturall, of the best sort we have in Ingland, with the edges of the leaves (petals) deeply cut . . .' More recently, Mr Will Ingwersen reported having seen *D. plumarius* growing about the limestone rocks on the western coast of Corsica where its bright pink flowers seen against the dark rocks created a lasting impression with him.

In his *Herbal* (1597), Gerard distinguishes (the name Dianthus was not in use until Linnaeus compiled his binomial system of plant classification) between the 'Carnation Gilloflower (the Great Double Carnation) and the 'Clove (or Pink) Gilloflower' from which it would appear that by then, the carnations had not the same clover perfume as the pinks, though of the Great Double Carnation, Gerard said its flowers 'had an excellent sweet smell' though it may not have been of cloves.

That there were many different species and varieties is confirmed by Gerard who said : 'A great large volume would not suffice to write of every one at large . . . and every year every climate and every country bringeth forth new sorts . . .'

Gerard also distinguishes between the 'wild (native) Gilloflowers' as they had smaller flowers than the 'Carnations and Clove Gilloflowers'. Earlier, Tusser had written of 'pinks of all sorts' and at a later date, Milton wrote of 'the white pink', possibly the Old Fringed and still obtainable, to be included amongst other fragrant flowers to strew over the hearse of Lycidas.

That there were at the time, 'streaked gillyflowers' is confirmed both by Shakespeare and in the *Book of Flowers* by Maria Merian, a copy of which is in the British Museum and in which there is a colour illustration which shows the 'streaked gillyflowers' much as we know the flaked carnations of today.

In *A Winter's Tale,* which Shakespeare wrote in lighter vein, upon his return to take up residence at his home, New Place in Stratford-on-Avon in the spring of 1611, Perdita speaks of

'The fairest flowers o' the season
Are our Carnations and streak'd Gillyflowers'

At the time of Shakespeare's death, carnations and pinks had become amongst the most popular of all garden plants. Gerard wrote that '. . . they are well known to most, if not to all' and William Lawson in *The Country Housewife's Garden* (1618) said, 'I may well call them the king of flowers, except the rose.'

Possibly for their hardiness were they so popular and though native of south and eastern Europe, quickly became acclimatised to English gardens for which they were most suitable for the small 'knots' of the time. John Fletcher has commented on their hardiness :

Hide, O hide, those hills of snow
Which thy frozen bosom bears,
On whose tops the pinks that grow
Are of those that April weares.

By the beginning of the seventeenth century, the pink and carnation had reached their peak of popularity. Parkinson writing
shortly after Shakespeare's death said, 'What shall I say to the
Queene of delight and of flowers, carnations, and gillyflowers, whose
bravery (hardiness), variety and sweete smell joyned together,
tyeth every ones affection with equal earnestness both to like and
to have them?' Writing a little earlier, Gervase Markham in *The
English Husbandman* (1513) said, 'Gilliflowers are of all other
flowers most sweet and delicate,' and in *The Complete Gardener's
Practice* (1664), Stephen Blake wrote, 'Carnation gilliflowers for
beauty and delicate smell and excellent properties, deserve letters
of gold. I wonder that Solomon did not write of this flower when
he compared his spouse to the Lilly-of-the-valley.'

Exactly when the dianthus received its name 'pink' is not known.
Mr Stanley B. Whitehead believes the name to be a derivation of
the Celtic 'pic' meaning peak, possibly the 'peak of perfection'
amongst flowers; on the other hand, Mr L. J. Brimble in his
Flowers of Britain suggests the name was obtained from
the verb 'to pink' or 'to pierce', indicating the extremely serrated petals of *D. plumarius* and its offspring, the Old Fringed
Pink and Mrs Sinkins. Again, it has been suggested that the
name is from Pinksten, German for Pentecost, for it is at
this time when the pink comes into bloom, a late Whitsuntide,
and on the Continent the plant is known as the Whitsun
Gillyflower.

The native pinks of the British Isles remained very much
neglected, until Parkinson (1629) said that ' . . . some grow upright
like gillyflowers or spreading over the ground'. It was from the
so-called Matted Pink, *D. caesius* that the modern Alpine Allwoodii
were evolved and which bear scented flowers. During the reign of
Charles I, a number of pinks were introduced from France by
Queen Henrietta Maria, for the pink is said to have been her
favourite flower. But by the time of the Restoration, John Rea in
his *Flora* remarked that 'there were few carnations to be found in
any of our gardens'. However, in a later edition of his work he lists
360 varieties of carnation and pink and wrote:

'But yet if "ask and have" were in my power,
Next to the Rose, give me the Gillyflower.'

THE LACED PINK

The early nineteenth century was perhaps the Golden Age of the
pink, and in *The Flower Garden* (1839) M'Intosh, has listed 192
varieties, including several which were introduced by such well-
known florists of that time including Barlow, Hogg and Keen.
M'Intosh mentions that 'it is pre-eminently the cottager's flower as
it takes less care and skill to cultivate than the carnation and other
florist's flowers'.

Thomas Hogg, a nurseryman of Paddington Green, writing in
1822, lists 121 varieties in his Catalogue of Pinks, and in addition,
a dozen Scottish pinks, one of which had the charming name of
Robertson's Gentle Shepherd. Another of the old pinks was called
Kilner's Cricketer. It was raised in Yorkshire as one would imagine
when recalling those stout-hearted cricketers the late Norman and
Roy Kilner. That there must have been many varieties of the pink
during Hogg's time is obvious in reading the introduction to his
Catalogue of Pinks for he says, ' . . . and if I have not published
a numerous list, let it be remembered that quality, in respect of
flowers, is always preferable to quantity'. And he then lists 121
varieties!

In the same way that the miners of Yorkshire and Derbyshire
took up the culture of the pansy, and the cotton workers of Lancashire devoted their hours of leisure to the Show auricula, so did
the weavers of Paisley, near Glasgow, toil to reproduce the
intricate oriental patterns of their shawls on the flowers of the
pink.

The object of the Paisley weavers was to impart the characteristic of rounded or smooth edges to the flowers, thereby eliminating
the serrated petal edges of *D. plumarius*. At the outer edge of the
petals was to be a band of black or red or purple, with which
colouring the blooms were also marked at the centre. The variety
was recognised by the degree of black, red (crimson) or purple about
the bloom.

Each group of florists had their own particular favourites which
they exhibited at the pink shows up and down the country, possibly the most highly valued variety being Lustre, a purple laced

pink which took the premier awards throughout the 1830's. It occupies first place in a list of awards won at the leading shows in Britain during 1832 :

Purple Laced	First prize	Total Prizes
Bow's Lustre	18	36
Bow's Suwarrow	16	30
Hackin's Sir John	8	16
Cheetham's Independent	4	14
Wigley's Beauty	4	10
Red Laced		
Barlow's George IV	10	25
Humphrey's Cheetham	10	21
Claudius	4	15
Jupiter	4	14
Black Laced		
Cicero	13	25
Perry's Union	10	13
Davey's Eclipse	4	13
Davey's Heroine	4	4
Duchess of Rutland	3	10

In 1836, Mr Thomas Ibbett of Woolwich, a celebrated grower of laced pinks of the time, selected those he considered to be the twelve best for exhibition :

Barrett's Conqueror
Bray's Invincible
Clark's Matilda
Dryden's Earl of Uxbridge
Hopkin's One in the Ring
Ibbett's Triumphant
Mann's Dr Summers
Seal's Miss Austin
Steven's George Cook
Unsworth's Omega
Westlake's Hero

Ten years later, at the Metropolitan Floral Exhibition held on 12th July, 1845, the premier award for Pinks was won by Mr

Norman, another Woolwich grower with almost an entirely new list of varieties :

Church's Rowena
Clark's Matilda
Creed's President
Fisher's Matilda
Fisher's White Warden
Garrett's Alpha
Hardstone's Prince Albert
Headley's Duke of Northumberland
Heath's Lord Byron
Hodge's Cyclops
Hodge's Mars
Jeff's Mary Ann

Kirtland's Beatrice
Kirtland's Dr Daubeney
Kirtland's Gay Lad
Norman's Henry Creed
Smith's Dr Coke
Thurtell's Mile-end Defiance
Unsworth's Omega
Wallis's Unique
Weedon's Queen Victoria
Wilmer's Duchess of Kent
Wilmer's Tom Davey

All have long since vanished.

THE PAISLEY PINKS

But it was the silk weavers of Paisley who first took up the pink and brought it to a degree of perfection not since attained. The exquisite lacing of their pinks ran complementary to the oriental designs woven into their famous Paisley shawls which were exported to India and the far east in large numbers. This was expressed by Loudon in the *Encyclopaedia of Gardening* (1828) when he wrote, 'their attention to raising flowers contributed to improve their genius for invention in elegant fancy muslins' and it is certain that the weavers drew inspiration from the beauties of floral art which they had also created by their own powers of genius. It was the appearance in 1772 of the wonderful laced variety Lord Stoverdale that excited the imagination of the weavers and by the end of the century, almost a hundred varieties were in cultivation. They were known to those south of the border as the Scottish pinks.

Though Lord Stoverdale is generally recognised as being the first of the fully double laced pinks, the first variety was in fact, Duchess of Lancaster. Its introduction is described in an article which appeared in *The Floricultural Cabinet* on 1st May, 1841 by Mr Thomas Ibbett of Bull's Field, Woolwich and is of considerable interest. He writes, 'I flatter myself that no person is in possession of better information upon this subject than myself, having been acquainted with the raiser of the first named pink, as also of having had access to his books, as well as personal information from him.'

'The first pink was raised in 1772 by Mr James Major, then head gardener to the Duchess of Lancaster. Mr Major, having saved some seed in 1771, reared several plants which, blooming next year, one proved to be a double flower with laced petals at which he was agreeably surprised . . . Mr Major informed me, that he made known his discovery to a florist who came to see it and offered him the sum of 10 gns for the stock, but this he declined until he had consulted more of his floricultural friends. Having done so, one gentleman told him he had done right in not accepting the offer and advised him to increase the stock for the ensuing year and then offer them to the public. He accepted the advice and sent out the variety at 10s. 6d. a pair under the name of Major's Duchess of Lancaster. One order to a single individual of 40 pairs was delivered at this price.' The writer added, 'no person has ever been able to make half that sum by any new pink since'.

In his *Treatise on the Culture of Flowers* published in 1792, James Maddock, florist of Walworth wrote 'We may venture to assert that a pink, called Major's Lord Stoverdale . . . was the first that deserves to be classed amongst such as are held in esteem by florists. It was raised about twenty years ago and was the first pink possessed of that singular and beautiful ornament called lacing, which is a continuation of the colour of the eye round the broad part of the petals, that gives it a most elegant appearance.' On being shown Maddock's work, Mr Major said that, Lord Stoverdale was not raised by him until two years after Duchess of Lancaster, which was a seedling from it.

It is said that 'no person could surpass him (James Major) for his knowledge in the culture of florists' flowers. He lived many years in the parish of Lewisham in Kent and died there on 18th March, 1831, aged 94'.

Thomas Ibbett has told of his being present at the West Kent Pink Society's Show, held at the Tiger's Head, Chislehurst in 1840, which he described as the finest show he ever attended, 'when no less than 70 persons sat down to dinner provided for the occasion'. He continues, 'eleven prizes were awarded, including one open to all England, which was awarded to me for a seedling I named Capt. Dundas and I have no doubt but that in the ensuing season, it will be the finest in all the kingdom. There has however, been a new pink sent out in the name of Ne Plus Ultra and should any grower of it feel disposed to show it against Capt. Dundas at the last named Society, I will with pleasure bring the gallant Captain into the field for the third time, and he shall be attended by my Prince Albert; and should he take the right, I will place my Queen Victoria on the left, who will not be afraid to show herself against any Victoria at present sent out'. The same friendly rivalry was seen in the single wicket cricket matches of the time and made for a most entertaining period in the history of England.

Ibbett was one of the famous Woolwich growers, of whom Norman, raiser of those excellent pinks, Queen Victoria and Defiance was, with Ibbett the most successful on the show bench. Writing in 1839, Mr Ben Williamson of Clapton said 'I never met with any to excel what are grown at Woolwich and its neighbourhood, proof of which I refer to the Metropolitan Show of 26th June when the three main prizes out of four went to the Woolwich men.' They were rivalled only by those of Paisley and strange as it may seem, Paisley was then a small town of several thousand inhabitants, its origins dating back to the 12th century from the founding of the Cluniac abbey by Walter FitzAlan. The weaving of the famous shawls began towards the end of the 18th century, originally to the designs of Eastern shawls in silk brought home by returning sailors. It was the time of the Paisley poet and weaver, Robert Tannahill who worked at home, composing his poetry whilst weaving the intricate designs of the east into his splendid shawls, in the same way that the weavers of Lancashire and Yorkshire tended their looms in their cottage homes whilst auriculas grew in pots in the long low windows in front of their watchful eyes.

Requiring a clean atmosphere, the Paisley pinks flourished until the factory took over from the hand loom, until the tall chimneys began to belch out their blackened smoke and dirt which was soon to cover the countryside and which has continued ever since.

By the middle of the 19th century, the Scottish pinks had disappeared entirely from Paisley with perhaps Dad's Favourite, re-discovered in a cottage garden in Berwickshire, the only survival. Or it may have been one of the laced pinks raised by the miners of Northumberland and Durham, possibly from varieties obtained from across the border. One of their raising was Lord Archibald Hamilton which made only a small flower but its lacing was almost perfection. Of this variety and of other laced pinks. William Harrison of the Felton (Northumberland) Floricultural Society had this to say (1841): 'Many of the kinds are surpassingly beautiful; indeed their ground colours are so pure and their edgings so perfect that the admirer of these flowers may with justice say that in their production, nature had employed her ablest and most favoured artist.' And he goes on to say : ' . . . many of the small kinds such as Lord Archibald Hamilton and Waile's Beauty, lace best, though are least esteemed by amateurs on account of the few petals they contain, whilst those which make large blooms such as Unsworth's Omega, though they have far more petals and consequently rise higher in the centre or to use a florist's phrase, crown better, and are more prized by exhibitors on that account, yet lace much more imperfectly . . .'

In his definition of a Fine Pink, Maddock said that the stem should be strong, elastic and erect, not less than a foot in height. The flower cup or calyx should be smaller than that of a carnation, but similar in form with the flower not less than $2\frac{1}{2}$ inch diameter. The petals to be broad and substantial with fine fringed edges, free from coarse, ragged or deep indentations. They approach nearest to perfection when the fringe is scarcely discernible. If the petals were entire, this would be desirable. The broadest part should be perfectly white, unless it be ornamented by a continuation of the colour of the eye (lacing) round it which should be clean, bold and distinct. The colouring should consist of bright or dark crimson or purple, resembling velvet. The nearer it approaches to black, the more it is esteemed. The proportion of the colour to white should be nearly equal.

CULTURE OF THE PINK

The florists of old, almost without exception, made mention of the pink's liking for a well drained soil and an open, sunny situation but surprisingly they made no mention of the plant requiring a soil containing plenty of lime. Large quantities of manure as for auriculas was the order of the day and this more than anything may have contributed to the rapid decline of the florists' pinks.

In a letter dated 30th July, 1821, addressed to T. Sabine, Esq. Secretary of the London Horticultural Society, Thomas Hogg said, 'I form my pink beds and plant them about mid-October; they are raised 6 inches above the alley to enable heavy rains to drain off in winter. The soil consists of a sandy loam, a mixture of yellowish loam; common black garden loam; road grit taken from the entrance to Paddington pond, washed before it is used, together with a good proportion of rotten horse dung . . . I top-dress the beds in May with a small quantity of one-year-old sheep dung, sweepings from the St. John's Wood Lane sheep pens.' Always it was manure, never lime which should be used as a top dressing. This made for a 'soft' disease prone plant and few varieties survived for long.

Hogg has told that 'florists contending for a prize and anxious to get the plants large, would leave three blooms only on each stem, and four or five stems to a plant . . . As soon as the pods are well formed, they tie a piece of raffia around them, to prevent their bursting irregularly and as soon as in bloom, place a glass and other covering over them to protect them from rain and sun, thus preserving their colours from being faded and tarnished'.

Hogg has told that a pink bed will continue to flower well for two years in succession (it will do so indefinitely if top dressed with lime), though most florists renew their plants yearly by 'piping the grass'. This is the old florists' term for propagation by pipings which are the non-flowered shoots. They are removed with two pairs of leaves by pulling them in an upwards direction. Pinks are also propagated by removing the shoots at a node, either by cutting them or breaking them off. Carnations are increased by layering.

Hogg began to take his pipings on 21st June and Joseph Paxton when head gardener at Chatsworth said that his pipings were taken 'about the middle or end of June, never later than the first week of July when they should be about 2 inches long'. Paxton recommended that they be inserted in beds of sandy soil, planting them about 3 inches apart.

M'Intosh in *The Flower Garden* said that Thomas Ibbett begins 'piping' (and it might be the band of the Black Watch) about the third or fourth week of June, choosing a southern aspect in the most airy part of the garden. Or they may be planted in a frame or in boxes, in a sandy compost, keeping them moist and shaded from the sun when they will root in about four weeks.

Pinks may also be propagated from slips. These are cuttings or shoots removed from the main stems at the base of the plant. They are taken with a 'heel' and will readily root in a sandy compost.

In *A Winter's Tale*, Polixenes describing to Perdita, the art of grafting fruit trees also exhorts her, 'to make (her) garden rich in gillyvors but Perdita, not liking the streaked gillyflowers of the time replies :

> 'I'll not put
> The dibble in earth to set one slip of them.'

The early pinks and carnations would have been well known to Shakespeare and of how to propagate and grow them, and he may have obtained his knowledge from Gerard who had his garden close by the playright's London lodging house.

The beds are made up in early autumn, planting 9 inches apart for pinks will spread rapidly and form large clumps. They require an open, sunny situation and a well drained soil containing plenty of lime rubble which is also given each year as a top dressing. Pinks can endure long periods without moisture and do better in the eastern part of England and Scotland than in the west. Only when the buds are forming and until the flowers have opened, do the plants need care with their watering.

To prevent those large flowering varieties from bursting their calyces, the florists assisted nature by 'letting down the pod', which is done with a penknife, to make slits around the calyx so that all parts of the flower will open at the same time and so preserve the symmetry of the bloom.

Another innovation was to place a circular card beneath the calyx so that when it opened, the outer or guard petals would rest against it, covering it entirely, thus giving the flower a symmetrical appearance.

Though many of the old garden pinks have survived since earliest times, few of the old laced pinks are now to be obtained, though one or two may be re-discovered in cottage gardens of the Scottish Lowlands and in those counties to the south of the border.

FOURTEENTH-CENTURY PINKS

FENBOW'S NUTMEG CLOVE. It is one of the oldest garden plants still in cultivation dating from the fourteenth century. It was re-discovered in 1960, by Mr Sanderson of Leeds, growing in the garden of Colonel Fenbow in whose family are preserved records to say that the Nutmeg Clove was growing in the same garden in 1652, planted there by a certain Julian Fenbow to impart its powerful nutmeg scent to flavour wines. It bears a small but fully double flower of crimson-maroon with slightly feathered petals and measures little more than 1 inch across. The leaves are blue-green and upright.

SOPS-IN-WINE. A plant of this name still survives and may well be the original of Chaucer's time for it is believed to have reached England during the early years of the fourteenth century, from a European monastery garden which is believed to be situated near Orleans. It flourishes in cottage gardens in Berkshire where it is still called by its ancient name. The white flower is extremely fringed and has a black central zone whilst its perfume resembles that of the Old Nutmeg Clove carnation which may have reached England at about the same time.

FIFTEENTH-CENTURY PINKS

CAESAR'S MANTLE. It is the Bloody Pink of early Tudor and Elizabethan times and may well date from the end of the fifteenth century. It bears a flower larger than a ten pence piece, of a dark blood-red colour, covered in a grape-like 'bloom'. The crimson-red becomes almost black at the centre whilst the petals are deeply toothed. It has a powerful clove scent.

SIXTEENTH-CENTURY PINKS

FOUNTAINS ABBEY. It resembles the equally old Queen of Sheba in appearance, the flowers being less than 1 inch diameter but they are semi-double. The petals are beautifully fringed whilst the black lacing on a white ground is the equal of the old Scottish pinks. To my knowledge it has no connection with the famous abbey.

NUNSUCH. It is of 'Painted Lady' type and is believed to have been discovered in the gardens of Henry VIII's palace of Nonsuch though it may have received its name from its great beauty. The petals are more deeply fringed than others of this type whilst the ground colour is pink with ruby-red flashes.

OLD MAN'S HEAD. Dating from the early seventeenth or late sixteenth century and rediscovered in a N. Yorkshire garden. It is a sturdy grower bearing white semi-double flowers, curiously spotted and splashed with purple and with a powerful clove perfume.

PAINTED LADY. It was rediscovered in 1950, growing in a Monmouthshire garden and resembles in all characteristics an illustration of 'Ye Gallant's Fayre Ladye' pink which appears in a book of garden flowers of the first year of James I's reign. It bears a bloom only 1 inch across and is semi-double with fringed petals which are white, flashed with purple. In his book *Old Carnations and Pinks*, Rev. Oscar Moreton tells that it grows in his garden at Chipping Norton and has the 'strongest and sweetest clove scent of all'.

QUEEN OF SHEBA. A pink of the 'Painted Lady' type, bearing single flowers 1 inch across, with neat serrated petals which are laced with magenta-purple on a white ground. Of the late Elizabethan era, either late sixteenth or early seventeenth century.

UNIQUE. Of the same age as those surviving members of the 'Painted Lady' type. The flowers are single and of outstanding beauty, the ground colour being red and covered all over with flashes of black and pink.

SEVENTEENTH-CENTURY PINKS

BAT'S DOUBLE RED. It is a pink which has been growing in the Botanical Gardens at Oxford since the end of the seventeenth century and is believed to be that raised by a Thomas Bat in London and has until 1950, believed to be lost. It has blue-green foliage and bears flowers with bluntly toothed petals of rich ruby red, over a long period.

BRIDAL VEIL. One of the old fringed pinks, possibly of the late seventeenth century, the double blooms of ice white, having a crimson patch at the base of each petal. They are heavily scented.

FIMBRIATA. Its origin is lost in antiquity but it is most likely a late Elizabethan pink, the creamy-white flowers with their fringed petals having pronounced perfume.

GREEN EYE. Also Charles Musgrave or Musgrave's Pink, named by the late Mr George Allwood after the owner of the cottage garden where it was rediscovered. It is said to be identical with plants which have been growing in the Palace garden at Wells since the end of the seventeenth century. The blooms are single, of 1½ inch diameter and are of purest white, with slightly fringed petals which overlap and they have a conspicuous green eye or zone. The blooms have outstanding fragrance.

OLD FRINGED. It is one of the oldest pinks in cultivation, most likely grown in gardens of the late Elizabethan period. It is a delightful plant of dwarf, compact habit, and bearing semi-double flowers of purest white with extremely fringed petals and of exquisite clove perfume. The seed-bearing parent of the first *allwoodii* pink.

PHEASANT EYE. One of several Pinks surviving from the early seventeenth century though each of them may be older. It is to be found in both the single and semi-double form with the petals deeply fringed whilst the ground colour is white or blush, with a conspicuous purple-brown 'eye' at the centre. Occasionally the flowers have lacing of the same colour.

EIGHTEENTH-CENTURY PINKS

BEVERLEY PINK. It was found in a cottage garden of a Mr Williams at Beverley where it had grown since at least early in the century. The small semi-double blooms of crimson-red are flaked with white and yellow and have the true clove perfume. It was first noted by Miss Gladwin who described it in the *Journal of the Royal Horticultural Society*.

CHELSEA PINK. Also Little Old Lady. It was to be found in Chelsea gardens early in the century. It is like a Painted Lady, with glorious perfume, the small double flowers of crimson-red being edged and splashed with white.

GLORIOSA. An old Scottish pink, possibly having a carnation for one parent for the flowers are of beautiful shape and fully double, being of pale pink colouring with a crimson eye and having outstanding fragrance.

INCHMERY. It makes a neat compact plant and bears a profusion of double flowers which open flat without splitting their calyces and are of an attractive shade of bright clear pink which are a pleasing foil for the silvery foliage. It has outstanding perfume, 'as heady as that of Mrs Sinkins but not so cloying', wrote Mr Ingwersen.

MONTROSE PINK. Also the Cockenzie Pink for it was discovered in the Scottish fishing village of that name and was found growing in the Garden of Montrose House where it has been since early in the century. It is still listed by Forbes of Hawick and is a beauty, growing 9 inches tall and bearing on stiff stems, fully double blooms of brilliant carmine-pink.

NINETEENTH-CENTURY PINKS

AVOCA PURPLE. It may be very much older for it is to be found in many Co. Wicklow cottage gardens. It bears a small purple flower, streaked with lines of darker purple and it is sweetly scented.

BLACK PRINCE. An old Irish variety now rarely seen and somewhat resembling Sops-in-Wine, its semi-double flowers being white with a large black centre or eye and with similar nutmeg scent.

EARL OF ESSEX. One of these much loved of garden pinks which always splits its calyx but is always welcomed in the garden. The clear rose-pink blooms with their fringed petals have a small dark zone and sweet perfume.

EMILIE PARÉ. One of the truly outstanding pinks, raised in 1840 in Orleans, France, by André Paré, probably having the Sweet William for one parent for it bears its double salmon-pink flowers in clusters and will survive only a few years so that it should be propagated annually.

LINCOLNSHIRE LASS. It has been known since the beginning of the century and may be much older. The flowers are of an uninteresting flesh colour but the delicious scent makes it worthy of cultivation.

MRS SINKINS. It was raised by a Mr Sinkins, Master of Slough Workhouse, and named after his wife. The plant, which has the distinction of being incorporated in the Arms of the Borough of Slough, was introduced by the Slough nurseryman, Charles Turner, one of the great florists of the time. It is a pink of great character, its large white cabbage-like blooms borne on 12 inch stems above a mat of silvery-green foliage, possessing an almost overpowering perfume.

NAPOLEON III. Raised by André Paré in Orleans in 1840 from a Sweet William crossing and like Emilie Paré will flower itself to death in two years. It bears on 10 inch stems, large heads of double clove-scented flowers of a striking scarlet-cerise colour.

PADDINGTON. It was raised about 1820 by Thomas Hogg, a nursery-man of that part of London on which now stands Paddington Station. Of dwarf habit, its double pink blooms have serrated edges and are richly scented.

ROSE DE MAI. It may be traced back to the beginning of the century and it is a beauty, the double blooms being of a lovely shade of creamy-mauve with fringed petals and glorious perfume.

RUTH FISCHER. Dating from the end of the century, it is a most attractive variety of compact habit and bears small fully double flowers of purest white with a rich, sweet perfume.

SAM BARLOW. At one time it was to be found in every cottage garden though is now rarely seen. Like Mrs Sinkins and so many of the old double pinks it splits its calyx but blooms in profusion, its white flowers having a maroon blotch at the centre and with a penetrating clove perfume.

WHITE LADIES. To the grower of cut flowers, it is with Scabious, Clive Greaves, the most profitable of all plants, bearing its sweetly scented blooms of purest white throughout the summer and they do not split their calyces. Obviously a variety of *D. plumarius,* for it has the same fringed petals, it is a plant of neat habit and is tolerant of all conditions.

TWENTIETH-CENTURY PINKS

DUSKY. The results of back crossing the Old Fringed pink with an Allwoodii seedling and it is free and perpetual flowering. The blooms have fringed petals and are of a lovely shade of dusky-pink.

ENID ANDERSON. A most striking pink, its semi-double clove-scented flowers of glowing crimson being enhanced by the silver-grey leaves.

FRECKLES. An Imperial pink, it bears a double bloom of unusual colouring, being dull salmon-pink flecked with red and with a penetrating spicy scent.

GUSFORD. An outstanding pink, bearing large double blooms of rosy-pink on 12 inch stems and which are deliciously scented.

HASLEMERE. Raised at the Ipswich nurseries of Thompson and Morgan, the large fragrant double flowers have a deep chocolate centre and fringed petals.

ICE QUEEN. A 'sport' from Dusky, it bears a highly scented double bloom of icy white which does not burst its calyx and which has fringed petals.

LILAC TIME. Raised by Mr C. H. Fielder of the Lindabruce Nurseries, Lancing, it is an Imperial pink and bears fully double blooms of a lovely shade of lilac-pink with a powerful scent.

MISS CORRY. Raised in Holland, it bears large double blooms of richest wine-red with the true clove perfume.

MODERN LACED PINKS

Several are thought to have survived from the time of their greatest glory in Scotland and from them, possibly re-named, a number of laced pinks were raised by the Allwood Brothers between the two world wars. They have the habit of the *Allwoodii* pinks and from them Mr F. R. McQuown continued the programme and raised a number of laced pinks to which he added the 'London' prefix. They had as parents, the laced *Allwoodii*, the *Herbertii* pinks and perpetual flowering carnations.

These laced pinks are still obtainable, though are rare :

CHARITY. The habit is short and tufted whilst the plant is free flowering. The semi-double blooms have a white ground with clearly defined lacing of bright crimson.

DAD'S FAVOURITE. Also known as A. J. Macself, for it was re-discovered by the one-time editor of *Amateur Gardening* growing in a Berwickshire cottage garden and may be that favourite of the Paisley growers, the variety Sir Walter Scott. The blooms which are semi-double open flat and circular, the pure white ground being laced with ruby-red.

FAITH. The first of the laced *Allwoodii* (1946). The blooms are small but fully double with the petals broad and fringed. The ground colour is rosy-mauve with lacing of cardinal-red.

JOHN BALL. Raised and introduced by Turner of Slough about 1880. The bloom is large and double with a white ground and has lacing and zoning of velvet-purple.

LONDON SUPERB. The large double blooms have a pale pink ground and are laced with purple. The fringed petals and perfume give it the old world charm.

MASTERPIECE. One of Turner's finest, it was first exhibited by him at the show of the Royal Botanic Society, held in Regent's Park on July 2nd 1844 when it received an award. It made a large flower, of perfect symmetry with broad overlapping petals, the ground being pure glistening white with a heavy edge of pale crimson. The lacing was regular and did not 'run' into the ground. It now seems to be extinct.

MURRAY'S LACED. A delightful pink, it was re-discovered in 1949 and whilst the semi-double blooms are small, the ground is pure white and the lacing clean, of a beautiful shade of mulberry-red. This may also be one of the old Paisley pinks.

REVELL'S LADY WHARNCLIFFE. Raised by John Revell of Pitsmoor, Sheffield in 1832 and it could be found in the district until the first world war and perhaps later. It was illustrated in *The Floricultural Cabinet* for 1st September, 1833, the Editor remarking that 'we are glad to learn that the raiser now has 100 plants for sale of this variety'.

It was the best laced pink of the time to be raised south of the border, the bloom having perfect symmetry and it never burst its calyx. The ground was pure white with an edge of crimson-purple. SMITH'S DR COKE. Raised by John Smith of Faversham, Kent, it was considered to be one of the finest laced pinks raised outside Paisley. The bloom was entirely circular, filled with broad petals which were glistening white, laced with dark purple.

SMITH'S SUPERB BLUSH. It was illustrated in *The Floricultural Magazine* for 1st June, 1835 and is believed to be named after Mr E. D. Smith, the artist of Sweet's *Florist Guide*. The bloom was large and of deep rose-pink with heavy lacing of deep crimson. The London florists sold it at 2s. 6d. a pair and as the magazine remarked, 'although sometime in cultivation, it is still in great request and is a favourite with the ladies'. It was to be obtained until recent times though may now be extinct.

VICTORIAN. A laced pink of early Victorian times bearing huge blooms which often burst their calyx but is a most attractive variety. The white ground is zoned and laced with chocolate.

WILLIAM BROWNHILL. It dates from about 1780 and is one of the best of the laced pinks, the beautifully formed blooms being white, laced and zoned with maroon and they do not burst their calyces. It is still obtainable.

CHAPTER X

The Carnation

The earliest carnations – Properties of a florists carnation – The early
growers – Old varieties of carnations and picotées – Culture of the Border
carnation.

Since earliest times the carnation has been a universal favourite
and whereas the laced pink was grown by only a few enthusiasts
and did not appear until a later date, the carnation was long
established for the exquisite beauty and perfume of the flowers had
no equal. Perdita speaks of

'The fariest flowers o' the season
Are our carnations and streak'd Gillyflowers'

Parkinson, writing in 1629 mentions several red striped forms known
as 'striped savadge' and 'blush and red savadge'. He also mentions
a gillyflower known as Master Tuggie's Princess and Master Tuggie
we know, lived in Westminster where he grew the most famous carnations of the time. Parkinson said that 'in the excellence and
variety of these delights, they exceedeth all that I have even seen'.

Ralph Tuggie grew his carnations during the time of James I and
of Charles I whose queen, Henrietta Maria considered it her
favourite flower. Later, the Empress Josephine, distinguished for
her taste and fondness of flowers had a collection of yellow
picotées in her garden at Malmaison and they also grew in
profusion in the Royal Gardens at Frogmore during the time of
Queen Charlotte.

PROPERTIES OF A FLORISTS' CARNATION

The carnation reached its peak of popularity and perfection at
the beginning of the 19th century when the Flake, Bizarre and
Picotée were most in demand. A Flake had a pure white ground
with distinctive markings of scarlet, purple or rose. Thus there
were scarlet Flakes, purple Flakes, etc. Likewise in Bizarres, but
here there were two colours on a white ground such as scarlet and
crimson, the flower being classed as a crimson, scarlet, pink or
purple Bizarre depending upon which colour predominated. The

ground colour should be pure, the flaking rich and well defined and in the case of Bizarres, it should be possible to distinguish between the two colours.

The Picotées had a white or yellow ground and were edged with scarlet, maroon, purple or rose. In the properties of a fine Picotée, the edge should be regular and decided, like that of the laced pinks and should not 'run' into the ground colour. The flowers are depicted in a water colour drawing by Johann Simula of about 1720 and now in the Natural History Museum, London. One variety, Admiral Tromp shows a bloom with a clearly defined rose edge whilst both flower and calyx have perfection of form.

The florists carried the remarkable edge colours of the picotées a stage further, dividing them into 'heavy' or 'light', depending upon thickness of colouring. Thus Abercrombie's Lady Louisa was classed as a heavy Rose-edged Picotée.

In his *Definition of a Fine Carnation*, M'Intosh quotes both Maddock and Paxton who considered that the stem should be strong, straight, and be not less than thirty nor more than forty-five inches high while the footstalks should be strong and elastic, neither too short nor too long.

The flower should be at least 3 inches in diameter and consist of large and well formed petals, neither too thin and empty, nor too crowded and confused.

The calyx should be strong, about 1 inch long, firm enough at the top to keep the base of the petals in a circular body and rising about half an inch above the calyx. The outer or guard petals should be long, broad and substantial and should rise perpendicularly about half an inch above the calyx, then turn off horizontally, supporting the interior petals and forming a convex and nearly hemispherical bloom, perfectly circular.

The inner petals (next to the guard petals) should decrease in size as they are nearer to the centre of the flower, which they should completely fill. The petals should be regularly disposed alike on every side, lying in a tiled manner upon each other, nearly flat but with a slight concavity at the circumference. The edges should be entire and free from fringe or notch, the picotée being an exception.

The colours should be distinct, each petal having a due proportion of ground colour, perfectly clear. The colours bright and equally marked all over the flowers; the stripes regular, narrowing gradually to the claw of the petal, there ending in a fine point. Almost one half of each petal should be white and free from spots.

Old laced pinks. A plate
from *The Florist* of 1848.
Top: Young's Double X.
Left: Mr Edwards

Laced pink, Murray's
Laced Pink

Flaked carnations – Jolly Dragoon (top) and Justice Swallow (from a coloured engraving of 1850)

As all the florists' flowers, carnations were sold in pairs, the average price of a fine show variety at the beginning of the 19th century being about 5/– a pair and amongst the most popular were:

Crimson Bizarres	s	d	Pink and Purple Bizarres	s	d
Booth's Squire Trafford	4	0	French's Duke of Kent	4	0
Fletcher's Stafford Hero	4	0	Gill's Bristol Hero	4	0
Lee's Duke of Kent	4	0	Kenny's Patriot	4	0
Medwin's Lord Eldon	5	0	Troup's Unique	4	0
Young's Earl Grey	5	0	Ashworth's Stranger	4	6
Cartwright's Rainbow	6	0	Hogg's Epaminondas	5	0
Ely's Jolly Dragoon	6	0	Jacques Iris	7	6
Hogg's Dr Lindley	10	0	Stone's Venus	15	0

Scarlet Bizarres	s	d	Pink and Rose Flakes	s	d
Cook's Duke of			Austin's Lady Paget	4	0
Wellington	4	0	Brook's Flora's Garland	4	0
Ely's Major of Ripon	4	0	Meesom's Invincible	4	6
Humphrey's Duke of			Davey's Tower of Babel	5	0
Clarence	5	0	Honey's Gen. Elliott	5	0
Pearson's Lord Bagot	5	0	Hufton's Queen Adelaide	5	0
Stewart's Cornelia	5	0	Hogg's Queen of the		
Strong's Duke of York	6	0	Roses	7	6

Scarlet Flakes	s	d	Purple Flakes	s	d
Barne's Lord Nelson	3	6	Kershaw's Royal George	5	0
Smith's Marquis of			Martin's President	5	0
Chandos	3	6	Wood's Princess Charlotte	5	0
Waterhouse's Earl Fitz-			Hogg's Mrs Siddons	5	6
william	3	6	Maltby's Emma	6	0
Fletcher's Beauty of			Taylor's Waterloo	6	0
Birmingham	4	0	Lascelle's Queen of		
Hufton's Magnificent	4	0	Sheba	10	0
Houseman's Pretender	4	6			

Purple Edged Picotée	s	d	Red Edged Picotee	s	d
Faulkner's Salamander	4	0	Bambury's Duchess of		
Douglas' Prince Leopold	5	0	Beaufort	4	0
Martin's Complete	5	0	Hall's Magnificent	4	0
Hogg's Minstrel	6	0	Russell's Incomparable	5	0
Wood's Agrippa	6	0	Tyso's Shepherdess	6	0
Ely's Dr Horner	7	6	Wood's Champion	6	0
Hufton's Drusilla	7	6			

The yellow ground picotée was never popular with the florists who preferred a flower with the purity of a white ground, whilst the yellow picotées were more tender and difficult to grow.

THE EARLY GROWERS

In *The Floricultural Cabinet* of December 1848, the Editor, writing of the yellow picotée said : 'It is desirable we should have fine-shaped flowers with a smooth petal edge, of good substance and of rich clear yellow, the lacing distinct and of both the light and heavy edged kinds. And Dr Horner of Hull, in the *Midland Florist* of the same year said, 'In the northern counties, a taste for the yellow picotée still lingers and many therebe that lament the want of good sorts. The demand is there, but no supply . . . Let the effort, too long delayed, be in earnest commenced, to raise the flower to its true position; the chiefest of the Dianthus class, and to constitute it the most perfect, as it is the most beautiful and attractive.' But the day of the florist was on the decline and the exhortations of the doctor were never fulfilled. There was no definite part of Britain where the carnation reigned supreme. Hogg grew his plants in London; Waterhouse in Sheffield; Wood in Nottingham; and Ben Ely, one of the most successful of the Northern growers lived at Carlton, near Wakefield. He began growing carnations in 1803 whilst carrying on his business as a master blacksmith at Carlton 'where he resided for twenty years, greatly esteemed by his neighbours for the honesty and integrity of his business transactions and for the sobriety of his personal conduct'. Whilst at Carlton he had twelve children and by his industry, cared well for them. In 1826, he purchased land at nearby Rothwell Haigh, built a substantial house into which he moved with his family the following year and gave up his blacksmith's business to become a professional florist. Ten years later, when he was sixty, he raised the famous picotée, Dr Horner, to be followed two years later by Grace Darling and Mrs Hemmingway. In 1842, appeared Mrs Ramsden and Great Western but these were his last for on 26th March, 1843, he died suddenly when at the height of his powers as a florist. He concentrated mostly on the picotée and those he raised reached the highest standards this flower had ever attained.

A number of the better known carnation growers lived in S.E.

London. George Edmonds, raiser of the famous picotée Jenny Lind, was an amateur grower who resided at Brooklands in the Walworth Road and at the Royal London Floricultural Show, held at the Surrey Zoological Gardens on 21st July, 1847 he was awarded 1st prize for 'the best stand of 12 distinct varieties of the picotée'. Amongst the twelve were several varieties of his own raising, including Regina, Clara and of course, Jenny Lind which during the summer of 1847 was causing quite as much comment as a flower and receiving honours similar to those accorded the popular Swedish operatic star of the same name.

In the same week, Edmonds also won the Large Silver Medal awarded for 24 distinct picotees at the (Royal) Horticultural Society's Show, held in Chiswick Gardens. Included amongst the twenty four were only two varieties which had earlier appeared at the Royal South London show which gives some idea of the number of varieties grown and of the quality of bloom from which he was able to select.

At the Horticultural Society's Show, almost all the main awards went to the London growers who had a big advantage in that they could display their blooms in a fresh condition and had no worries with transport. The large Knightian Medal for twenty-four blooms was won by John Edwards of Holloway and the Bronze Medal by Mr Ellis of Woolwich. Of the awards to nurserymen, Messrs Norman's of Woolwich took the Large Silver Medal; Turner's of Slough the Silver Knightian; and Keynes' of Salisbury, the Silver Banksian Medal. All were names well known as raisers of fine picotées which at this time seemed to be concentrated in N. London.

OLD VARIETIES OF CARNATION AND PICOTÉE

White Ground Picotées

EDMOND'S JENNY LIND. Raised by Mr George Edmonds, it was first exhibited in 1847 when it attracted the attention of all who saw it. The medium sized blooms were of perfect form with beautifully rounded petals and a wire edging of rose pink 'with not a single spot upon the ground colour'.

It was named in honour of the famous Swedish operatic singer who came to England early in 1847 for the summer 'season' and had her cottage home in Old Brompton, then the centre of the market gardening industry. Miss Lind soon endeared herself to all and she was to remain in England until her death at Malvern forty years later. She is buried in Great Malvern Cemetery.

ELY'S DR HORNER. One of the finest varieties raised by Ben Ely, it was sent out by him in 1838 at 7s. 6d. a pair. The bloom was of enormous size, being the largest carnation ever raised up to that time with beautifully rounded petals of great substance which enabled the bloom to hold its form for many days. The ground was a brilliant white, the edging deepest purple, free from striping. The flower high and well crowned, filled at the centre with imbricating petals. It was named in honour of Dr Horner of Hull.

ELY'S EMPEROR. One of the last of Ben Ely's wonderful picotées and thought by many to be his finest. The enormous bloom appeared from a long calyx (pod) which did not burst, the petals being beautifully formed with a heavy edging of crimson on a brilliant white ground.

ELY'S FIELD MARSHALL. Raised in 1842, it was thought by some to be finer than Dr Horner for the bloom was large with a perfect calyx, the petals broad with a glittering white ground and heavy edging of purple confined to the margin of the petals.

ELY'S GREAT WESTERN. The bloom was more than 3 inches in diameter, the petals broad and symmetrical, of purest white with a heavy edging of deep purple.

ELY'S MRS HEMMINGWAY. A purple-edged picotée, it was introduced in 1840 and was from the same seed pod as Ely's Grace Darling. The bloom was of medium size with the petals strong and substantial and beautifully rounded so that it retained its form for many days. The ground was brilliant white with the edging a lovely shade of rosy-purple.

ELY'S MRS HORNER. A scarlet-edge picotée of almost the same quality as Dr Horner, the bloom being large but it did not burst its calyx, whilst the ground was glistening white with the edging clearly defined.

ELY'S MRS RAMSDEN. It was later into bloom than most, measuring 3 inches across and was of perfect form with light lacing of rosy-purple on a spotless white ground.

GIDDING'S BEAUTY OF HEMMINGFORD. It made a medium sized bloom of charm with petals of great substance and of glistening white. The pretty light edging was made up of pencil markings of rose-pink.

MANSLEY'S MISS JANE. The flower was large but did not burst its calyx. The petals broad with glistening white ground and a heavy edge of rich crimson.

MANSLEY'S NULLI SECUNDUS. Raised by Robert Mansley of Halifax and introduced in 1840, it stood without a rival for many years as an exhibitor's favourite. The blooms were of great size and of perfect symmetry, the ground being glistening white with a heavy edging of soft purple which did not run into the ground at any point. For years it took first prize in its class wherever exhibited.

MARTIN'S PRINCE GEORGE. An excellent picotée of good size with the petals beautifully rounded. The ground was glistening white with a heavy edging of crimson-red which tended to extend down the centre of each petal and detract from its merits on the show bench.

MITCHELL'S BEAUTY OF WARLEY. The flowers were large and of perfect form, well filled with broad petals, the ground pure white with a heavy edge of deep purple.

NORTH DURHAM TRIUMPHANT. It was raised by the gardener of the Hon. H. T. Liddell M.P. and named in honour of his election as Member for North Durham after the Reform Bill. It was a picotée of great beauty, the edging made up of pencillings of dark purple which went completely round the petals.

SHARP'S RED ROVER. One of the best of the heavy scarlet edged picotées for the petals were free from any other markings. Though the blooms were small, it was a sweet and popular variety.

TALFORD'S FANNY KEMBLE. A purple-edged picotée that contained 63 petals and made so large a bloom that unless great care was taken with it, it often burst its calyx and appeared in great disorder. Florists would nick the calyx all the way round and tie around it waxed thread. It was also necessary to dress the petals into concentric circles with the central petals forming the crown.

WELL'S JENNY JONES. The flower was of medium size with beautifully rounded petals, the ground pure white with a wire edge of brilliant scarlet which gave it a light and pleasing appearance. It was one of the best picotées ever raised.

WILLMER'S ALCIDES. A picotée introduced about 1840 with petals of great substance and beautifully rounded. The ground was pure white with a heavy edging of ox-blood red which sometimes extended down the centre of each petal, this being its only fault.

WOOD'S AGRIPPINA. Raised by Wood of Nottingham, it was considered to be one of the very finest of the picotées, the bloom being large and perfectly round, delicately edged with bright purple.

WOOD'S CHAMPION. A scarlet edged variety of outstanding quality, the shape excellent, the ground pure white and though the red edge was described as being dull, 'even with this imperfection it would be difficult to find a better red picotée'.

YOUELL'S MRS R. BLAKE. Its flower was one of the largest with broad petals and a well filled crown, the edging light and clearly defined and of bright purple.

Yellow Ground Picotées

BURN'S ST CUTHBERT. It made a large coarse flower, valuable only in the border but of arresting colouring, with a ground of deepest yellow, pencilled at the edge with pale purple.

GROOM'S FAVOURITE. The bloom was large, with the crown filled with petals, the edging light but clearly defined.

HOGG'S PUBLICOLA. Like most of the yellow ground picotées it originated in the south of France and was grown in Hogg's garden at Paddington and listed in his catalogue at 5s. a pair. It was possibly the best of all in its colour, making a large full bloom of golden yellow heavily edged with brilliant scarlet which does not run into the petals below the edging.

PRINCE OF ORANGE. In spite of a tendency to burst its calyx, Hogg thought it the best of its group, the orange-yellow ground colour being unique and enhanced by the brilliant red edging. The petals were of perfect shape. Like all the yellow picotées, it was slightly tender and confined to southern gardens.

Flakes

BROOK'S FLORAS GARLAND. In size and form it had few equals, 'requiring but little assistance from the most skilful dresser to set it off'. The ground was pure white, the deep pink flakes being equally divided with the ground. It was a consistent winner for many years.

CHADWICK'S BRILLIANT. It took Premier award in its class at the 1843 London Floricultural Exhibition and it could not be faulted with its good calyx, full crown, pure white ground and brilliant scarlet flaking.

COSTER'S SQUIRE CLARKE. The flower was not large but had a bold crown and broad smooth petals with a pure white ground and small flakes of brilliant purple. It was distinct from other purple flakes.

DALTON'S LANCASHIRE LASS. It grew to a large size with the crown well filled with central petals, the ground pure white, flaked with bright pink.

ELY'S BRIGHT VENUS. The scarlet flaking was brilliant, the ground pure white, the flower symmetrical but unless grown really well, it was rather thin of centre petals so that the bloom had a flat appearance.

ELY'S LADY HEWLEY. The flower was large and symmetrical, the ground pure white with flakes of bright purple. Writing in 1842, William Harrison said that in his opinion it was the best purple flake cultivated in the north of England.

HOGG'S FOXHUNTER. In 1840 it was considered to be one of the finest scarlet flakes in all England. Its bloom was of considerable size with plenty of centre petals to form a good crown and a calyx which did not burst. The ground was of purest white, the flaking of brilliant scarlet.

HOGG'S SYLVIA. A magnificent rose flake of vigorous habit and bearing a large broad petalled bloom which did not burst its calyx. The ground was glistening white with bold flakes of bright rose-pink which gave it a most showy appearance.

HUDSON'S MISS THORNTON. The flower was large yet did not burst its calyx. The ground was pure white with distinct purple flaking.

HUFTON'S MAGNIFICENT. Producing a large flower, it needed help in the nicking of the calyx so that it opened evenly. When it did so, its brilliant red flaking and perfect symmetry won it the highest honours.

JONATHAN MARTIN. It was raised by an unknown amateur of Sunderland and its culture was confined to the florists of Northumberland and Durham. The bloom was one of the largest with a large number of central petals to give a high crown. The ground was glistening white, the scarlet flaking being heavy which gave it a fiery appearance so that its raiser named it after the notorious incendiary who set York Minster alight.

LEIGHTON'S BELLEROPHON. A Cambridgeshire flake, it was described in 1842, as being 'an old variety but there are few purple flakes better worthy of cultivation even yet'. It had a fine calyx and bore a large flower of perfect symmetry, the ground being spotless, and with flakes of pale purple.

LOW'S DUCHESS OF WESTMINSTER. One of the best rose flakes of the 1840's, it made a large flower well filled with petals, the ground being pure white, the flaking bright and distinct.

MARTIN'S PRESIDENT. The bloom was large and full but as it opened high above the calyx, it required careful dressing when exhibited. The flaking was deep purple, equally divided with white ground.

MILLWOOD'S PREMIER. The flower was of medium size and of perfect symmetry with a brilliant white ground and flakings of bright purple.

POPE'S QUEEN. Though an older variety it was considered to be little inferior to Leighton's Bellerophon in 1850 for it formed a first rate flower with a good crown, the ground glistening white, the flaking of deeper purple than any other.

PRINCESS CLEMENTINE. Its raiser is unknown but it was named in honour of the youngest daughter of Louise Philippe, King of France and was one of the best of all exhibitor's carnations, the bloom being large, well filled at the centre, the petals strongly marked with broad flakes of rich rosy-mauve.

SIMPSON'S MARQUIS OF GRANBY. A top class exhibition flake, making a large symmetrical flower with a clean ground, beautifully marked with brilliant scarlet.

TURNER'S PRINCESS CHARLOTTE. It bore a large flower of ideal exhibition form with a pure white ground and deep purple flaking.

WILSON'S WILLIAM IV. It made only a small flower and needed good cultivation but the petals were broad and well placed, the ground pure white, the flakes a vivid scarlet.

Bizarres

BOOTHMAN'S HARKAWAY. One of the best in its class, the outer petals being beautifully rounded and well filled at the centre, the ground pure with the pink and crimson striping evenly distributed.

CARTWRIGHT'S RAINBOW. It was said to be the most widely grown of all carnations but was shy in producing shoots for propagation. The flower was large, of ideal exhibition form with the crimson and purple markings clearly defined and unequalled in the purity of the ground.

ELY'S COLONEL WAINMAN. A bizarre of outstanding merit, the petals broad and well rounded, the centre well filled. The white ground unblemished, the scarlet and maroon markings evenly distributed.

ELY'S JOLLY DRAGOON. Introduced in 1840, it was for years the premier scarlet bizarre, the bloom being large, of perfect symmetry and with broad overlapping guard petals. The ground was pure white with crimson and scarlet markings alternating regularly which gave the flower a particular brilliance. One writer (1842) said, 'it seems to me to be one of the few carnations that will gratify almost any florist'.

ELY'S MRS GOLDSWORTHY. An excellent show variety, bearing a

large flower of fine form with the white ground remarkably pure, the pink and purple stripes alternating regularly.

FLETCHER'S DUCHESS OF DEVONSHIRE. The bloom was rather small and it required to be grown well to have it at its best but its scarlet and purple markings were almost perfect and the flower was filled with broad overlapping petals.

JACQUES GEORGIANA. Like Woodhead's Spitfire it bloomed late and so usually missed the shows but it was one of the most handsome crimson bizarres ever raised, bearing a large flower of brilliant colouring, free from any running into the ground.

RAINFORD'S GAMEBOY. A scarlet bizarre of great beauty, the petals broad and symmetrical, the markings bright and evenly distributed.

STONE'S VENUS. A pink and purple bizarre of great beauty and 'few could boast of both colours as distinctly marked' but though so popular, it was difficult to strike and always held its price, in 1837 being valued at 15s. a pair.

WAKEFIELD'S PAUL PRY. Introduced in 1839, it was one of the finest pink and purple bizarres, bearing a bloom of perfect symmetry, of medium size with glistening white ground and regularly alternating flakes.

WILMER'S CONQUERING HERO. 'Were it possible to combine the merits of the two flowers, I should only desire to rob Fletcher's Duke of Devonshire of its brilliancy and Conquering Hero would be the best scarlet bizarre ever raised, wrote Wm. Harrison in 1837. The bloom was large, distinctly bizarred with a pure white ground.

WOODHEAD'S SPITFIRE. The flowers were large and of ideal exhibition form, one writer of the time describing it as being 'quite distinct from all others I am acquainted with. The ground is remarkably fine, the stripes of pink beautiful with a good deal of dark purple-maroon colouring, giving it a darkish appearance'. But it was late into bloom and in some seasons was too late for the main shows.

WOOD'S WILLIAM IV. Noted for his picotées, this was Wood's finest bizarre, resembling Earl Grey but of more brilliant colouring whilst the bloom was large and symmetrical.

YOUNG'S EARL GREY. One of the outstanding bizarres for many years, one to have in any collection for the flower was of perfect form, the ground colour pure, the markings clear and bright.

Picotées of more recent introduction

If not of the same quality as the picotées of the early 19th century, several varieties introduced towards the end of the century possess many of the qualities of those of earlier introductions and a beauty which endears them to carnation lovers everywhere. They may be found in cottage gardens and at the nurseries of a few specialist growers.

E. M. WILKINSON. A white ground picotée with a light edge of claret-rose.

EVA HUMPHRIES. The finest picotée introduced since the mid-19th century with broad overlapping petals and glistening white ground. The thin wire edge is of beetroot purple and it is clean and neat.

FASCINATION. A variety of beauty, the ground being deep yellow with a thin edging of soft purple-mauve.

FIREFLY. A yellow ground picotée of excellent habit with a heavy edge of crimson.

GANNYMEDE. It makes a large flower filled with petals at the centre, the white ground being clean and with a heavy edging of crimson-red.

LINDA. A refined white ground picotée with a heavy edge of rose-pink.

NEPTUNE. It bears a large bloom of perfect symmetry with a pure white ground and heavy edge of purple-blue.

PAULA. The blooms are large with broad overlapping petals. The ground is pure white with a light edge of pansy purple.

PERFECTION. The blooms have ideal exhibition form and glistening white ground with a deep edge of scarlet.

PURPLE GEM. The bloom is large and refined with a ground of brilliant white and an edge of deep purple.

SANTA CLAUS. The bloom is of ideal form with a pale yellow ground and light edge of deep purple.

TOGO. It bears a flower of perfect form with a deep yellow ground and heavy edge of dark crimson.

Flakes and Bizarres are now grouped under white and yellow ground fancies but those with two colours (Bizarres) are now almost unknown. A number of the white and yellow ground fancies are still to be found in cottage gardens and may be obtained from a few specialist growers :

FLORENCE GRISBY. It is a bloom of ideal exhibition form, the ground of golden yellow being flaked with red.

LORD LONSDALE. One of the best of the yellow ground fancies, the colour being clear lemon yellow, the flaking deep scarlet.

MRS GOODFELLOW. It bears one of the largest blooms, opening to 4 inches across with a pure white ground and flakings of deep pink.

RAVENSWOOD. The flower is of medium size and beautiful form, the ground pure white, the flakings deep maroon.

ROBIN THAIN. It makes a small but beautifully shaped bloom, the pure white ground being flaked with crimson.

WILLIAM NEWELL. It bears a bloom of beautiful symmetry with broad petals, the ground glistening white with distinct flakings of geranium-red.

A number of self-coloured varieties dating from the late 19th century remain to be re-discovered and have a beauty all their own :

BEAUTY OF CAMBRIDGE. The best yellow self with sturdy stem and non-bursting calyx and bearing a bloom of soft sulphur yellow.

CONSTANCE PULLEN. A handsome pure white of great size and substance.

MONTROSE. An old favourite bearing flowers of geranium-red with such freedom that it was planted by cut flower growers everywhere.

W. B. CRANFIELD. It bears a large flat bloom with broad petals and is unsurpassed as an exhibition self. The colour is brilliant pillar box red.

Culture of the Border Carnation

The advice of 'Innovator' writing in *The Floricultural Cabinet* of 1834 holds good today when considering purchasing plants : 'You had better pay a little more to a florist of standing than risk being cheated by the allurements of cheapness', and so careful were the old florists to obtain true stock that the writer goes on to say, 'I would also recommend your attending the removal of the layers from the parent plant yourself :'

To uphold the constitution of the plants, carnations are propagated by layering. This is done during July and early August, to allow the shoots to root before the arrival of the frosts. June is not a satisfactory month as it is usually too dry. Unflowered shoots are selected close to the ground around the outside of the plant and where their stems may be brought into contact with the soil without severing them. First, the lower leaves are removed, then a strong joint immediately below is selected. About 1 inch in below the joint, a cut is made into the stem in an upwards direction. The shoot will be partly held to the main plant whilst the tongue is opened up to the joint to allow a small stone to be inserted to prevent it from closing. The partly severed shoot is then pressed into the soil, just covering the joint and is held in position by a layering pin. The soil, into which some peat should have been worked, must be kept comfortably moist when rooting will take place in about six weeks. The shoot is then severed from the main plant and set out in the open ground or in a pot where it remains throughout winter. Early October is the most suitable planting time for this will allow the plants to become established before winter.

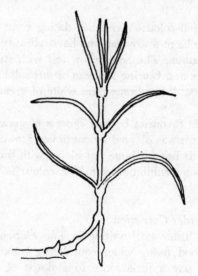

Fig. 6. Propagation by layering

Carnations (and all dianthus) require a fibrous loam, enriched with some hop manure or old mushroom bed compost, or a soil which has been manured for a previous crop. It must be well drained and if lime is not present naturally, this should be given as lime rubble or in the hydrated form. The old florists' usually omitted the lime and in order to have the blooms as large as possible, would use fresh manure which caused the plants to grow 'soft'. Sometimes, just before coming into bloom, the plants would collapse. Innovator has described this trouble, when the soil had become too acid. 'The cure is easy', he wrote. 'Water them three times a week with lime water for a fortnight or so, and they will quickly recover.' The writer also advises mixing gypsum in the soil 'which greatly invigorates their growth and causes the white to be perfectly clear'. This is the only occasion I have been able to discover in the records of the old florists when it was suggested that lime was to be used in the diet of carnations. The plants flourish and remain healthy almost indefinitely in a calcareous soil or if dressed with lime (in some form) every autumn.

Use pot grown plants and set them out about 20 inches apart, to allow space for layering and to attend to staking and disbudding. Plant firmly but not too deeply, only just covering the soil ball. The old florists would erect glass frame-like structures over their plants as they were more tender than where grown 'hard' but border carnations are extremely hardy and protection is not necessary except to protect the bloom as show day approaches. In spring, hoe the ground between the plants and by early May, the flowering shoots will have appeared. Almost daily the stems will lengthen and the buds begin to swell.

To prevent the pods or calyces from splitting and which will cause the blooms to open unevenly, the florists employed one of several methods. Either they would place a piece of circular card cut with a central opening which would fit over the calyx, or they would tie a piece of linen thread around the calyx. Another method was to fix around the pod or calyx a narrow slip of pig's bladder which when first made damp with gum water, dried secure. Or growers would nick the calyx all round with a sharp knife, to enable all parts to burst open at the same time.

At this stage, it is also necessary to disbud, removing those secondary buds which cluster around the main or central bud. This is done either with the fingers or with a pair of scissors. Staking is also necessary and is done by using small green stakes and around both stem and stake and resting on the uppermost pair of leaves, a wire carnation ring is placed.

Where growing for exhibition, the blooms should be shaded from the sunlight and protected from rain by erecting above them, an awning of canvas or polythene supported on stout stakes. As soon as flowering has ended, layering commences as described.

CHAPTER XI

The Pansy and Viola

Varieties of the early florists pansies – The Fancy pansy – The Viola –
Classes and forms of the Viola – The Violetta – Culture – Growing for
exhibition – Exhibiting the blooms – Propagation.

It is a native flower, one of the loveliest of the countryside
and has been held in esteem by poets and writers since earliest
times. *Viola tricolor* or wild heartsease, to be found growing about
undulating meadowlands and hedgerows, bears only a small flower,
the two upper petals being of deep purple, the three lower petals
pale yellow with orange rays or markings at the centre, hence its
old country name of flamy, for it was made up of the colours of a
flame when wood is burning. The blooms bear their nectar deep
down in the spur of the lower petal and it is believed that the
ray markings around the eye act as a guide for bees. When sugar
was unknown in England, nectar-bearing plants were greatly
prized.

Another native species is *Viola lutea,* which grows in hilly
grassland in the north. It bears a tiny pale yellow bloom, devoid of
purple colouring and was used in raising the Tufted pansy or viola.

Spenser in *The Shepherd's Calender* (1480) called *V. tricolor,*
'The pretie paunce' and by the time Shakespeare began writing his
plays, it was known as the pansy, from the French pensées,
'thoughts' as in *Hamlet* when Ophelia says :

'And there is pansies, that's for thoughts.'

Parkinson called it *Viola flammea tricolor,* alluding to the likeness
of the colours of the flower to a flame and he tells us that heavy
manuring resulted in 'fairer colours and a better scent than where
they grow wild'. He describes *V. lutea* as being better able to
'abideth our winters'. In other words, it was more perennial and
for this reason, when used in breeding the viola, the result was a
plant of greater durability and compactness.

Little was done to improve the pansy until 1814 when two
enthusiasts succeeded in creating attention with their hybridising at
the same time and in the same part of the country. In the garden

of Lady Bennett, a daughter of the Earl of Tankerville, at Walton-on-Thames, James Lee, a nurseryman of Hammersmith, saw what he believed to be the first notable advancement in the wild heartsease. He advised William Richardson, Lady Bennett's gardener, to continue with his work, of hybridising and selection, and within a short time, as many as twenty new varieties were raised at Walton, which were a great improvement on our native heartsease. They were to play an important part in the future of the flower.

Fig. 7. Improvement of the pansy

Less than ten miles away, at Iver in Buckinghamshire, Lord Gambier was instructing his gardener, William Thompson, to improve upon a number of forms of the wild species, especially *V. luteus,* which were found growing in the grounds at Iver. Thompson tells, in an article to the *Flower Gardener's Library* which appeared in 1841, that he had help in his work by obtaining the first true all-blue viola from a nurseryman at nearby Slough by the name of Brown. M'Intosh writing in his book *The Flower Garden* published in 1839, relates that James Lee of Hammersmith had about the same time obtained a plant of the large blue flowering variety from Holland, which Richardson used in his hybridising at Walton. It would appear that this was a similar plant to that used by Thompson and that both pioneers were making use of it at the same time.

It passed on its brilliant blue colouring to one of Thompson's first seedlings which he named Beauty of Iver. It was illustrated in colour in *The Floricultural Cabinet* for 1st May, 1835 and was described as 'surpassing every other of its kind that has yet been seen; indeed nothing equal to it has before come under our notice; it is really a gem, and must be coveted by every grower and admirer of this pleasing and fashionable flower'. The writer adds : 'we are given to understand that it will be difficult to obtain a plant of it this year.' It was indeed a beautiful flower with a broad 'face' of brightest yellow, completely enclosed by a distinctive edging of sky blue. It was the first step forward in raising a circular bloom that was the object of all the florists whilst the contrasting edging had a similar appeal.

Four years later, the first blotched pansy appeared and was named Thompson's Medora. It was discovered by Thompson quite by chance growing amongst some heathers where it had seeded itself. The appearance of the now familiar blotched pansies led to a tremendous interest in the plant, and in 1841 the first Pansy Society was founded. This was the Hammersmith Heartsease Society and was followed four years later by the Scottish Pansy Society, the viola as we know it today then being unknown. The definition of a Show pansy as set down by the Societies was that the bloom should be circular with a white or cream ground or band to the lower petals (the centre portion being covered by a large blotch), the two upper petals being of the same colour as the ground.

The blotched pansies made their way onto the Continent and in 1849, a Hammersmith nurseryman, John Salter was amazed at the quality of bloom of the pansies he saw on a visit to Belgium, many of them the result of M'Intosh's hybridising. Salter was later able to obtain seed and raise a new strain of pansy having much richer colouring and with the lower petals almost completely covered with that attractive black blotch we know so well. The first Fancy pansies had appeared and in that year were referred to in the *Gardener's Chronicle* for the first time. They were quickly to displace all other pansies in the affections of the public when during the 1840's, plants were first offered for sale at high prices.

But it was in the cooler temperatures of the north that the new pansies were happiest, blooming more freely and over a longer period, and it was there that the work of raising new varieties continued. In Yorkshire, William Dean one of the famous trio of brothers who did so much in the raising of new plants, introduced a number of varieties and over the Border, Alex Lister, and William Cuthbertson of Dobbie and Co. were raising and exhibiting some magnificent new varieties. As yet, however, the pansy was grown entirely for exhibition, its straggling habit making it unsuitable for bedding, whilst in the words of M'Intosh the plants were 'imperfectly perennial', propagation from cuttings and replanting each year being a tedious business.

Considerable improvement was made in the bloom from the time of the early introductions of Wm. Thompson and those which appeared less than four years later when such as Beauty of Edmonton and King of the Heartsease, raised by Mr Page at Edmonton and the variety Lord Durham, raised by Mr Burley at Simpsfield in Surrey which by then had attained a standard which has since been difficult to maintain.

Within a few years of Thompson's early introductions, the interest in pansies had spread to all parts of Britain. In a letter dated 1st August, 1834, Mr Wm Barratt of Wakefield told of his having 170 varieties in his collection and he lists a number of them, classifying them into several distinct groups. Several were of his own raising :

Bicolours, composed of two strikingly different colours:
Mr Mapleton, Barratt's Odora, Lass of Richmond Hill.
Tricolours:
Earl Grey, Lee's Favourite, Barratt's Lady Kaye.
Edged, the upper petals edged yellow or white:
Jane Shore, Silver Belted, Mrs Grimstead, Othello.
Purple selfs:
Grand Purple, Lady Bath, Louise Philippe, Bluebeard.
Upper petals dark, lower white or yellow:
Barratt's Emperor, Prince George, Lady Ackland.
Ruby Coloured:
Mrs Ladbrooke, Amanda, Copper Captain.
Striped :
Barratt's Chancellor, Ajax, Lord Gambier.
Light coloured :
Fair Rosamond, Lady Grenville, Venus.
Sky blue, lower petals of various colours :
Maid of the Mill, Pallida, Lady Althorp.
Yellow :
Lord John Russell, Waverley, George IV, Bang Up.

In M'Intosh's book, he states that good varieties may be obtained from 1s. to 4s. each which is the price range for top quality pansies and violas of today. It is interesting to recall M'Intosh's *'Characters of a fine Heartsease'* in which he says that the chief object to be desired is symmetry of flowers. He writes, 'the petals should be large, broad and flat, lying upon each other as to form a circle. The top petals should not wave nor bend back, whilst the lower petal should be broad, the eye not too large.' It is only where M'Intosh suggests that the bloom be not less than 1 inch in diameter that the modern requirements of a Show pansy differ from the standards of more than a century ago.

VARIETIES OF THE EARLY FLORIST'S PANSIES

BURLEY'S GENERAL WOLFE. It appeared in 1839, the bloom forming a complete circle and being of deep pansy-purple with a 'face' of brightest yellow.

BURLEY'S LORD DURHAM. Introduced in 1838, the blooms were now completely circular with a broad lower petal and were bright yellow with purple blotches around the eye.

DUKE OF MARLBOROUGH. A beautiful pansy with a large yellow face surrounded with purple-black, the two upper petals being also black.

HOGG'S ROYAL CRIMSON. An unusual variety, bearing blossoms of bright crimson with a 'face' of brilliant gold.

MAJOR'S BLUE FRINGE. Raised at Knostrop, Leeds in 1847 by Mr James Major, it remained for many years outstanding on the show bench and was in every collection. The bloom was circular and of purest white with a broad edging of mid-blue, the eye surrounded with similar colouring.

MARSDEN'S KING WILLIAM IV. The lower petals were deep yellow, the upper navy-blue to provide striking contrast.

NEILSON'S BLACKLEY HERO. A fine deep purple self, perfectly round, of excellent substance and with smooth edges.

NEILSON'S MAGNIFICENT. Introduced in 1848, it was one of the outstanding varieties of the time. The ground colour was deep rose, with an edge of wine-red, the edging of the three lower petals being of white. A flower of superb form : 'Its contrasted colours render it particularly handsome'.

NE PLUS ULTRA. Introduced in 1837, the bloom was almost circular, the three lower petals black, the two upper being dark blue with a pale blue ring around the eye.

PAGE'S ECLIPSE. Introduced in 1839, it bore a most handsome flower, the three lower petals being cream, surrounded with a thick edging of pansy-purple, the upper petals navy blue.

PAGE'S KING OF THE HEARTSEASE. The bloom measured more than 2 inches across, the lower petals being white edged with blackish-purple, the two back petals being of similar colouring. 1839.

ROLLISON'S PRINCESS VICTORIA. A very early and beautiful variety, the three lower petals being white edged pale blue, the two upper petals being of deep purple-blue.

THOMPSON'S BEAUTY OF IVER. Though still retaining much of the form of the wild heartsease, this was a great step forward and was one of the most beautiful pansies ever introduced. The blooms were of clearest golden yellow, entirely surrounded with a distinct edging of deep blue.

By 1840 the pansy had reached so complete a degree of perfection that with the formation of the first Pansy Society (Hammersmith) in the following year, it was possible to set a standard for exhibition. The definition of an exhibition variety said that 'the bloom should have a white or cream ground to the lower petals, with the upper petals of the same colour'. Since that time however, the pansy has been extensively developed so that it may now be divided into two main classes :

(a) The Show and (b) The Fancy pansy.
Again, the Show is sub-divided into
(a) Belted or Margined (bi-colours) and
(b) Self colours

The blooms should be thick, smooth and circular, with no waviness in the petals, whilst they should possess a glossy, velvet-like texture.

The face of the bloom should be slightly arched or convex, with a small eye. The two centre petals should meet above the eye and reach well up the top petals. The lower petal should be sufficiently deep and broad to balance the others and each should lie evenly upon each other. To elaborate further, the top of the lower petal should be straight and horizontal, with the two centre petals arranged evenly on either side of an imaginary perpendicular line drawn through the eye. The tops of these petals should reach to the same height on the upper petals so that the whole of the bloom is evenly balanced. As to the correct marking of the Margined or Two-colour varieties, the ground colour should be the same throughout, with the margin well defined and of uniform width, and the same colour as that of the two upper petals. The blotches should be dense, solid and as near circular as possible. The eye should be well defined and circular and be of a bright golden yellow colour. It is important that there is no suffusion of colour of the margin into the ground colour.

The Self colours may again be sub-divided into light and dark self-coloured varieties, where the upper and lower petals are of the same dark colour, free of any blotch. The same remarks as to smoothness of petal, form, and texture of bloom apply equally with the selfs as with the belted bi-colours.

Here is a selection of the true Show pansies which should be grown where open competition is desired. The plants, however have not the habit which makes them suitable for bedding and where this is required, the modern hybrid strains raised from seed, will prove more satisfactory in this respect.

SHOW VARIETIES

ALICE RUTHERFORD. A deep golden yellow self of great beauty.

BLUE BELL. A dark blue self colour of great beauty.

CHARLES MCCRERIE. A belted variety, the ground colour is pale sulphur, with a margin of violet.

GOLDEN GIFT. The ground is rich yellow, the belting and upper petals being of violet.

JAMES FERGUSON. The ground is of rich Jersey cream colouring, the belting and upper petals being of violet.

JAMES GRAME. The ground is deep creamy-yellow, the belting and upper petals being deep purple.

JAMES RUTHERFORD. This is a pure yellow self.

JAMES THOM. An old favourite having a bright yellow ground, the belting and upper petals being of a chocolate-violet colour.

MAGGIE MYERS. A pure yellow self of fine form.

MRS PETER THOMSON. The ground is primrose-yellow with the margin and upper petals being rosy-purple.

THE FANCY PANSY

As with the Show pansies, the Fancy or Belgian pansies should bear a circular bloom with smooth, velvet-like petals, lying evenly over each other. It is in this respect that the Exhibition pansies made most headway during the 19th century. The earliest introductions had a ragged appearance, the petals being spaced apart whilst the blooms were oval or long in shape rather than circular, which is the hall-mark of the Exhibition pansy. The two centre petals should reach well up on the two upper petals, whilst the lower petals should be broad and deep to give a balanced or circular effect to the bloom. There is no definition as to colourings. The blotch, of violet or chocolate colour should almost cover the whole of the three lower petals with the exception of a wide margin which may be of any colour or of more than one colour. The top petals need not be the same colour as that of the margin of the lower petals and may be rose, cream, gold, purple or intermediate shades. The eye should be bright yellow and clearly defined.

Inharmonious colourings and a bloom which is less than $2\frac{1}{2}$ inches in diameter, or is of poor shape and substance, will detract from obtaining maximum points. The following Fancy pansies have enjoyed considerable success on the show bench. The selection is far greater than that of the Show pansies, which they supplanted in popularity.

VARIETIES

ADAM WHITE. The large blotches are of chocolate, the edges and top petals being of golden-yellow, suffused with violet.

ALDERLEY. The large refined blooms have circular blotches of deep plum, the lower petals being margined rosy-pink. The upper petals are white, flushed with purple and edged white.

ALEX LISTER. The dense blotches are of chocolate, the edges rose and cream with the top petals rosy-purple.

ALEX WATSON. The large blotches are deep purple, the margins lemon shading to blue.

ANNIE LISTER. The bloom has a large almost black blotch and a margin of cream. The upper petals are of violet mauve also with a broad margin of cream.

BETTY SHEPHERD. Outstanding with its jet black blotches and brilliant golden margins.

DAN THOMPSON. It has large blotches of mahogany brown with pale primrose margins.

DAVID DUNCAN. The blotches are black with lemon and carmine margins.

CATHERINE. The blotches are violet, the edges ruby with the upper petals a rich shade of purple.

DR MCKINNON. The blotches are violet, the petals being edged with cream, with the upper petals cream and rosy violet.

ELSIE WILKINSON. It has large mahogany blotches and crisp yellow margins.

ENA WHITELAW. The blotches are chocolate, the petals being edged with gold with the upper petals soft purple.

ERNEST CHEETHAM. A variety of great size with deep plum blotches and a narrow edging of white round the lower petals; the upper petals being plum coloured.

GEORGE CLOSE. The blotches are parma violet, the margins old rose.

HENRY STIRLING. The bloom is large with a chocolate blotch and belting of yellow flushed with crimson. The top petals are yellow, margined with crimson.

JAMES GARROW. The blotches are jet black, the edges crimson.

JAMES MCMURTRIE. The blotches are dark brown, the lower petals being margined with yellow. The upper petals are yellow, suffused light blue.

JANET NORRIS. A most striking variety having deep purple blotches with a thin margin of ivory round the lower petals.

LORD RUTHERFORD. The blotches are deep purple, the edges pure white.

MRS A. B. COCHRANE. A huge bloom with purple blotches and cream margins; the upper petals being purple and cream.

MRS CAMPBELL. A grand yellow self with huge circular claret-coloured blotches.

MRS J. YOUNG. The blotches are deep violet with pale lemon margins.

MRS R. PUGH. It has crimson blotches and edging of deep yellow.

NEIL MCCOLL. The blotches are plum, the lower petals margined with rose and white. The top petals are cream and purple.

STEPHEN MCLAUCHLIN. It has plum purple blotches and light purple margins.

T. B. COCHRANE. The blotches are dark blue, the lower petals being margined white with the top petals purple and white.

TOM HUNTER. The blotches are jet black, the margins pale lemon yellow.

W. B. CHILD. A variety of refined form having a huge purple blotch with a margin of gold. The upper petals are deep golden yellow with purple blotches.

WENDY RUTHERFORD. It has crimson blotches and maroon margins.

For garden decoration, a number of the favourites of the 19th century are still to be found and though they have not the refined qualities of the show and fancy varieties, they will prove colourful for long periods where used for summer bedding :

VARIETIES

ADONIS. The blooms are pale blue with a large dark blue blotch.

EMPEROR WILLIAM. The large blooms are of rich mid-blue with a darker blotch.

FIRE KING. The lower petals are golden-yellow, the upper petals crimson scarlet.

GOLDEN QUEEN. The large blooms are pure yellow throughout. One of the best bedding pansies.

KING OF THE BLACKS. The medium sized blooms are purple-black throughout.

LORD BEACONSFIELD. The large blooms are deep violet at the centre, shading to white at the margin.

ORANGE KING. One of the best, the blooms are not so large as the others but are of a rich shade of apricot-orange.

PRINCE HENRY. The blooms are deep violet-blue throughout.

SNOWFLAKE. The huge refined blooms are pure white.

THE VIOLA

The interest being taken in the pansy as a show or florist's flower, brought about a keen desire to use it for garden decoration and in 1840, John Fleming, head gardener at Cliveden, succeeded in crossing the Sweet Violet with the new Belgian Fancy pansy. The result was that he obtained four varieties of distinctive colouring. These proved suitable for bedding and received much publicity from the press.

It was this success which prompted James Grieve of the Scottish firm of Dicksons to commence improving the pansy, to bring about its suitability for bedding. This was in 1867 and James Grieve, of apple fame, was to become the father of the bedding viola as we know it today. He made use of a number of species which were either native to Britain or had reached our shores from Europe at the end of the 18th century. Crossing *Viola cornuta*, the Horned

Violet of the Pyrenees with one of the Fancy pansies, he obtained a variety with tufted and more perennial habit which he called Vanguard. Using *V. striata* as the seed bearer, as he also used *V. cornuta,* the result was the yellow bedding viola, Bullion, which has retained its popularity until the present day. The plants were short jointed, of compact bushy habit and were extremely free flowering. They were quickly to prove a sensation for they were required by every gardener, and nowhere did they do better than in the cool climate of the north.

At the same time as James Grieve was raising his famous tufted pansies now called violas, John Baxter, head gardener to Col. M'Call at Daldowie was working on similar lines, possibly inspired by Grieve's work. He was to adopt the now familiar method of displaying blooms on the show bench individually, rather than in bunches. Amongst his well known introductions were Blue Cloud and Duchess of Fife, the latter being an entirely new 'break' in the habit of this plant for it was of almost creeping form, whilst the primrose-yellow bloom was strikingly margined with blue. It has retained its popularity for a century though is now rare.

But the raising of new violas was not only to be Scotland's glory, for in his tiny garden at West Ealing, Richard Dean was achieving similar success. Possibly his most important introduction was a seedling of close tufted habit and was better able to withstand the warm conditions of the south than any viola previously introduced. The blooms were neat and round and were of a lovely shade of mid-blue. Dean named it Bluebell and it quickly became popular for bedding.

Dean writes that 'at about this time, I got from Mr Grieve several varieties that he had raised and which were described in the *Floral Magazine* of 1872 but only The Tory did well in the warm climate of the south'. In fairness to James Grieve, it should be stated that several of his later introductions e.g. Bullion and Sovereign, the latter raised from Henderson's Show pansy, Golden Bedder, proved well able to withstand the southern climate. This fact Dean confirmed when he stated that, 'I always looked upon Sovereign, sent out in 1874 as one of the most useful bedding violas of the day'. Together with White Swan, each of these bedding violas are grown to this day and should not be allowed to pass out of cultivation.

At the time, the Royal Horticultural Society held extensive trials at the Chiswick Gardens and amongst 20 varieties to receive an

Award of Merit were The Tory, Sovereign and Golden Gem, raised by Grieve; and Bluebell and White Swan from Richard Dean. Another variety to receive an Award was Novelty, raised and submitted by James Cocker of Aberdeen, raiser of the Bon Accord double primroses and who now concentrate on raising some magnificent new roses like the 1970 introduction, Anne Cocker.

The viola or tufted pansy may be divided into two sections, apart from the numerous hybrids grown from seed – varieties suitable for exhibition, and those used for bedding. It may be assumed that exhibition varieties are those which bear a larger and more refined flower, yet not all of such form come within the requirements set down by the various societies. The bloom should be circular with the petals lying evenly over each other. The centre petals should meet above the eye, whilst the lower petals be deep and broad, to give balance to the bloom. The colour may be self, mottled, suffused or margined, but must be entirely free of any blotch or rays. Thus, of the more popular varieties, whilst Moseley Perfection with its refined golden yellow bloom, entirely rayless may be used on the show bench, Bullion which is free flowering and of similar though slightly richer colour, would not be accepted for exhibition, for the bloom is anything but refined in form and is heavily rayed. As with all Show pansies and violas, the eye must be bright and clearly defined whilst the bloom must be more than $2\frac{1}{2}$ inches in diameter. Flowers which have gaps between the petals or where the petals are thin at the edges, also where the eye is too large, will not be suitable for exhibition. Colour is given greater prominence, by those judging, than any other point, and a bloom which tends to fade or with margined varieties, where this is ill-defined, will fail to win maximum points.

It is interesting to record that James Grieve said, where the Show or Fancy pansy was the seed bearer, the plants took on the habit of the pansy, possessing the same straggling habit and being biennial rather than perennial as is the viola.

CLASSES AND FORMS OF THE VIOLA

Exhibition Varieties
ADA JACKSON. A new colour break. The large white blooms have an edge of rosy-mauve on the three lower petals, the upper petals being suffused rosy-mauve.

AGNES COCHRANE. The lower petals are crimson-purple; the top petals are rich mauve splashed with purple.

ANDREW JACKSON. The refined bloom is of a rich shade of purple, striped with amethyst and pale mauve.

A. S. FRATER. An excellent variety the large blooms being creamy-white, margined with mauve.

BARBARA BENNETT. A crimson purple self of massive, but refined form.

BEATRICE CHALMERS. A most handsome variety, the large cream blooms being edged with blue.

CATHERINE WILLIAMS. A magnificent deep cream, edged with mauve.

DORA MCGILL. A plum self of great size and substance.

DOROTHY STEIN. The large lemon yellow blooms are edged with mauve.

DOUGLAS UPTON. The rose-pink blooms are striped and marbled with crimson.

ELIZABETH WILLIAMS. The huge blooms are of deep mauve with an atractive cream centre.

GRACE MOORE. The flowers are deep cream, heavily belted with violet.

HELEN COCHRANE. Possibly the finest pure white ever raised.

H. H. HODGE. A fine variety having a lemon ground with a wire edge of lavender. Excellent habit.

JEAN LISTER. The blooms are large and of rich cream edged with blue.

JOHN ADAMSON. A pure golden-yellow of outstanding form.

KATHLEEN HAYLE. A pure cream self of high quality.

KATHRYN. The large blooms are white, shaded fuchsia-pink at the centre.

LADY TENNYSON. An outstanding pure white. The habit of the plant is ideal in every way.

LESLIE KEAY. A fine large cream, attractively edged with heliotrope.

LOIS MILNER. A lovely yellow, edged bright blue, the two upper petals also being suffused with blue.

MADGE MCKNIGHT. The large white blooms have a wire edge of rich mauve.

MARY ANDERSON. An outstanding viola, the pale sulphur-yellow blooms are edged with mauve.

MAY CHEETHAM. A new variety of superb form and likely to be the most popular viola of its colour on the show bench for many years.

The huge bloom is pure primrose yellow, rayless and of great substance.

MAY JACKSON. The primrose yellow petals are edged with mauve, the upper petals suffused mauve.

MILNER'S FANCY. The bloom is most striking, being large and of deep purple-red, striped with rose.

MIRA WALKER. An exhibition favourite, the rosy-mauve blooms having a creamy-white centre.

MOSELEY PERFECTION. The beautifully formed golden-yellow blooms are entirely rayless.

MRS A. BLEARS. An exceptional variety, the pale cream blooms having a wire edge of purple.

MRS A. COCHRANE. The large blooms have a cream centre and are edged and suffused pale lavender.

MRS ALEX FOREST. The large deep cream bloom is suffused with violet on all petals.

MRS A. STEVENSON. The large flowers are pale yellow, suffused at the edges with heliotrope.

MRS BOWMAN. A pure yellow self of outstanding quality.

MRS JAMES ANDREWS. The large blooms are palest cream with a contrasting edge of pale blue.

MRS J. H. LITTLE. The primrose-yellow blooms are heavily banded with an unusual shade of slate-blue.

MRS J. ROBERTSON. The sulphur-yellow blooms have an attractive picotée edge of lavender. The top petals are also pencilled lavender.

MRS. M. WALLACE. Unusual in that the bloom is lavender, speckled or marbled with purple.

MRS T. BATES. A fine pure yellow self of fine form.

PEACE. One of the finest of all exhibition violas but now rarely to be seen. The large circular rayless blooms are creamy-white, slightly flushed with lavender.

PICKERING BLUE. One of the most popular of all violas for exhibition and bedding. The large, sweetly scented blooms are of a lovely shade of deep sky-blue.

R. N. DENBY. An outstanding variety, the pale lemon yellow bloom being edged with pale blue.

ROBERT WEBB. A dark flowered blue 'sport' from Pickering Blue, and possessing the same excellent qualities.

ROSIE BELL. The blooms are large and of a deep magenta pink colour.

ROWAN HOOD. The large well formed blooms are deep chrome-yellow belted with lavender.

RUTH FISHER. The flowers are blue, streaked with white at the centre.

SIR EDWARD GREY. The blooms are of pure crimson-red throughout.

SUE STEVENSON. One of the finest varieties ever raised, both for exhibition and bedding. The large blooms are of a rich shade of violet with a large clear yellow centre.

SUSAN. A superb viola for exhibition, a seedling from the popular Ada Jackson. The white bloom has a margin of mid-blue on the lower petals, the top petals being suffused blue, whilst the bloom is extremely large.

WILLIAM JACKSON. The large refined blooms are brilliant golden-yellow with a picotée edge of white.

Bedding Violas

The qualities of a bedding viola are such that the plants should possess a dwarf, compact habit and be free flowering, the flower stem to be erect and of sufficient length to maintain the blooms above the foliage. Where used for exhibition, the blooms should be, like the Exhibition varieties, quite free of rays and blotches, though this generally adds to their attraction when used for garden display e.g. Bluestone, Pinkie, Dobbie's Bronze and Palmer's White.

The viola in all its forms is always more satisfactory in the south than is the pansy, proving better able to withstand warmer and drier conditions. For this reason, it has increased in popularity to the exclusion of the Show and Fancy pansy. William Robinson, who did much to popularise the viola, has written that in the south the margined varieties such as Goldfinch aand Duchess of Fife were never as reliable as the self-colours, for their margins were not so clearly defined as when growing in the north. There is some degree of truth in this statement though modern varieties are more reliable in this respect, whilst planting in partial shade will do much to provide the cool conditions which all members of the family love best.

Bedding Varieties

ADMIRAL OF THE BLUES. A fine old Exhibition variety, now used chiefly for bedding. The mid-blue flowers suffused with crimson and with a striking yellow eye make this one of the best violas ever introduced.

AMY BARR. A fine bedding variety. The blooms are deep pink with a white centre.

ARABELLA. A beautiful viola, the bloom being pale mauve deepening to violet at the edges.

BARBARA. A colourful variety, the top petals being mauve-blue, the side petals mauve pink, the lower petals being yellow, edged with mauve.

BLUESTONE. An old variety of most compact habit. The clear mid-blue colour of the medium sized blooms with their striking golden eye surrounded by a small purple blotch make it unbeatable for bedding. Very long in bloom.

BRENDA RUSHWORTH. An unusual variety, the large lemon yellow blooms being flushed with lilac at the edges.

BULLION. Almost a hundred years old and for its freedom of flowering is still widely planted. The bloom is brilliant golden yellow and rayed. It is of compact habit and is early to bloom.

CRIMSON BEDDER. The blooms are of a rich crimson-purple shade, produced with great freedom.

DOBBIE'S BRONZE. Probably the best bronze for bedding. The blooms are bright, with a terra-cotta flush, and with a bronze blotch at the centre.

IRISH MOLLY. The colourings are so diverse as to make it difficult to describe. It may be said to be bronzy-yellow, with a copper centre but the bloom has an unusual green appearance.

JACKANAPES. A very old variety, the upper petals being crimson-brown, the lower petals bright yellow.

JAMES PILLING. A fine belted pansy, the white bloom being margined with lavender-blue.

J. B. RIDING. An old favourite, a 'sport' from William Neil, the bright slightly rayed purple blooms being produced with freedom.

KATHLEEN. The white blooms have a thick edge of reddish-mauve and have a mauve-pink blotch on the upper petals.

MAGGIE MOTT. Extremely long and free flowering, bearing silvery mauve blooms of great beauty. One of the best violas ever introduced.

MISS BROOKS. A uniquely coloured viola, the large blooms being of a deep cerise-pink self colour.

MOSELEY CREAM. The large refined blooms are of a lovely Jersey cream colour.

PALMER'S WHITE. A fine white for massing, the blooms are medium-sized, the habit of the plant being most compact.

PINKIE. The large blooms freely produced are of a bright shade of raspberry-pink, pencilled with mauve.

PRIMROSE DAME. Most freely flowering, the primrose-yellow blooms have a bright golden eye.

REDBRAES BRONZE. An old variety of excellent habit, the bronzy blooms being beautifully shaded old gold.

RUTH ELKINS. The large rich yellow blooms are attractively edged with deep purple-blue.

SKYLARK. The blooms are produced with freedom and are creamy-white edged with soft rosy-mauve.

SOVEREIGN. Fine rayless deep yellow, similar in colour to Bullion but a better shaped bloom. One of the best violas ever introduced.

T. E. WOLSTENHOLME. A grand variety, the medium sized bloom being of rich chestnut-bronze throughout.

WHITE SWAN. The pure white blooms are rayless and have a striking orange eye.

THE VIOLETTA

At the same time that James Grieve was raising his violas from *Viola cornuta,* the Horned Violet of the Pyrenese which is a fibrous rooted plant of tufted habit, Dr Stuart of Chairnside was also using the plant in his hybridising. By crossing it with pansy Blue King, he obtained a new strain of rayless violas which he called Violettas. The plants have the same tufty habit as *V. cornuta,* yet the blooms are larger, being longer in shape and rayless whilst possessing the fragrance of vanilla.

In *Pansies and Violas* published in 1892 by Messrs. Dobbie and Co. there appeared in Dr Stuart's own words, a short account of his hybridising, which is worthy of reproduction. He writes, 'In 1874, I took pollen from pansy, Blue King, a bedding variety then in fashion, and applied it to *V. cornuta.* There was a podful of seed which produced 12 plants and which were all blue in colour, but with a good tufted habit. I then took pollen from a pink pansy and fertilised the flowers of the first cross. The seed from this cross gave more variety of colour and had the same tufted habit (of *V. cornuta*). The best were sent to R.H.S. for trials as Chiswick. After being in the ground for some time, I received a letter from a member of the Floral Committee enquiring how they had been raised as they were all different in habit from all other violas sent for trial. I heard no more until the autumn of 1875 and was surprised when informed that I had received six First Class Certificates.

'It was, however, ten years before I succeeded in finding a really rayless viola. In Queen Victoria's Jubilee Year whilst walking round a seed bed, I found what I had for long been seeking – a pure white rayless self. It was a warm night and the perfume from the blooms attracted my attention. The plant was pulled to pieces and every bit propagated.'

The box of bloom was sent to Mr William Robinson, then editor of *The Garden,* who at once recognised a new strain. It was given the name of Violetta and quickly became a favourite in the cottage garden. It was Robinson who wrote in *The English Flower Garden,* 'No family has given our gardens anything more precious.' Almost a century later, the same may be said of it and yet it is known to few gardeners. D. B. Crane continued with violettas where Dr Stuart had left off towards the end of the century, and amongst his finest introductions were Diana, with its lovely clear primrose-yellow blooms; Eileen, pale blue with a gold eye; and the blue and white Winifred Phillips. Though longer flowering than any of the pansies and violas, and being of more perennial habit it is surprising that these charming plants have never become as popular as the ordinary bedding violas. They come into bloom in April, with the primroses and continue until the frosts, the dainty flowers hovering like butterflies over the dark green foliage. On a year-old plant, as many as 60 blooms have been counted at one time. Also, with their fibrous roots and tufted habit the plants present no difficulty in their propagation, being lifted and divided in March like any other herbacious plant whilst they are extremely long lasting. Above all is their delicious vanilla perfume.

VARIETIES

ADMIRATION. The larger than usual flowers are of a rich shade of purple-violet.

BABY GRANDE. The oval-shaped blooms are pale crimson-pink.

BUTTERCUP. One of the loveliest of all the violettas, the oval blooms being a rich orange-yellow colour.

COMPACTUM. The pale lavender blooms have a bright yellow eye.

DAWN. Lovely for planting with Iden Gem or Jersey Gem, for the blooms are of a pale shade of primrose-yellow.

DUCHESS. A lovely variety, the cream coloured blooms being margined with lavender-blue.

GERTRUDE JEKYLL. A lovely bi-colour with the upper petals pale primrose; the lower petals golden-yellow.

HEATHER BELL. The blooms are of rich mauve-pink.

IDEN GEM. The dark blue flowers are held on long stems.

JERSEY GEM. Also known as Blue Gem. The dainty flowers are of deep aniline-blue.

LE GRANDEUR. The blooms, which are rather larger than usual, are of a lovely shade of mid-blue.

LITTLE DAVID. The cream-coloured blooms held well above the foliage possess the rich fragrance of freesias.

LORNA. The blooms are of a lovely shade of deep lavender-blue.

LYRIC. An original variety, the pale lilac blooms being attractively marbled with lavender-mauve.

MAUVE QUEEN. The flowers are reddish-violet borne in profusion.

MRS GRIMSHAW. A recent introduction, bearing blooms of a lovely shade of rose-pink.

VIOLETTA. The original hybrid and still obtainable. The blooms are white, suffused yellow on the lower petals, and are produced over a long period.

CULTURE

Pansies and violas enjoy cool conditions. That is why the modern pansy florists are to be found near Leek and Macclesfield and Biddulph Moor, high above sea level, in the cool damp climate of the Pennines. The plants also enjoy shade and are never happy in a sun-baked situation. They require a soil well enriched with hop manure, old mushroom bed compost or decayed cow manure and as much humus as possible as such clearings from ditches, peat or leaf mould. During summer, the soil should be cool and moist, entirely opposite conditions to those enjoyed by the pink and carnation but similar to those required by the primrose and polyanthus. Pansies are deep rooting and the ground should be prepared to a depth of 18 inches.

If the soil is well drained, planting may be done in autumn,

Picotée-edged carnations – Duchess of Sutherland (red) and Lorina
(purple). From a coloured engraving of 1849

Dahlia, Levick's Beauty of Sheffield (from a coloured engraving of 1834)

otherwise April is the most suitable time, especially for those plants raised from cuttings which have been removed in July and August and which should remain in the frame over winter. Whether to plant in raised beds or on the flat will again depend upon how well the soil is drained. If the soil is light, plant on the flat, otherwise plant in beds raised 6-8 inches above the surrounding ground.

Plant 9 inches apart with the roots and lower portion of the stem covered with soil and make quite firm. Plant only when the soil is in a friable condition and water in, keeping the ground moist throughout the summer. If possible, sprinkle a little peat about the roots at planting time and if growing for exhibition, add a small quantity of bone meal or used hops. If growing in frames, ventilate freely and make sure that the plants are well hardened before planting out.

Pansies and violas used for bedding should have their early blooms removed so that the energy of the plant may be concentrated in building up a strong rooting system. In this way they will come into bloom early in June and will continue colourful to the end of summer. But the plants will remain long in bloom only if the dead flowers are constantly removed. If allowed to set seed, they will soon stop flowering. They will also remain longer in bloom if given a peat mulch in July and this should be worked with the fingers right up to the base of the plants. Regular watering during dry weather is also essential whilst the plants will appreciate a daily syringing with clean water.

GROWING FOR EXHIBITION

Plants grown for exhibition bloom will demand greater attention to detail than where grown only for bedding. For example, timing of the blooms calls for experience, it being one thing to be able to grow blooms of prize-winning quality and another to have them in perfect condition on the day of the show.

The number of shoots allowed to each plant will be determined by the vigour of a particular variety, also by planting time. For example, Christine Williams is a variety of great vigour and so may be allowed to form five of six shoots without fear of reducing the quality of the bloom. Less vigorous varieties should be confined to no more than three or four stems from which all lateral shoots should be rubbed out as soon as noticed. If bloom is required for

I

an early show, two or three stems should be allowed to form and these are disbudded until a fortnight before the event, for this is approximately the time taken for new buds to form and for the bloom to attain perfection. No hard and fast rule, however, can be made, for the weather will play a large part in the opening of the bloom. If a period of dull weather be experienced, it may be safer to allow about 16 days for the buds to open, for it is quite a simple matter to retard the blooms for a day or so, but difficult to bring them on when the weather is cool and sunshine absent. An additional day or two should be allowed in the north where blooms open more slowly but where the cooler conditions are more suitable for growing exhibition quality bloom than the warmer climate of the south.

Plants grown for the later summer shows will be planted out in April, and throughout summer they must be given all possible help to bear bloom of top quality. The soil between the plants must be constantly stirred either with a hoe or with a hand fork, taking care not to cultivate too close to the plants. And towards the end of June a mulch should be given which should consist of a mixture of finely pulverised turf loam, peat and decayed manure which is spread over the beds to a depth of from one to two inches. It is important to work the compost with the fingers around the crowns of the plants, for it is here that it is most required. The compost must be in a moist friable condition when applied. Ten days later the beds should be given a dressing of weathered soot whilst the plants are still being disbudded. From this time until the end of August, whilst show quality blooms are being formed, the plants will benefit from additional feeding. This will enable them to bear bloom of considerable size and over a period of two months. Most exhibitors make up their own mixture, but for general purposes diluted manure water into which has been dissolved some dried blood will prove safe and adequate. One pint of dissolved dried blood should be added to every three gallons of diluted manure water, and this is applied once every week, preferably during showery weather. If not, it should be well watered in immediately it is applied.

If the plants appear backward by early July, due possibly to continued cold winds, or to the plants being rooted late in the season, they must be given a stimulant. The mixture should consist of four ounces each of sulphate of potash, sulphate of ammonia and superphosphate of lime, and two ounces of steamed bone flour and dried blood, making one pound altogether. This will be sufficient for approximately 60 to 70 plants of the Show or Fancy pansies, or for almost 100 exhibition violas. The mixture may be applied in the powder form during a showery day, or it may be dissolved in water. Care must be taken with its application. It is important to apply it evenly over the bed, whilst care must be exercised, so that the mixture, either in its powder or liquid form, does not come into direct contact with the plants, or the foliage may be scorched. As a precaution for those using the mixture for the first time, it may be advisable to reduce the sulphate of ammonia by a half. There will also be less chance of damaging the foliage if the stimulant is applied during damp weather.

Timing of the blooms for the show dates must be carefully done so that in between, the plants may be given periodic rests, the feeding of liquid manure and dried blood continuing even when the plants are bearing no bloom. To ensure adequate bloom on show day all buds must be allowed to develop from about 15 to 16 days before required, and if the weather proves unduly warm, which frequently happens in July and August, the plants will require shading. For this reason pansies and violas are more easily managed for show purposes north of a line drawn across England from Worcester to the Wash, where the weather rarely becomes unduly warm. Help may be given the plants by way of a deeper mulch where they are growing in full sun and in warm southerly districts, for this will help to keep the roots cool. Even so, the blooms often open more rapidly than expected, and must in some way be retarded if they are to be at their best on show day. Where the blooms have been timed to perfection, it will be advisable to give protecttion against showery weather which may cause unsightly marking or if unduly warm, the blooms may become slightly faded and this will be noticed by the judges. After a full 12 months of care in their culture and with the blooms showing every appearance of reaching perfection on show day, it is most disappointing for them to become spoilt at the last moment. When the buds are being allowed to come into full bloom, the plants should be watched with the greatest care.

To protect the blooms from strong sunshine, and from heavy rain as they reach their best, a cloche may be used, shaded on the inside and which should be placed over the plant, suspended on two small stakes. Alternatively, a cardboard cone may be placed on a stick and held several inches above the plant, or a square piece of tin or wood nailed to the top of the stake may be placed 12 inches above the plant. The amount of shading will depend upon situation; plants growing in dappled shade requiring protection only from heavy rain.

The bloom should always be removed in the early morning whilst it is in a crisp condition, refreshed by the dew and the coolness of the previous night. The bloom should be cut with as long a stem as possible, severing near to the leaf joint. Some growers prefer to break the stem away at this point so that not even the smallest amount of stem remains on the plant. The removal of the bloom in this way, however, calls for experience, for the shoot may quite easily be broken too. To obtain the bloom in as fresh a condition as possible, it is advisable to water the plants at the roots on the previous evening, taking care not to splash the blooms.

EXHIBITING THE BLOOMS

The bloom is exhibited either in glass tubes or from specially constructed 'boxes' or trays which are square in shape and made of metal, and into which a dozen holes have been made approximately 3 inches apart each way. Beneath each hole is a small metal tube which is filled with water. The stems should be shortened to about two inches so that as much stem as possible remains attached to the bloom, yet the bloom should lie flat on the tray which is white or green to reveal the true colours. The sides of the tray extend to one inch above the blooms so that they may remain in position and can be covered with a lid without damage to them. In this way they may be transported to the show, taking care not to tilt the tray, or the water will be spilled, causing the bloom to wither. Trays may be obtained to hold 6, 12, 18 or 24 blooms, and each bloom must be neatly named.

The blooms may also be exhibited in glass test-tubes filled with water, as long a stem as possible being inserted. Foliage may be judiciously used, placing this in first, with the stem of the bloom behind, and threading it through in such a way as for the bloom to show in front, the leaves holding the back petals in position. The tube is then placed into a small tin bucket, painted green and filled with moist sand. Where it is required to exhibit six blooms, three should be arranged in fan-like fashion to the front of the bucket, which should be placed in a basket to present a more pleasing appearance, and at the back in longer tubes three more blooms are placed. The back tubes will be almost completely hidden by the bloom in the shorter tubes. Green moss should be placed over the sand around the base of the tubes. Three tiers of blooms will mean that three sizes of tube must be used, one behind the other.

PROPAGATION

Named varieties of pansies and violas may be increased by : (a) Cuttings and (b) Root division (with violas). Cuttings may be rooted either in a cold frame or under cloches. It is possible to root them in a shady bed in the open. Non-flowered shoots should always be used and they should be removed when between two and three inches long. The first shoots will be ready for rooting in July and will be found growing from the base of the plant where they are nipped off with the fingers and removed to a cool room to be prepared for insertion. The stem should be cut immediately below a leaf joint, for here the cutting will root most quickly. The lower pairs of leaves will be carefully removed by pulling in an upwards direction so as not to tear the stem, and the cutting will then be made ready to insert. So that the maximum amount of moisture may be absorbed by the shoot, the plants should be given a thorough soaking of water previous to the cuttings being removed, but in any case they should always be kept well supplied with moisture so that the maximum number of shoots may be obtained.

After the cuttings have been prepared and it is advisable to take only one variety at a time so that the cuttings do not become mixed, they should be inserted in the rooting medium without delay. If the shoots lose moisture they will tend to droop and will take longer to form roots. For this reason cuttings being sent through the post should always have the base of the stems packed in damp moss, and upon arrival they should have their stems placed in cold water for several hours before they are prepared and inserted in the rooting compost.

After the first batch of cuttings have been taken, the plants will benefit from a mulch of peat and decayed manure given during early August and worked around the crowns of the plants. This will encourage the formation of numerous new shoots and so that they will have made sufficient growth for them to be removed during September, or in the south, until mid-October. They should have formed their roots before the year end and the advent of severe weather. For this reason, all cuttings should be removed by 1st October in the north and ten days later in the more favourable districts.

The cuttings may be rooted either under frame lights, which is the most suitable method where large numbers are being handled; or in deep boxes covered with a sheet of glass; under cloches, either tent or bell-shaped; or in a sheltered bed outdoors where early cuttings can be taken. But whatever the method, the rooting medium and the maintenance of the cuttings will be the same in each case.

The frame is prepared by removing the top 2 inches of soil and working in to the underneath soil some humus in the form of leaf mould, spent hops or peat, together with a small quantity of decayed manure. Where this is unobtainable, use 2 ounces per square yard of bone meal. This preparation of the lower soil is done so that when rooted, the cuttings will be able to obtain additional moisture as well as a supply of plant food. When the bed has consolidated, over the top is added a 2 inch layer of sand and peat. Both are almost sterile and will contain neither disease spores nor weed seeds, and should be used where sterilised soil is not available. Cuttings of most plants root more readily in a sand and peat mixture than in soil. The peat should be made moist before mixing with the sand, for dry peat is difficult to make moist when once the bed is made up. The grittiness of the sand will help the cuttings to root quickly, whilst the peat is used to maintain moisture and to prevent the sand from drying and panning, thereby cutting off air from the roots. Being almost sterile, however, there should be available some plant food for the roots to assimilate when once rooting has taken place, and this is provided by the compost underneath. This will permit the cuttings to remain in the frames for as long as necessary if for any reason it is not possible to move them as soon as rooted. In any case, autumn rooted plants will remain in the frame until April and possibly longer. Where rooting in boxes or under cloches, the same procedure should be adopted.

The cuttings are dibbled into the sand and peat 3 inches apart each way. Closer planting is not advisable for fear of encouraging mildew. Make the cuttings quite firm so that the base of the stem comes into contact with the rooting medium, by pressing with the fingers. Then name each row clearly. After inserting, give a thorough watering and put the frame lights into position.

It will be found that when removing the shoots, some will have formed small rootlets where a peat mulch has been given and these, which should not be trimmed, are best planted in a separate frame, for they will form additional roots more quickly than unrooted cuttings. Or they may be planted into sheltered beds of prepared compost outside, protection not being necessary unless during the period December to February, when boards may be erected around the beds and lights used for covering the plants.

Where the cuttings are unrooted, care must be exercised in providing correct moisture and ventilation. To keep the cuttings too dry will mean that they will droop before they have formed roots. Rooting will be delayed, whilst they may not form roots at all if lacking moisture. On the other hand, an excess of moisture may cause 'damping off', when whole batches of cuttings may die. This will usually prove troublesome during winter and as a precaution the cuttings, upon inserting, should be watered with Cheshunt Compound.

After watering in the shoots, dust with flowers of sulphur to prevent mildew and close up the frame. If the sun's rays prove too strong, it is advisable to shade the lights by applying lime-wash on the inside, or the lights may be covered with hessian sacking during midday. Diffused light, however, is better than total darkness which may result in loose-jointed plants and the whiting should be washed off as soon as the cuttings are well rooted. To prevent the cuttings from drooping, they should be syringed with cold water about midday and if the weather is hot during July and August, again in the evening. The rooting compost should be kept moist. It will be found that cuttings inserted in mid-summer will require more attention as to supplies of moisture than those inserted early in autumn. Apart from watering, cuttings will require little more attention other than shading, if the autumn sunshine proves troublesome. With late struck cuttings, little or no ventilation will be given until early March when the frame may be first raised an inch or so, then removed during all sunny days until finally by the month end the lights are removed entirely.

With summer cuttings, the lights should remain in place, apart from when the plants are sprayed, until they have begun to form roots which will be in about three weeks time. This will be observed by the appearance of the fresh pale green leaves at the top of the plant. Additional moisture and ventilation should then be given, the sides of the outer lights being propped open. After about 12 to 14 days they may be removed altogether, replacing them only when heavy rains occur. During the remainder of summer, possibly from the second week of August until the beginning of September, the plants must never be allowed to lack moisture, and regular daily syringing should continue, whilst any buds which may form should be carefully removed. The plants will be ready for lifting in September. Cuttings inserted during autumn will take a full month to form roots. When lifting the plants from the frames, take care that the roots are not severed from the base of the stem.

Violettas and a number of species from which they have been evolved, e.g. *V. cornuta* and *V. gracilis*, also those bedding violas which closely resemble them in their habit, may readily be increased by lifting and dividing the roots. This is the easiest and most reliable of all methods of propagation, for when carried out at the most suitable times, the divided plants will make rapid growth and there will be few difficulties in their culture.

Possibly the ideal time to divide is late in spring, when the plants have made some fresh growth and before they come into bloom. The new shoots are formed around the outsides of the plant in the same way as other herbaceous plants, and they are divided by pulling the plants apart into as many divisions or pieces as necessary. Where it is required to propagate a variety as quickly as possible, then the plants may be divided into very small pieces each containing a few fibrous roots. These are planted out during early May into beds of prepared soil enriched with some humus-forming materials and a little decayed manure. It is important to provide humus to retain summer moisture. The offsets or divisions are planted six inches apart each way, and especially for the first weeks after moving must be kept thoroughly moist. An established clump will break up into dozens of small pieces, but because these plants are of perennial habit and will form large clumps it does not mean they should be left too long without being divided. Frequent division will maintain the health of the plants and planting in fresh ground will also maintain their vigour. If the plants are allowed to remain too long without attention, the centre portion may tend to die back through lack of food and moisture.

CHAPTER XII

The Violet

Propagation – Rooting cuttings – Division of plants – Planting – Feeding and mulching – Growing under glass – Frame management – Picking the bloom – Single Varieties – Double Varieties.

Closely related to the pansy and though never a florist's or exhibitor's flower, varieties of *Viola odorata,* the Sweet Violet, have during recent years become much in demand and have attained the status of antique plants. They are now as difficult to find as the old laced pinks and double primroses but they do exist in cottage gardens, chiefly in the west country, their culture extending from Cornwall to Hampshire where they were once grown in large numbers to supply the plant trade and the markets with cut blooms to make into posie bunches for the ladies to wear.

The sweetly-scented violet was in commercial cultivation in ancient Athens before the birth of Christ for the blooms were used for sweetening. So highly regarded was the flower that it became the symbol of Athens. In France, the violet has been held in equal reverence, the bloom being produced in large quantities both for the cut flower trade and for the perfume industry. Shortly before his exile, Napoleon picked violets from the grave of his beloved Josephine and which were found in a locket he was wearing on his deathbed.

In England, before the importation of sugar, violet flowers were used as well as honey for sweetening, both meat and game being made more palatable in this way, whilst the blooms were in demand to strew over the floor of church and manor house, to counteract the musty smell. Thomas Tusser, in his *Five Hundred Points of Good Husbandry*, mentions the flower as being suitable for 'windows and pots' under the heading 'For those who have no garden' and this is how the plant was grown in early times, in earthenware pots in a sunny window for the perfume of the flowers was much appreciated in the home. Where flowering in a bedroom, the blooms were thought to relieve melancholia and bring about contented sleep. The bloom, dried and crystallised has been used as a decoration for cakes and as a sweetmeat since medieval times. Today, the candied flowers are used to flavour chocolate filled with a violet-coloured cream.

Lending itself admirably to cultivation in the small rectangular beds of the mediaeval garden, the plants were to be found in the early monastic gardens until the mid-17th century, when landscape gardening first received prominence. It was Gerard who wrote of the violet in so charming a manner when he said, '. . . gardens themselves receive by these the greatest ornament of all chiefest beautie and most gallant grace, and the recreation of the minde which is taken thereby cannot but be very good and honest; for they admonish and stir up a man to that which is comely and honest for flowers, through their beauty and exquisite form do bring to a gentlemanly minde the remembrance of honestie, comeliness and all kinds of vertues. For it would be an unseemely and filthie thing for him that doth looke upon and handle, faire and beautiful things and who frequenteth faire and beautiful places, to have his mind not faire, but filthie and deformed.'

Certainly no garden flower possesses greater charm or a more delicious fragrance. In his delightful essay *Of Gardens*, Sir Francis Bacon has said, 'That which above all yields the sweetest smell in the air is the violet, especially the double white violet which comes twice a year, about mid-April and about Batholomewtide', which almost all violets do. Indeed, the violet is cleistogamous, in that in spring the blooms are sweetly scented but then rarely set seed, whilst in autumn the blooms are much smaller, possess little fragrance but set some seed, the flowers being self fertilising.

From the time of the sixth century poet bishop of France, Fortunatus, poets have honoured the violet above all other flowers, but it was Shakespeare who gave it most prominence, alluding to the plant on eighteen occasions. In *Henry V* it is Henry who says :

> I think the king is but a man as I am; the
> Violet smells to him as it doth to me

It was the fragrance of the bloom, rather than its colour to which Shakespeare most frequently alludes. At the very beginning of *Twelfth Night,* we have Orsino, the Duke making his famous entry with :

> If music be the food of love, play on;
> Give me excess of it, that, surfeiting,
> The appetite may sicken and so die.
> That strain again ! It had a dying fall;

> O, it came o'er my ear like the sweet sound,
> That threathes upon a bank of violets,
> Stealing and giving odour!

and again in *Hamlet* where, in a room in Polonius' house, Laertes says:

> A Violet in the youth of primy nature,
> Forward, not permanent; sweet, not lasting.
> The perfume and suppliance of a minute;
> No more.

This reference to the fleeting fragrance of the bloom is interesting, for violets do possess the strange quality in that their powerful fragrance is not lasting. This is due to a substance known as ionine, a name from the ancient Greek ion, from which the word violet is derived. This substance possesses the ability to dull the sense of smell within a short time, and so it is not the flower which, as some believed, loses its fragrance when cut, but it is our own powers of smell which are lost. If after a few minutes the bloom is again smelled, the perfume will return only to disappear again. It is this which has contributed to the charm of the violet, for it is never possible to enjoy an excess of its fragrance.

The poet Barton has alluded to its humility and perfume:

> 'Beautiful are you in your lowliness,
> Bright in your hues, delicious in your scent;
> Lovely your modest blossoms, downward bent
> As shrinking from your gaze.

To add to its mysterious qualities, the violet is often associated with death. The poet Milton in his lament to *Lycidas* says:

> Bring the rathe primrose that forsaken dies,
> The tufted crow-toe, and pale jessamine,
> The white pink, and the pansy freaked with jet,
> The glowing violet . . .
> And every flower that sad embroidery wears.

And at almost the same time (1674), Henry Vaughan so beautifully expressed the short life of the violet bloom, which reveals its charm for but a few hours before another takes its place:

'So violets, so doth the primrose fall
At once the spring's pride and its funeral,
Such early sweets get cut off in their still prime
And stay not here to wear the foil of time.'

In a letter of April 13th 1819 sent by John Keats to his wife Fanny, he writes 'I hope you have good store of double violets – I think they are the Princesses of flowers, and in a shower of rain almost as fine as barley sugar drops are to a schoolboy's tongue.'

For centuries violets have been sold in the streets of London. 'Buy my sweet violets' was for long a cry, though this is no longer applicable to the modern posies made up most often of the scentless Governor Herrick. The use of modern insecticides, however, should once again see a return to perfumed varieties, more troubled by pest and disease but which are still grown in large quantities to supply the perfume industry in the making of soaps and scent, which like that of the lavender always retains its popularity. Surprisingly almost all those violets sold in the streets up to 1920 were imported from France, the home of the commercially cultivated violet. The rest reached our cities from the countryside. The tariff placed on flowers after the first World War, brought about the growing of violets and anemones on a commercial scale in England for the first time.

It was Queen Victoria who set a new fashion in violets, the bloom being used as posies not only for evening wear, but for daytime occasions. During the latter part of her reign it was said that over 4,000 plants were grown under frames at Windsor, to supply the Queen and the ladies of the Court with bloom.

The violet is a plant for the specialist, and is generally grown by small family concerns. Here the removal of runners and picking and bunching of the bloom is done by members of the household, for this is a crop of high labour costs, which today makes its culture profitable only where grown as a sideline, or where household labour may be obtained. This is the chief reason why the violet is grown for market in small plots of less than a quarter of an acre, the fishermen of Devon and Cornwall contributing to the quantity of bloom sent to Covent Garden in winter and spring. Gone are the days when large West Country nursery firms could find continuous employment for more than a dozen men on the planting and marketing of violets alone.

Situation too, plays an equally important part as the problem of labour. In the south-west, the single varieties will bloom in the open from early in the year, and requiring no glass protection, prove most profitable though the distance of marketing the bloom makes considerable inroads into these profits. In Hampshire, Pembrokeshire, along the Bristol Channel coast and the banks of the Severn, from the borders of Devon and Somerset to Gloucester, plants grown outdoors will not come into bloom until the early spring, and to obtain winter bloom they must be given some protection. Farther north, plants required to bloom during early spring should be covered with glass otherwise they will not bloom until mid-April, when prices will have become less remunerative.

The plants must also be confined to those districts which are away from heavy industry, for in no way will they tolerate a polluted atmosphere. This is yet another reason why violets flourish in the West Country. Those growing in favourable districts might find this a crop worthy of specialisation, perhaps together with primroses and anemones, raising plants for sale and anemone corms from seed. Such a scheme, whereby there would be bloom and plants to sell almost all the year round would be particularly attractive to a woman, for the work is light, interesting and profitable. Catalogues with descriptions of the various plants and a good postal trade both for plants and bloom, quite apart from the use of the wholesaler and florist, would help to build up a substantial business. But violets are an exacting crop and must be grown well for them to be profitable.

PROPAGATION

To perpetuate the stock of named varieties, violets are propagated (a) by cuttings; (b) by division of the plant; (c) from runners.

The first runners will be ready for removal in early spring immediately after plants in frames have finished flowering; or where plants have been flowering out of doors, the first runners will have formed during April and May. Not all will be suitable for propagation and only those which form a rosette or cluster of leaves along the string should be used for reproduction. Those which form only an odd leaf or so rather than a crown, will never make suitable flowering plants and should be destroyed. It will be found that the strings or runners will have formed roots along the underside portion of the stem and beneath the rosette or crown so that they should be removed with about an inch of the 'string.' This will help the rosette to grow away vigorously, especially during dry weather. Runners removed in spring will grow into plants suitable for moving to cold frames in September, and in the more favourable districts these same plants will come into bloom early in winter. Elsewhere the plants are grown on outdoors until the following spring, when they will come into bloom in March in the normal way. It will be advisable to remove any flower buds which appear during the summer and all runners must be removed as they form. A plant required to bear large quantities of bloom during winter and early spring cannot be expected to be allowed to reproduce itself at the same time. If allowed to do so, then it will bear less bloom. So as to obtain as large a number of rooted runners as possible from those plants which have flowered, rooting will be hastened and will be more reliable if some of the strings are pegged down with carnation layering pins, though generally there will be large numbers that will root without any help whatsoever.

Propagation in this way may continue throughout summer, at all times keeping the soil thoroughly moist about the plants which should be partially covered with a mixture of peat and soil, or with leaf mould when they will form additional runners with renewed vigour which may be removed until the middle of September.

Unrooted runners from young plants which have been set out in spring should be removed as they appear. They should either be planted in cold frames, where they will quickly root, or where they may have already formed rootlets. Make up into beds outdoors, spacing the plants 4 to 5 inches apart. At the end of summer every third plant should be removed to form a new bed, the others remaining to bloom in early spring.

When the runners are removed will determine the flowering time of the plants. Those removed in early spring will come into bloom in October in the south or early in spring in the less favourable districts. When removed between June and October, either from the old plants or from runners set out in early spring, they will bloom later; in the south early in spring, in the north late in spring. Provided some runners are removed during March and April to build up into sturdy plants to bloom in winter, additional beds should be made up with later runners and cuttings, to provide bloom when those growing in frames or outdoors early in spring are coming to an end. In this way heavy pickings will continue from the early winter months until well into May, when the demand for violet bloom begins to fall away.

ROOTING CUTTINGS

Though the planting of rooted runners will be the most reliable way of propagation, those rosettes which have the appearance of growing into strong plants though they may not have formed roots, should be retained. They will be obtained from runners set out early in spring. These cuttings as they are called should be rooted in a cold frame, or under cloches exactly as for viola cuttings. The same rooting medium should be used and the frame prepared in a similar way. The cuttings are inserted 3 inches apart and until rooting has taken place, the frame lights must remain in position whilst the cuttings should receive some shade from the mid-day sun. Rooting cuttings may take place from April until October, those rooted early in summer being hardened and planted out in July – often a damp month – to bloom late the following spring, whilst cuttings rooted during mid and late-summer should be planted out in early autumn to bloom either outdoors or in frames the following winter. The more tender varieties such as La France and most of the doubles would in any case be best left in the frames until the spring, when they may be set out in beds to grow into sturdy plants during summer. They are removed to the frames again in September for winter and early spring flowering.

It is interesting to recall the method by which Mr John Dunn raised large quantities of violets for Queen Victoria at the turn of the century. Propagation was always from cuttings, taken in September from plants which were to bloom the following spring. It was important that each cutting should possess a crown and these were inserted in frames containing sandy soil 4 inches apart. The plants remained in the frames over winter and were planted out during April. Throughout summer they were syringed every evening to keep down red spider and encourage new growth, whilst all runners were removed as they formed. In this way, plump crowns were ready for planting in the frames by the first week of September, to come into bloom about November 1st.

As with violas in frames, violets must be given ample ventilation or there may be a serious outbreak of mildew, and watering must be done with care, especially during winter. The plants should be regularly sprayed against mildew and aphis and any buds which form must be removed.

Cuttings taken from those varieties growing in frames during February and early March when flowering may be coming to an end, may be rooted in boxes or pans in a warm greenhouse or frame. At the bottom of the box should be placed a layer of compost to a depth of 2 inches. This should be composed of peat, a little decayed manure and some fibrous loam. Over this is placed an inch layer of the moist peat and sand rooting medium. By this method the rooted cuttings may remain in the boxes until ready to be planted out in beds during May. A temperature of 50–55° F. should be maintained and the cuttings kept frequently syringed, and shaded from strong sun when necessary. When rooting has taken place, the boxes should be moved to cold frames where the plants are gradually hardened before being planted out.

DIVISION OF PLANTS

For the amateur and also for the commercial grower, propagation by division is an easy and reliable method of increasing stock and maintaining its vitality. After the plants have flowered and a number of runners and cuttings have been removed during spring, they are allowed to produce additional runners and cuttings throughout summer, or they may be lifted and divided in exactly the same way as herbaceous plants. They may be allowed to produce runners throughout summer and may then be lifted and divided, but their future vigour will be greater if not allowed to over-produce before being divided. Again, if the dividing is done before the end of June, the divisions will form sturdy plants for winter flowering, either under glass or outdoors. As April and early May is often a period of showery weather, this is a suitable time for dividing where growing commercially, or as soon as the plants have finished blooming. The amateur, possibly where the plants come later into bloom, may prefer to divide in early autumn, replanting into prepared soil. It should be said, however, that dividing should not be delayed so late that the plants have not time to become established before the hard frosts. September is a suitable time for dividing and if the weather continues dry as it so often does at this time of the year, the plants must be kept well watered until established.

To divide the plants they should first have all runners removed and they should then be lifted with care, using a garden fork. The plants will be seen to have formed new crowns around the original plant, held together by short strings or runners. These should be removed so that each rosette is composed of two or three crowns. All soil should be shaken from the roots, and like all runners, should be dipped in a nicotine solution, ½ oz. to 10 galls. of water, before replanting. The amateur may use soft soap solution instead. It will be found that the original or centre piece of the clump will have become woody and this should be discarded. Before lifting and dividing, newly prepared ground should have been made ready to take the new divisions so that they do not have to remain out of the soil for a moment longer than necessary.

The divisions may also be potted into 60 size pots containing a compost of fibrous loam, decayed manure and either peat or leaf mould in equal parts, and in the pots the plants may be allowed to bloom in a frame, in a cool greenhouse or in a sunny window in the home, being removed indoors during October. Both divisions and runners of the double varieties, removed during mid-summer should be grown on in pots if they are needed for flowering under glass during winter, for with a richer diet and the fact that the plants do not receive a check when moved to the frames, will enable them to come early into bloom. Plants grown in pots will require greater care with their watering throughout summer, and it will be advisable to pack moist peat round the pots whilst in the open frames.

Mr Oldaker, head gardener to the Emperor of Russia during the early years of the 19th century, grew his violets in pots and it is said that from 400 pots he would obtain as many as 12,000 blooms, or 30 from each plant, produced from October until early May. After flowering, the plants were divided into several portions, each of them containing two or three crowns, for it was Mr Oldaker's opinion that small crowns would not make substantial plants in time to commence flowering in October. Where large numbers of early bloom are required, this is sound advice.

It is mostly the double-flowered plants which are grown under glass and these possess a more compact habit than the singles, forming tight clumps of numerous crowns which lend themselves to division rather than to propagation by runners.

M'Intosh in *The Flower Garden* relates how Mr William King, head gardener at Wenvoe Castle, Cardiff, grew his violets. Against

Mr Dunn's method of striking cuttings in September and giving his plants a full year's growth before they came into bloom, Mr King followed Mr Oldaker's method of propagating by root division, setting out the plants in a north border where they remained until September. Whilst both are entirely different methods, it must be assumed that as both were experts, the results would be similar. There is the same difference of opinion today, for violet culture has not appreciably changed and for those who may wish to know of any differences in quality or freedom of flowering, it may be said that divided plants produce bloom early and of outstanding quality, though the plants do not possess quite such vigour as where grown from runners or cuttings, and so are not quite as free flowering.

The selection of a suitable position for planting a bed of violets is of equal importance to the amateur as to the commercial grower. The ideal position should be one where the plants receive some shade from the summer sun and protection from winter and spring winds. Enjoying exactly the same conditions as the strawberry, for both are plants of the hedgerow and deciduous woodlands, the two may be grown together. For the commercial grower they present an ideal combination, the strawberries coming into fruit when the violet bloom is coming to an end. If the perpetual or autumn-fruiting strawberries are also grown, these will bear a heavy crop during the late summer and early autumn months, before frame-grown violets come into bloom, thus giving an all-year-round income. The strawberry too, enjoys exactly the same soil conditions with ample supplies of humus and a soil which is slightly acid, having a pH value of 6.5.

Of the utmost importance to violets is a pure atmosphere. For this reason small beds made up in town gardens rarely prove successful and the commercial culture of the crop should never be attempted other than where the atmosphere is free from pollution.

Beds or plantations made up in April or May, the most suitable time for planting, must receive protection from the mid-summer sun, even where the soil has been enriched with ample supplies of humus. Dappled or partial shade is essential if the plants are to make vigorous growth during summer, without which they cannot be expected to yield an abundance of bloom the following winter and spring. It is also important to provide protection against the cold winds of winter and spring, for like most plants, and especially the anemone which is often grown commercially with the violet, the sweet violet will not tolerate them. Under such conditions the blooms become burnt or browned, or the buds may not open. Before the plants come into bloom, they must be given adequate protection, if this is not already provided by nature.

An excellent idea is to place branches of evergreens, such as cupressus, in rows along that side of the beds which may be troubled by cold winds. The branches are held in place by strong stakes placed opposite each other and 2 inches apart at regular intervals along the row. Some protection from winter winds and summer sun will be provided by the dense, partially evergreen foliage of the perennial scabious, planted in strips at regular intervals along each bed, allowing room for a small path down each side. The amateur, growing several small beds and even the small market grower, may provide simple and valuable protection by placing 9 inch boards, held in position by strong pegs, around each bed.

Though in the south-west planting is generally done in rows 18 inches apart which permits mechanical hoeing, a method is to make up each bed to the measurements of the frame lights, 4 feet lights are used and the plants are set in staggered fashion, in rows just under 12 inches apart so that with the advent of cold winds, or where winter bloom is required, all that is necessary is to board up the beds and cover with the lights at the appropriate time. A distance of 15 inches is allowed between each plant in the rows and between each bed an 18 inch path is made which will permit cultivations and picking to be performed with ease.

PLANTING

To bloom profusely and over a long period, violets require a soil containing plenty of humus and plant food. Humus is provided by incorporating peat or leaf mould, shoddy or used hops though where obtainable nothing is more valuable than decayed cow manure. It should be dug in to a depth of 12 inches for they are deeply rooting and soil which does not retain moisture during the dry summer months will not grow good violets.

For spring planting, prepare the ground in autumn or early in March and prior to planting, rake into the top 3 inches, 2 oz. of bone meal and 1 oz. each superphosphate of lime and sulphate of potash per sq. yd.

Planting is done with a trowel, making the runners or divisions quite firm. Where divisions are used see that the crowns are planted level with the soil. It is a controversial point as to whether the plants should be set out in rows or in beds. With the bed system, as previously explained, planting in beds of four rows, each row 12 inches apart, they may be covered with boards and lights whenever necessary. There is also less work in transplanting where the plants are to be grown under glass. Though a path is made down each side of a bed, it must be agreed that cultivations are more difficult and are best done by hand. Also picking the bloom off, and attending to those plants growing in the middle of the beds calls for more time than where the plants are growing in rows. Against this, however, is the larger number of plants per acre, and so the larger amount of bloom obtained by the bed system. Where planting in rows allow the plants 15 inches both in and between the rows, though 18 inches should be allowed for strong growers such as Governor Herrick and Mrs Dwight. Too close planting should be avoided, or mildew may break out not only where growing in frames, but on plants growing outdoors during wet, humid seasons. To remain vigorous and healthy, the plants must receive sunshine and air, though the strong sunshine of mid-summer and the cold winds of winter must be guarded against.

After planting, keep the surface soil between the plants aerated by constant hoeing, which will also suppress annual weeds. In addition, carefully observe the foliage for attacks of mildew, leaf spot or red spider and treat accordingly. Better still, the troubles may be prevented by routine spraying. It should never be taken for granted that the plants will remain healthy no matter what weather conditions prevail. A dry season may cause an outbreak of red spider, a wet summer may mean an outbreak of mildew or leaf spot.

FEEDING AND MULCHING

Early July the plants should be given a weekly application of dilute manure water, which is best given during a showery day, or failing this it should be well watered in so that the manurial value reaches the roots. The commercial grower will apply a dressing of artificial fertiliser during mid-July and again during mid-August. This may consist of 3 parts superphosphate, 3 parts sulphate of potash and 1 part sulphate of ammonia, applied during showery weather at the rate of ½ oz. per yard row. The fertiliser should be applied to the ground between the plants so that it does not come into direct contact with the foliage, otherwise 'burning' might take place, especially in dry weather.

Immediately after the first application of fertiliser, the plants should be given a mulch. This will help to retain moisture in the soil during the height of summer, besides keeping down weeds. It will be amazing how well the plants respond to a feed and a mulch; an abundance of new growth appearing as if by magic. The closer to the plants the peat mulch is given, the better they will respond and by the end of summer when the plants are ready for the frames, or for covering where they have been planted in the open, they will have made large clumps composed of a number of crowns and in consequence cannot fail to give an abundance of bloom. Peat mixed with a small quantity of decayed manure, especially cow manure will prove excellent as a mulch. Old mushroom bed compost is also valuable. Spent hops and bark fibre may also be used. After the mulch has been given, hoeing should stop, for by then the plants will have made considerable growth and their roots will be reaching out over a wide area and may be damaged if hoeing is done too close to the plants. In any case, the mulch will do the work of the hoe.

The amateur could use a mixture of peat, decayed manure and loam with which to mulch the plants, and an occasional dusting of the soil with weathered soot will prove a splendid tonic.

GROWING UNDER GLASS

The more tender Parma and the double violets will bloom through winter and spring if given under glass culture and it is at this time that the bloom is most profitable. Unprotected, early flowering singles such as Princess of Wales and Admiral Avellan will in more favourable parts, commence to bloom out-doors early in autumn and continue almost without a break until the end of April.

Violets are one of the easiest plants to be brought into bloom under glass and one of the least expensive. The easiest way to protect them is to place frame boards around beds of plants where they have been growing since planted out in spring, and covering them with lights as soon as the weather becomes cold. Where this method is followed, the plants should be provided with plenty of food during the growing season and particularly during the latter weeks of summer. There should be liberal mulchings with decayed manure, peat and leaf mould which may be carefully forked into the soil between the plants. There will be no bottom heat where this method is followed, but this is not necessary except in cold districts, and where employed particular care must be taken to prevent mildew, which will frequently attack plants under glass.

Where making up a frame, the position should be well drained. If not, remove the soil to a depth of 15 inches and at the bottom place a 2 inch layer of crocks or crushed brick. Over this should be placed 9 to 10 inches of prepared compost. In cold districts this should be still in the process of fermenting although gradually losing heat. Decayed leaves, mixed with some moist peat and fermenting manure, frequently turned about for several days so that the materials are thoroughly mixed to ensure that correct fermentation takes place, will prove suitable, but must not be placed in the frame until peak heat has been passed. To help the compost to retain some warmth, it should be trodden to make it quite firm and immediately afterwards a 4 inch covering of friable loam mixed with some peat and leaf mould should be placed over the compost and made level. A small quantity of cow manure or old mushroom bed compost may be mixed with the top soil. The level of the soil should not be more than 7 to 8 inches from the lights, so 9 inch boards must be used. For the plants to be farther away from the glass will tend to draw the stems, making them soft and floppy. It is also of extreme importance to see that the glass, whether of lights of cloches, is perfectly clean so that the maximum of light rays reach the plants. Failure to observe this will result in a 'drawn' plant and blooms which lack depth of colour.

After making up the frames, give the top soil a thorough watering, and allow the compost forty-eight hours to settle down before planting. The plants should be watered thoroughly before moving if the weather proves dry, as it so often does during the last days of September when transplanting. Before moving, all runners should be taken from the plants if this has not already been done, likewise any open flowers, for it is better for the plants to become established before opening their bloom. Lift with as large a ball of soil as possible so that the roots receive little disturbance. In this respect pot-grown plants will prove an advantage where runners or cuttings have been taken later than advisable. Set out the plants about 10 inches apart and plant firmly, watering them well in afterwards. At first keep the frames closed, then for possibly a fortnight the frames should be kept open during all sunny days, closing them in the evening from mid-October onwards.

FRAME MANAGEMENT

The actual management of the frames (or cloches) calls for the greatest attention to detail; it is in fact the most exacting part of violet culture, for if the plants are too dry, an outbreak of red spider or aphis may result; if a too damp and stuffy atmosphere is maintained, a serious attack of mildew may occur. Dusting at regular intervals with sulphur, which should be done between flushes of bloom, will prevent an outbreak of mildew. On rainy and misty days, the latter especially proving troublesome in winter where growing plants close to the sea, the plants should be covered, though air must be freely admitted by opening the sides of the lights at the end of the frames so that there will be a free circulation through the frames. It is because of winter fogs that winter-flowering violets are rarely successful when growing near industrial areas.

Only when the weather is really cold should the lights be closed and where it is required to maintain a supply of bloom, or to give protection to the less hardy Parma violets, sacking or hessian canvas strips should be placed over the frames, to be removed on all inclement days. Warmth may be maintained in those districts where severe weather may be experienced by banking hot-bed manure or even ordinary soil around the frame boards.

As soon as the cold mid-winter period has ended, more air is admitted, and if additional moisture is given to the plants, they will make fresh growth and recommence bearing bloom in abundance. Water should be withheld from the plants during the period of cold, damp weather when they will benefit from being kept on the dry side.

Never at any time must the plants be coddled, even the Parmas require a liberal amount of fresh air, and to keep the frames closed a moment longer than necessary may be to bring on an attack of mildew, whilst the plants will become drawn and sickly. All dead and malformed blooms must be removed at the base of the stem, together with decayed foliage and any runners, until the crop is nearing its end. Runners may then be allowed to form for removal and making up new beds in spring. If the plants are in any way forced, only weakly runners will result.

Plants, grown in frames, which have given large quantities of bloom in autumn and the early part of winter, will benefit from a weekly application of dilute manure water from mid-February until the finish of the crop. The plants will also appreciate a mulch with decayed manure carefully worked around the plants, and will respond by producing another heavy flush of bloom during early spring. The doubles Marie Louise and Madame Millet, and Mrs Lloyd George and Coeur d'Alsace are varieties which respond to such treatment and provide heavy pickings of bloom again in spring.

To prolong the pickings, so that there will be an abundance of bloom from early in the year, additional frames may be made up and planted in October, or the plants may be covered with cloches in February. Joseph Paxton, when gardener to the Duke of Devonshire at Chatsworth would always ensure an abundance of spring bloom by covering a number of plants with hand lights which remained over the plants until the end of March. Rows of plants may be covered with cloches to bloom from October whenever weather conditions permit, whilst the spring flowering varieties, or where it is required to have large pickings in spring, cloches may be used to cover the plants early in February.

Where barn-type cloches are to be used for covering the plants, they should be set out in single rows in the ordinary way as when growing by the row system, rather than in beds. The same remarks appertain to plants which are to come into bloom in early autumn and are to be covered with cloches, as for those grown in frames, they must be propagated as early in spring as possible to enable them to enjoy a long season to build themselves up into sturdy plants. A number of varieties lend themselves more to cloche culture than others by way of their compact habit. This not only reduces the incidence of mildew but enables slightly closer planting, the aim being to get as many plants as possible under cover, will most probably cause trouble. Varieties suitable for cloche culture are California, Coeur d'Alsace, Mrs Lloyd George, Princess Alexandra, Luxonne and Semperflorens.

It will be important to keep clear the glass of the cloches, washing with soapy water before the plants are covered. To provide ventilation, cloches should be removed at regular intervals along the rows on all suitable days. If the weather continues dry for any length of time, the cloches should be removed and the plants syringed and the soil given a soaking. Every so often they should be uncovered to allow them to receive gentle rain. Though the plants must be treated as hardy as possible, the cloches should be in position during wet and misty weather, also during periods of hard frost. It is advisable to keep the plants covered just before a flush of bloom is ready to be gathered, whilst any spraying or dusting for pest disease attack should be done between flushes of bloom.

Whilst only a few of the numerous varieties of the violet are grown commercially, a large number, many almost unknown, are suitable for garden culture. To the commercial grower a variety must be free flowering over as long a period as possible, whilst the plants must show a certain resistance to disease. Again, the more delicate or tender varieties, and this includes many of those bearing double blooms, demand that extra care with their culture which the professional grower can rarely find time to give them. All of which means that the most beautiful varieties, those bearing a bloom of unique colouring and those having a rich perfume are now known to only a few enthusiasts. Few of these varieties will measure up to the standards required by the commercial grower, who more and more tends to place his trust on these varieties descended from *V. hirta,* e.g. Governor Herrick and Bournemouth Gem, which are resistant to red spider and are free flowering yet possess no perfume. The cut flower grower must play safe, but it is unfortunate that so many charming varieties, many of them known for a century or more are fast becoming extinct simply because the modern generation of amateur gardeners know only those varieties grown and sold by commercial growers.

Owing to the difficulty in fertilisation and setting seed, very few varieties of the sweet violet are known in comparison with other forms of the viola family. The late Mr J. Kettle of Corfe Mullen enjoyed success as a raiser during more recent times, but those varieties we know well have generally been found growing either in the wild state, or have appeared amongst other named varieties by accident.

It is difficult to give any exact figures as to yield and financial returns when growing violets commercially, but it may be said that an average yield would be around 6,000 bunches of about 25 blooms per bunch from $\frac{1}{4}$ acre spread over a period of about five months, where picking commences early December in the south-west. The amount of bloom picked gathers momentum until a peak is reached during March, after which the bloom begins to diminish.

PICKING THE BLOOM

The fact that violets are naturally short stemmed in comparison with most other cut flowers, does not make their bunching the easier. Where growing in the more favourable districts, it will be necessary to look over the plants, whether growing outdoors or in frames, every day except when the weather is dull and cool, when alternate days will suffice, also for plants growing in the less favourable parts. But no definite rule can be given in this respect for it depends entirely upon the weather and the season.

William Turner in his *Herbal* of 1568 said, 'The violet is better that is gathered in the morning whose virtue neither the heat of the sun hath melted away, neither the rain has (been) washed away.' Commercial growers would not quarrel with this opinion for as early in the morning as possible is by far the most suitable time to pick the bloom. No blooms should be picked unless fully open when they should be removed with a pair of small scissors and with as long a stem as possible. They should be placed with care into large baskets or trays and removed without delay to a cool room for sorting. There the bloom is made up into bunches of approximately twenty to thirty-six blooms, depending upon variety and quality. Those varieties bearing a large bloom, such as Princess of Wales and where of top quality, will be made into bunches of twenty to twenty-four blooms. Bloom of second quality should be made up into bunches of about thirty blooms. Each box must be graded, two dozen bunches of first quality bloom, or three dozen of second quality being placed in each box. So that grading may be done, and that there will always be at least one full box to send to market, too many varieties should not be grown.

When sorting, all badly shaped or soiled blooms should be removed, likewise any that may have become faded or which have curled petals which will show them to be past their best. The experienced sorter will be able to make up over a hundred bunches an hour, and the best way is to have one person cutting the blooms whilst another does the bunching. In this way the blooms are not out of water longer than necessary. Where in short supply, bunch up the best as one grade and see that the bunches are as uniform in size and quality as possible. An average size bunch should contain from twenty-four to thirty blooms, backed by four fresh leaves and held securely by a small rubber ring which will be so much easier to manipulate than raffia.

After bunching, place in shallow trays of water for three to four hours, before placing in non-returnable cardboard boxes. The size of box will be 20 inches long by 17 inches wide, the bunches being placed between each other so that the stems will not show. Where two dozen bunches are to be placed in a box, two rows each of six bunches should be placed at each end of the box. Immediately in front of these should be placed six more bunches beneath the bloom across the box, a small wooden stick is fixed to hold the bunches in position. Where three dozen bunches are being placed six rows to a box, the inter-locking stems should hold the bunches in position without the aid of a stick.

It is important that the bunches are quite dry before being placed in the boxes. If allowed to remain in water in a cool, airy room for several hours before boxing, the blooms will be quite dry even where picked damp. The stems, however, must be dried with a clean cloth before placing in the box.

SINGLE VARIETIES

(F) denotes suitable for frame culture

ADMIRAL AVELLAN (F). This old variety remains one of the best of all violets. The blooms are large, freely produced and are of a rich reddish-purple colour, whilst they are amongst the most strongly scented. It is hardy and does well in all soils and in all districts, coming early into bloom.

ASKANIA (F). An excellent violet, bearing a long pointed bloom of a lovely shade of violet-blue. Not quite as hardy as some, it blooms freely under glass and possesses a powerful fragrance. The blooms are held on long wiry stems.

BARONESS DE ROTHSCHILD (F). Introduced early in the century, it has become quite a popular commercial variety. The blooms which possess fragrance are large and of deepest purple. Under glass it is not one of the the earliest, but remains in bloom when others have finished.

BOURNEMOUTH GEM. Due to its resistance to red spider, it is rapidly gaining in popularity. It is free flowering, the blooms being of rich purple-blue. The blooms possess slight perfume where grown in a cool, moist climate; elsewhere none at all.

CALIFORNIA (F). The rich violet-purple blooms are held on long stems and are of attractive form with pointed upper petals and they carry a rich perfume. An excellent variety for frame culture and for the open ground, for it is quite hardy.

COEUR D'ALSACE (F). A charming old variety which blooms well under glass in winter, bearing its sweetly perfumed rose-pink blooms on long stems. Though not a popular commercial variety, it should be so. It is the first to open its blooms in the open and excellent for a rockery.

CZAR (F). Excellent under glass, the large reddish-purple blooms are freely produced on long stems, and carry a strong perfume. Sets seed well but the plants are subject to disease.

DEVONIENSIS. Fifty years ago this was a popular variety with the West Country growers on account of its lateness, for it greatly prolonged the season. Extremely free flowering, the large blooms are of a lovely shade of deep purple-blue, but carry little perfume.

GOVERNOR HERRICK (F). Though devoid of perfume, the plants are so resistant to pest and disease as to make this the most popular variety with commercial growers. The blooms, freely produced, are large and handsome and are of a bright purple-blue colour. Does well on shallow chalk soil.

JOHN RADDENBURY (F). This little known variety is one of the loveliest of violets, the blooms being of a shade of bright china blue, sweetly perfumed and held on long, sturdy stems. In certain soils the blooms may have a rose flush. Should be more widely grown for the bloom sells well.

LA FRANCE (F). The rounded blooms, the largest of all violets are a lovely shade of metallic blue borne on long, erect stems. Though making a large plant and blooming freely, it is not one of the hardiest and away from the south-west the plants should be given the protection of a frame in winter. It is very fragrant.

LUXONNE. This hardy violet is not so well known as it deserves to be. Not only is it hardy, but is very resistant to pest and disease, whilst it is one of the most prolific of all. The large blooms, held on long sturdy stems are of deep navy blue.

MADAM SCHWARTZ. For northern growers this is one of the hardiest, for it will come into bloom unprotected early in March, earlier if the weather is kind. The blooms are large and of a bright shade of violet-blue, borne on long stems.

MRS F. W. DWIGHT (F). It blooms well under glass and is free flowering outdoors. It is now widely grown in the Falmouth district of Cornwall for the large violet-blue flowers are borne on tall, erect stems over a long period.

MRS LLOYD GEORGE (F). This lovely old blue violet with its striking pale yellow centre, may be classed as a semi-double variety and is one of the best of all. The blooms, borne on long stems carry a sweet woodland perfume, and are freely produced during winter given the protection of glass. Also known as Cyclops on account of its unusual eye or centre.

PRINCESS ALEXANDRA (F). It bears a larger bloom than Admiral Avellan and of a similar colour, and whilst it is as free flowering, it is not so hardy. Excellent under glass and where grown in the south-west.

PRINCESS OF WALES. But for its susceptibility to red spider this would be the most popular of all violets. It is free flowering, does well under glass and in the open, bearing its large rich violet-blue flowers on long stems. The blooms are similar in size and shape to *V. gracilis,* and possess outstanding fragrance. The habit of the plants is robust, the blooms being borne on long, sturdy stems. It was first sent out from the gardens of Windsor Castle.

SOUVENIR DE MA FILLE (F). Raised in France, it possesses all the qualities of a first rate market violet. The blooms are almost as large as those of Princess of Wales and are of a lovely dark blue colour, produced with freedom. It does well under glass and comes early into bloom.

SULPHUREA (F). This is the only yellow violet and though it may not be a favourite with the public and is rarely planted commercially, it is delightful in the garden. With its compact habit it is ideal for the rockery, whilst in partial shade its brightly coloured blooms reveal their true beauty. The blooms are not a true yellow and may be described as being of a Jersey cream colour, flushed with apricot-buff. A form known as Irish Elegance bears a bloom of a slightly deeper shade of creamy buff.

TRIUMPH (F). Similar in colour and size of bloom to Princess of Wales, but it is of more compact habit, making it an ideal variety for planting under cloches or in frames. The blooms freely produced, carry a rich perfume.

VICTORIA REGINA (F). Valuable for cloche culture in that it makes a tiny, neat plant yet comes early into bloom and flowers profusely. The blooms are large, delicately perfumed and are of a bright violet-blue colour.

WHITE CZAR (F). The large, sweetly fragrant blooms are of purest white, but occasionally revert to the reddish-purple of Czar, from which it 'sported'. This is an excellent variety for growing under glass.

DOUBLE VARIETIES

COMTE DE BRAZZA (F). Also known as Swanley White or the White Parma violet, and has the same tender habit. It should be grown in frames even in the south, and where this is possible it bears its pure white, sweetly fragrant blooms in profusion and which look most attractive backed by a leaf of the violet or ivy.

COMTE DE CHAMBAUD. Sometimes listed as French Gray, for the very large blooms are of a greyish-white colour, attractively scented. It bears profusely in spring but not during autumn or winter.

COUNTESS OF SHAFTESBURY (F). Free flowering, of vigorous habit and reasonably hardy away from the south, it bears one of the loveliest of all semi-double violet blooms, the colour being pale lavender-blue with rose-pink centre petals and attractive green stamens. The blooms, borne on strong, erect stems carry a delicate, but sweet moss-like fragrance.

DUCHESS DE PARMA (F). In favourable districts it comes into bloom in frames before Christmas, the lavender coloured blooms, with their delicious perfume being amongst the loveliest of all. Native of S. Europe, the plants are tender and it should not be grown outdoors away from the warmth of the south-west, where the plants prove most free flowering.

KING OF THE VIOLETS. Not grown commercially, for its bloom is of poor quality in comparison with other doubles. However, being hardy and free flowering it is a useful outdoor violet, the deep indigo flowers being most striking and possessing a distinct perfume. Not used for frame culture, for it blooms in March and April.

LADY HUME CAMPBELL (F). With Marie Louise this is one of the finest of all for frame culture, and possesses additional value in that it is the last of the doubles to come into bloom, so extending the season. It is also one of the hardiest of the doubles and with Mrs J. J. Astor, is perhaps the most free flowering. The plant is of vigorous habit and bears a bloom of an attractive shade of lavender-blue.

MADAME MILLET (F). Raised by the famous violet grower Millet, this is one of the finest of all Parma-type violets and when better known is certain to become widely used for frame culture. It makes a compact plant and bears with freedom a sweetly scented bloom of a lovely rose-lilac, the identical colour to the bloom of the double primrose Bon Accord Lavender.

MADAMOISELLE BERTHA BARRON (F). A hardy variety of strong, vigorous habit, though forming a compact plant making it ideal for under glass culture. It bears a lovely deep purple-blue flower which is sweetly scented, though not too freely produced.

MARIE LOUISE (F). Like most of the doubles, the plants do not possess the hardiness of single violets, and the plants should be given glass protection. For market, this is the most popular double, the lavender-blue flowers with their conspicuous white centre possessing a powerful fragrance.

MRS ARTHUR (F). It is hardier and more free flowering than Marie Louise, which the bloom closely resembles though it is not so sweetly perfumed. It is an excellent variety for frame culture, for which it is widely planted commercially, in fact it does well anywhere and may be classed as one of the easiest of the doubles.

MRS HIGGINS (F). Extremely free flowering, the richly scented blooms are of a lovely pure shade of lavender. One of the hardiest of the Parmas.

MRS J. J. ASTOR (F). Extremely free flowering, either in the open or under glass, the very double flowers are of a distinct and lovely shade of rose-pink. The blooms, held on erect stems, possess a powerful fragrance. Away from the south-west it should be given under-glass culture.

CHAPTER XIII

The Chrysanthemum

As a florist's flower – Old varieties of merit – Its culture.

Though held sacred in the gardens of China and Japan since earliest times, the chrysanthemum, the most popular flower after the rose, is a comparative newcomer to our gardens, the Old Purple flowering for the first time in Britain at the nursery of Mr Colville in the King's Road, Chelsea, in 1796. It had been brought to Europe from China several years earlier by a sea captain named Blanchard of Marseilles but there is on record that plants grew in the Chelsea Physic Gardens about 50 years before, though they were soon lost and may never have flowered.

The purple-flowering chrysanthemum was *C. morifolium;* it had double flowers and a tall habit and it became, with *C. indicum,* a single yellow-flowered variety, the ancestor of all the now so popular early and late-flowering varieties. Two other forms of *C. morifolium* were found in China, a yellow and a white. Both were mentioned in *The Book of Odes,* revised by Confucius in the fifth century B.C. during the Sun dynasty, which coincided with the Norman invasion of Britain. The monograph recognised 35 forms of the flower and by 1700, an encyclopaedic work on flowers of China recognised 300 kinds. The Chinese regarded the chrysanthemum as a medicinal plant, one which promoted long life and the dews from the leaves were collected and drunk. From the flowers, a wine was made and which was thought to increase vitality in man.

Plants had reached Japan by the fifth century A.D. and two centuries later the flower was taken by the Emperor for his emblem and was incorporated into the flag of the country.

In 1846, Robert Fortune introduced into Britain the Chusan Daisy, *C. rubellum* and in 1866 Mrs Beeton wrote that 'this little favourite had tended in no small degree to resuscitate the cultivation of the chrysanthemum.'

Able to withstand severe cold, the plant had a neat habit and bore small circular double flowers resembling the pompons on the caps of French sailors, hence its name of Pompone chrysanthemum and it quickly came to be planted in every small garden in Britain and in France. Careful hybridising saw its gradual development until today there are some varieties which grow less than 12 inches tall and during autumn, cover themselves in a mass of flowers no larger than a 10p piece.

By 1822, J. C. London said that 'The Chinese are supposed to have 50 kinds or upwards; and there are 14 described by Mr J. Sabine as having flowered in this country in the garden of the Horticultural Society.' These were :

Buff flowered	Quilled White
Changeable White	Quilled Yellow
Golden Yellow	Spanish Brown
Large Lilac	Sulphur Yellow
Pink flowered	Superb White
Quilled Pink	Tasselled White
Quilled Flamed Yellow	The Purple

By 1826, the Horticultural Society had 48 varieties growing in their gardens.

AS A FLORIST'S FLOWER

The first chrysanthemum to have any appeal to the florist was a variety called the Gold-bordered Red. It appeared about the year 1830 and was classed as an Incurved Ranunculus-flowered. It was described as having 'the most perfect and beautiful flower of all the genus. The red petals are striped with gold beneath and are golden-tipped; the tips incurving strongly to show the gold.' Writing in *The Floricultural Cabinet* of 1st June, 1833 Mr A. H. Haworth of of Chelsea said, 'Chinese chrysanthemums have not hitherto ranked with the true flowers of the florist because, however well formed, they are all, save the Gold-bordered Red of self or uniform colours; and the florist requires yet another colour or colours to be distinctly depicted upon the first or ground colour of every petal, to constitute his favourite flakes and picotées .... This will eventually come from the so-called Ranunculus-flowered group, one of that section, the Gold-bordered Red having already a fine form whilst its broad-edged border, base, and tips, often leaving when blown, a single flake of red in the central length of every petal .... Their unequalled sportiveness will reward us by a countless number of new forms and colours surpassing all we at present know.'

The writer said that the finest collections of the time were to be found in the gardens of Canon Ellacomb Ellacomb at Bitton Vicarage, Bristol; and at the nursery of Mr Tate of Sloane Street, Chelsea and that of Mr Dennis in the King's Road.

It was Mr Haworth of Chelsea who suggested the first classification for the various types of chrysanthemum. This was in 1833 and he described 48 varieties, dividing them into six groups :—

i. Ranunculus-flowered.

The best known were : Park's Small Yellow, the blooms being small and very double, about the size of a golf ball and of perfect symmetry.
Colvill's Pink. A pale pink 'sport' raised at Colvill's Nursery, the blooms being small and globular.
Expanded Light Purple. The flowers were twice the size of Colvill's Pink and were of perfect symmetry.

ii Incurved Ranunculus-flowered.

Quilled Pink. By many, thought to be the finest variety of the day, the blooms being ball-shaped with quilled incurving petals.
Gold-bordered Red. The first two-colour variety, the quilled petals being red, tipped with gold.
Superb White. A pure white incurving variety of globular form.

iii China Aster-flowered.

The blooms were large and had a central disc. They were later known as Anemone-flowered.
Two-coloured Red. The flowers were of two tones of red, the bloom having a central aster-like disc with outer rayed petals resembling a pyrethrum.
Clustered Pink. The flowers were large and resembled the former variety except that they were of two shades of pink.

iv Marigold-flowered.

The blooms resembled the Calendula or marigold, being of similar size and shape, somewhat shaggy with quilled petals and they opened flat.

King's Yellow. The flowers were brilliant yellow, shaded with bronze on the underside. It was early flowering.

Starry Purple. Very late, the flowers opened star-like and were fully double, the petals spoon-shaped at the tips, deep purple at the centre shading out to pale mauve.

v Tassel-flowered.

The blooms were large, the flowers drooping with quilled petals and they were of shaggy appearance.

Tassel Flamed Yellow. The blooms were large and double, being more than 5 inches across and composed of quilled petals, 'hanging more or less downwards, at their best resembling a flame-coloured tassel'.

Tasselled Purple. Also known as Old Purple, it was the first chrysanthemum to bloom in Britain which it did at Mr Colvill's Nursery, in the King's Road, Chelsea in 1796. The flowers were described as 'drooping, of middling size, at first of reddish-purple colouring, becoming paler with age'. It was illustrated in the *Botanical Magazine*

Great Tasselled White. Late into bloom, the flowers were more showy and were longer flowering than any other white, lasting until the end of January.

vi Half Double Tassel-flowered.

The flowers were only half-double with quilled petals and were drooping. Few had any garden value. The best was Half double Quilled White. Here, the flowers were large with a double row of petals, as in a pyrethrum and were 'singularly waved', as if pursuing each other from right to left, making a pleasing animated appearance.

Mr Haworth's paper on *The Classification of Chrysanthemums* first appeared in the *Gardener's Magazine* which was at that time edited by J. C. Louden. Mr Haworth advised planting them in a border against a sunny wall when they would bloom from about 1st November until late in January. After flowering, they were cut back, divided and re-planted like any other border plant.

The old florists also layered the shoots, selecting several from each plant towards the end of summer and pegging them into the ground, having first made a cut and tongue below a joint, as for carnations. By mid-September, roots will have formed when the stem is cut away from the parent and potted, to be grown on under glass to bear a large flower at the end of the year. This was the way in which Mr George Harrison of Downham in Norfolk grew his plants and in 1831 he told of having raised 900 plants in about 38 varieties which 'eminent florists came from Town to see when in bloom'.

Possibly due to the energies and enthusiasm of George Harrison, the first chrysanthemum show was held at Norwich in 1843. This was three years before Robert Fortune introduced *C. rubellum,* in which year the Stoke Newington Chrysanthemum Society which later became the National Chrysanthemum Society, was inaugurated. Though a large number of varieties were introduced from China at this time and there appeared numerous 'sports', it was *C. rubellum* and its varieties which really caught the imagination of the florists and the gardening public for the plant possessed a compact habit and great freedom of flowering, moreover it was ideally suited to pot culture and in the home, remained in bloom for many weeks. Again, the small symmetrical blooms appealed to those who for long had cultivated the carnation, pink and ranunculus. Later came the pompone dahlia, descended from *D. variabilis,* which was taken up by the florists for the same reason.

Of the early growers, Isaac Wheeler of Oxford exhibited some flowers before the Horticultural Society in 1832, likewise John Freestone of Watlington Hall, Downham who was the first to ripen seed and raise new varieties in England. At this time too, Messrs. Chandlers of Vauxhall Bridge were raising seedlings from seed sent from Versailles by John Slater who in 1848 returned to England and continued his occupation as a florist in Hammersmith.

James Douglas in *Hardy Florist's Flowers* has some harsh words to say about the manner in which chrysanthemums were grown and exhibited at the time (1880). 'The usual way of growing specimens is to pinch and tie out the young shoots until the plant is quite dwarf; and in the case of the large flowered specimens, each shoot is allowed to carry one flower only, with a stick placed in the pot to support it . . . Pompones also have to be tied down to cause a dwarf habit but this system of dwarfing is carried too far.'

He contends that 'nearly all plants exhibited near London are too severely trained; the growths are tied down and twisted during summer to obtain an unnatural dwarfness and this has also a tendency to dwarf the flowers. Some of the best specimens of the large flowered section I have seen were obtained by pinching back the leading shoot in May, when some five of six shoots were thrown up and allowed to grow on naturally. Such plants should, in the opinion of competent judges be placed before those which have been dwarfed and which would carry flowers not half the size.' Douglas also said 'that some varieties of the Japanese section make good specimens and a class for these, grown in pots would make an interesting feature.' Shortly after, the National Chrysanthemum Society inaugurated a section for the Japanese varieties which ever since has taken pride of place in the exhibiting of the chrysanthemum.

By the time Douglas' book had appeared, the plant had been classified into seven groups which have a modern look about them and which, with only slight modifications, they have retained until the present day :

Section I Incurved exhibition varieties
Section II Very large flowering varieties
Section III Anemone-flowered
Section IV Japanese
Section V Anemone-flowered pompones
Section VI Pompones
Section VII Early flowering (outdoor)

OLD VARIETIES OF MERIT

A number of the early pompones and anemone-flowered varieties are still to be found. One of the finest pompones was Model of Perfection, illustrated in *Hardy Florist's Flowers* in which is also mentioned Bob, brownish-red and Mdlle. Marthe, white as being amongst the best pompones. These varieties were also listed by Walter P. Wright in *Popular Garden Flowers* published 30 years later and they are still obtainable after almost a century. Bob, also known as Little Bob for it grew no more than 12 inches tall was included in the catalogue of John Forbes Ltd. of Hawick, Scotland, as recently as 1960 and as with so many of the old florist's flowers, it is in Scotland that many of the pompones survive. Others are :

CLARA CURTIS. The flowers are borne in profusion and are of deep strawberry pink.

CRIMSON PRECOCITE. Growing 3 feet tall, the blooms are of brilliant crimson.

DUCHESS OF EDINBURGH. The flowers are large and globular and of deep fiery red.

ELMIRANDA. Early and free flowering, the blooms are of a lovely pastel shade of lavender-mauve.

J. B. DUBOIS. In bloom early August, the flowers are of a most attractive shade of soft shell pink.

MADAME LEFORT. A very old variety growing 2 feet tall and bearing flowers of rich orange-bronze.

MARY STOKER. The blooms are small and dainty and of a lovely shade of lemon yellow.

MIGNON. Early and free flowering, the blooms being of brightest yellow.

PAUL BOISSIER. A French introduction bearing large poms of deep orange-bronze.

PIERCEY'S SEEDLING. Early to bloom, it bears flowers of rich golden-bronze, deepening to terra cotta with age.

PURPLE GEM. The large flowers are of deep rosy-purple, lovely under artificial light.

ST CROUTS. Like so many of the poms, it originated in France and is a charming variety, growing only 16 inches tall and bearing tiny poms of softest pink.

TOREADOR. The best of its colour, the flowers being of pale moon-light yellow.

WHITE BOUQUET. The best white, the large poms being shaded at the centre with green.

ITS CULTURE

The pompones are admirable plants for the small garden for almost all grow less than 2 feet tall and are completely hardy. They may be planted with the polyanthus which blooms in spring, the pompones coming into bloom in August and remaining colourful until the year end. Or plant them to the front of a border to extend the display into winter. They require a rich deeply dug soil which is well supplied with humus to retain summer moisture. During winter, dig in some decayed manure or used hops and some peat or leaf mould, incorporating it to a depth of 18 inches.

Young plants should be obtained towards the end of April and planted 20 inches apart, either in beds or in the border. Where growing in the border, set them near those plants which bloom early and which will give spring protection. These plants will have finished blooming and will have begun to die back before the chrysanthemums make their bushy growth. Firm planting is essential and, as the plants will be small when set out, mark their position with a stick. It is essential that the young plants do not suffer from lack of moisture during their early days in the open ground, and during July and August weekly applications of manure water will enhance the size and colour of the blooms.

After flowering, give a mulch of peat or decayed manure, which is placed around the roots, but not over them; by November next year's flowering shoots will have appeared, a second batch following in May when the soil begins to warm.

For two or three years the plants may remain undisturbed, after which time they should be lifted and divided in the usual way by using two forks. The old woody centre should be discarded. The plants may be lifted early in November each year, or in alternate years, when propagation may be carried out in several ways. Those who do not possess a greenhouse, and when it is not desired to propagate on a commercial scale, may remove the green shoots with a portion of root attached. These are planted 4 inches apart in a frame, over which is placed a glass light or a piece of Windowlite. There the young plants remain throughout winter, and will be ready for planting out again in April. The plants should be given almost no water during winter and, to prevent mildew, should be treated once a month with flowers of sulphur. Just before the plants are set out they should have the growing point removed to encourage them to build up a bushy plant. Chrysanthemums may also be propagated by division.

This method was recommended by Mr Nevin, who in *The Irish Farmer's and Gardener's Magazine* of 1832 said, 'Any time from the end of April to early July, I detach the young shoots from the old crowns. These are generally furnished with a few small fibres and at this season are about 12 inches or so in length. With a dibber I then proceed to plant as I would cabbages, into any warm border, allowing 2 feet between the plants and 18 inches in the rows, having previously pinched out the top of each plant. Then give one or two good waterings.' They are amongst the easiest of plants to propagate and grow well.

295

CHAPTER XIV

The Dahlia

The early introductions – Famous growers – Character of the dahlia –
Its culture.

The first notice we have of the dahlia is given in a *History of
Mexico* by Francisco Hernandez, botanist to Philip of Spain and
published in 1651. In it he describes two species which he found
growing on the mountains of Quauhnahuac, the tubers being used
by the natives for food. It was not mentioned again for almost a
century and a half when it was described by Mons. Menoville in
the history of his journey to Guaxaca which he made on behalf of
the French Government for the purpose of stealing the Cochineal
insect from the Spaniards for it is upon the dahlia that the insect
feeds. Three years later, in 1790, a plant bloomed in the Royal
Gardens at Madrid from seed sent to the King by Cervantes,
keeper of the Botanical Gardens in Mexico City. The Marchioness
of Bute, whose husband was our Ambassador in Madrid, obtained
seeds or roots and sent them back to Britain. However, they failed
to survive but in 1804, seeds were re-introduced from Madrid by
Lady Holland and during the autumn of the following year, the
plants bloomed in the gardens of Holland House, one of crimson
colouring, *D. coccinea*, being reproduced in the *'Botanist's Reposi-
tory'*.

It was not until the peace which followed Waterloo that any real
interest was taken in the plant when new varieties began to arrive
from Holland and France and shortly after, Joseph Wells of Tonbridge raised the first double variety. This was followed in 1830 by
Levick's bright red double, Commander-in-Chief which was
featured in the first issue of *The Floricultural Cabinet* and it clearly
shows the enormous improvement in the flower during the inter-
vening years. Levick had his nursery in Pinstone Street, Sheffield
now a busy shopping centre and he was to introduce a number of
dahlias of merit including beauty of Sheffield, the large white
flowers being tipped with purple.

THE EARLY INTRODUCTIONS

But the most decided advance came in 1832 when George Lynes, gardener to Mr J. Perkins at Springfield in Surrey, introduced the famous Springfield Rival which was a dark red self of perfect form.

In a letter dated 10th June, 1833, Thomas Hogg has described the advent of this dahlia which was to bring the flower into line with the other florist's flowers of the time. The dahlia, which takes its name from that of the Swedish botanist, Andreas Dahl, now made rapid progress and with the appearance of Springfield Rival became, as Louden's *Encyclopaedia of Gardening* tells us, 'the most fashionable flower in the country.' But let Hogg in his own words, tell the story of this outstanding novelty.

'The Rival,' he says, 'was raised from seed by Mr Lynes and was purchased in the seed bed where it bloomed, by Mr Inwood, a dahlia grower of Putney Heath for the sum of £5. The fame of it soon spread and several growers went to view it and wished to buy the root, but it was then sold. Amongst these was a person of the name of Glenny (soon to become one of the best known of the florists) who was very desirous to purchase it and offered 7 guineas but the answer he received was that the offer had come too late, and that it was sold. Nevertheless, Glenny returned a few days after, in the company of a Mr Hopwood of Twickenham and advanced his bid to 10 guineas, saying that as Mr Inwood had paid not deposit, he was not legally entitled to claim it. Lynes then told Inwood of what had passed saying, that he had no wish to run from his bargain but he hoped that Inwood would advance something more. In consequence of this, Inwood complied with his request and got the root for 7 guineas, being the amount of Glenny's first offer. From this you may judge that Springfield Rival is no common flower and as such I trust will not disappoint the expectations of the florist.'

Indeed, it did not. In 1840, it was exhibited by Turner of Slough at the Cambridge Show and was one of 24 distinct varieties which won for him the premier award and six years later it was the only variety included in a display of 24 blooms that had won at Cambridge previously and again he won first prize. This was at the Metropolitan Society's Show held on 25th August, 1846.

Lyne's Springfield Rival quickly made its mark and in a list of the best show dahlias for 1835, it was premier winner at all the autumn exhibitions, Widnall's Perfection and Pothecary's Cedo Nulli running it close to occupy second place :

Variety	Awards
Lyne's Springfield Rival	23
Widnall's Perfection	21
Pothecary's Cedo Nulli	21
Squible's, Hon. Mrs Harris	20
Harding's Lilac Perfection	19
Elphinstone's Polyphemus	19
Widnall's Granta	18
Douglas's Criterion	17
Paul's Clio	16
Brewer's Beauty of Cambridge	16
Montell's Newick Rival	16
Widnall's Apollo	15
Salter's Peronia	15
Pothecary's Village Maid	15

Shortly after the appearance of Springfield Rival came Dodd's Mary, a flower of similar qualities. Mr Dodds was then gardener to Sir George Warrender and was a breeder of fine dahlias. Of this variety, one report said : 'It was considered by all who have seen it to be unrivalled in its class; wherever it is exhibited, either in the country or metropolitan shows, its superiority is so evident, that the most inexperienced in the knowledge of the properties of a first rate flower have been struck with its beauty, whilst those capable of ascertaining its merits, without a single exception, state that it is in its class, superior to any other exhibited this year (1836).'

The most sought after varieties then cost a guinea each, this price being asked for Harris's two famous introductions, Lady Knox (white, tipped with maroon) and Acme (white, laced crimson); and also for Ansell's Unique (yellow, tipped maroon). Dodd's Mary and Penny's Publicola cost 15s.; and at half a guinea came Lynes' Springfield Rival; Page's Conquering King of the Yellows; Squibb's Purple Perfection; Dennis's Emperior (purple, edged yellow); and Bartlett's Desdemona (white, edged mauve). Less expensive were Heale's Defiance (white, edged pink); Brown's King of the Fairies (yellow, edged rose) and Cormack's Memnon (orange, tipped with brown) which were priced at 7s. 6d. each. All were of the pompone or honeycomb type, bearing flowers about 4 inches across and they were mostly of two colours which appealed more to the florists than did the pompone chrysanthemums which were without the contrasting edge. The dahlias were taken up by the Paisley growers which they exhibited after the June and July exhibitions of the laced pinks.

FAMOUS GROWERS

Michael Brewer and Thomas Widnall were Cambridge men, the latter having his nursery at Granchester and they showed their dahlias throughout the length and breadth of the country, no small feat in those days of stage coach travel. On 12th September, 1836 Tom Widnall was exhibiting at the Grand Dahlia Show at Salt Hill, Windsor when Her Majesty 'named two splendid seedlings, one a yellow belonging to Mr Widnall which she named Superba'. At this show Widnall, Brewer and Brown of Slough were the judges of the amateur growers' exhibits; and, Glenny, Salter and Wheeler of Warminster judged the nurserymen's flowers. All were highly competent to do so.

Two days later, Widnall attended the Sheffield Grand Horticultural Society's Show held at the Botanical Gardens on 14th and 15th September. 'Beautiful as were many of the exotics exhibited, particularly the orchids,' said the report, 'the point of attraction was the dahlia tent.'

For his stand of 50 blooms, Mr Widnall won the premier award which was a silver cup valued at £15 and Mr Levick of Sheffield took 2nd prize, a silver cup worth £10. A prize of a snuff box was awarded to Mr Harrison for an unnamed seedling and the sum of 2 guineas was presented to Joseph Paxton for a single specimen of an orchid which he was exhibiting on behalf of his employer, the 6th Duke of Devonshire.

At the Birmingham Dahlia Show, held on 12th and 13th September, 1838, Mr Widnall again took the Premier award for 24 blooms and the prize on this occasion was £100, this being the largest sum awarded for any florist's exhibit up to that time. Eight of the varieties were of his own raising and amongst the others were Springfield Rival and Dodd's Mary.

Of the other famous dahlia growers of the time, Harris, Pothecary, Squibb, Wheeler and Keynes were West Countrymen, natives of Dorset and Wiltshire for it was in those parts and in Cambridge, away from the industrial north (Paisley was the exception) that the dahlia was mostly grown. In Dorset, it was possible to treat it as almost a hardy plant, the roots being allowed to remain in the ground during winter. It was thus easier to preserve them than if lifted in autumn and stored away from frost during the winter months.

John Keynes was with Turner of Slough, considered to be the best of the dahlia growers and exhibitors of the 1850's and 60's. The two were firm friends and often exhibited together. Keynes lived in Salisbury and took up dahlia growing in 1845. 'The first really good seedling introduced into Salisbury was a variety called The Queen,' he wrote. 'This I had from my old friend Pothecary of Upway near Dorchester, and was the first light-edged I had ever seen. Well do I remember going into Squibb's garden, where it grew, to see this pet; and I dare say Charles Turner will remember the occasion too. There it was – and there, it is now in my mind's eye; time, place and circumstance as vivid as ever, the exact spot where it grew, the umbrella with which it was shaded, and its profusion of lovely flowers. It was worth a life of toil to raise such a dahlia. Poor old Pothecary. He was one of our first great seedling growers, though he never received the credit due to his productions.' Keynes continues : 'The first good dahlia I ever raised was Ovid, the root of which I sold for £50. I think we had never seen a nearer approach to a blue dahlia.'

Keynes raised his plants from seed sown as he said, on 10th March of each year. He sowed over a hot bed to encourage rapid germination and by early April, the seedlings were ready to move to small pots in which they were grown until planted out about mid-May when they would bloom the same season. Often, the best were sold for prices of up to £100 a root and were lifted late in autumn when they had finished flowering. Amongst his best were Constancy (yellow, edged crimson); Lady Gladys Herbert (white, edged crimson); and several self-coloured varieties such as Julia Wyatt (cream), Rifleman (scarlet), James Cocker (purple) and John Downie (claret), the last two being named in recognition of famous Scottish florists of the day.

Amongst Charles Turner's finest was Scarlet Gem which when shown at the Metropolitan Floral Exhibition of 1846 won a Certificate of Merit. It was described as being 'deep and bright in colour; in shape first rate, the outline perfect. It had a bold, large flower without coarseness'. Another was Figaro, a yellow lightly edged with scarlet whilst Toison d'or was pure yellow.

Another of the old Show dahlias raised by Turner is Mrs Saunders, introduced in 1872 and listed by Alexander Lister and Son of Rothesay to this day. Its flowers measure 4 inches across and are of soft lemon-yellow, tipped with white. It is one of the most beautiful of all dahlias.

Equally outstanding is Peacock, also a Turner introduction and happily still with us. It was handsomely painted by Mr John Farleigh and appears in Mr Sacheverell Sitwell's *Old Fashioned Flowers* published in 1940 and what a glorious flower it is, measuring about 5 inches across and of deep crimson-purple tipped with white. And there are others waiting to be discovered in those white walled cottage gardens of Western Scotland where in the mild climate, they are allowed to occupy the garden all winter. For this reason, they have survived.

Penelope bears cream coloured flowers suffused with pink; Model bears pale pink flowers edged with rosy-purple and Duke of Fife bears large flowers of glowing cardinal red. Of earlier date is Nulli Secundus, the blooms of old gold being tipped with bronze, mellowing tints of fading autumn.

CHARACTER OF THE DAHLIA

The Character of a Good Dahlia was first defined by M'Intosh in *The Flower Garden* (1838). Three criteria were taken into consideration, namely form, colour and size.

I. FORM. The front view of the bloom should be circular with the petals rounded and smooth at the edges, slightly concave. One of the most perfect in this respect is Springfield Rival.

When the petals are pointed, notched, fringed, piped, quilled, concave or convex, the circle is broken. Also when the eye is shown in the full-blown flower, it is also a defect.

The side view should be of a perfect hemisphere, like the upper half of an orange.

II COLOUR. This is looked upon by florists as an inferior consideration to form. In flowers of one colour (selfs), the colour should be bright and distinct, without breaking or blotching. When there are stripes or edging, they should be clear and uniform, without clouding or running. One-colour flowers of good form and bright colours are superior to badly formed and imperfectly coloured sorts.

III SIZE. Although large flowers of good form and clear distinct colours are superior to small flowers with the same properties, yet with florists, size alone is looked upon as nothing, when colour and form is defective. Few of the largest flowers are sufficiently hemispherical.

A grower of the time has suggested the following as being well tried and 'known to be good and constant'. They were all repeatedly successful at the major exhibitions held during the early years of the show dahlia :

> Beauty of Wakefield, white edged purple
> Defiance, white tipped scarlet
> Dodd's Mary, pale yellow tipped rose
> Essex Rival, dark red
> Eva, creamy-white
> Frances, white tipped rose
> Knight's Victory, crimson
> Marquis of Lothian, purple
> Ne Plus Ultra, yellow tipped crimson
> Springfield Rival, crimson
> Unique, deep yellow tipped red

The dahlia with its flamboyance and freedom of flowering is one of the few florists' flowers to have increased in popularity during the past hundred years. Its ease of culture has had much to do with this and which may account for the survival of a number of the old Show dahlias to be found to this day in nurseries and gardens of southern Scotland. Unlike the show auricula and other florists' flowers, it is a plant of enormous vigour, a well grown tuber (root) producing several dozen cuttings each year and without any noticable loss of stamina.

Since the beginning of the century, the Show dahlia has been developed to bear larger or smaller blooms as the case may be, those bearing larger flowers now being classed as Giant and Large Decoratives whilst the Small Decoratives more nearly resemble the old Show dahlias in size. The scarlet Shirley Westwell and the lilac-purple Florist are examples of the Small Decorative to achieve popularity in recent years. Further down the scale are the Large and Small Pompones, those having flowers measuring more than 3 inches across being classed as Large Pompones. This section has with amateurs, reigned supreme on the show bench during the past 50 years for they are ideal plants for the small garden, growing less than 3 feet tall whilst the flowers, neat and symmetrical and produced in the widest colour range, have endeared the flower to all exhibitors. The bloom resembles those of the ranunculus and pompone chrysanthemum in their long lasting qualities when cut, and have a firmness of texture which enables them to be transported a distance to market or show ground without adverse effects for they do not easily bruise. Another point in their favour is their freedom of flowering over a period of at least 16 weeks when there will usually be some bloom to cut each day.

ITS CULTURE

Dahlias need copious amounts of water to build up a large tuber and to make plenty of top growth. Prepare the ground in March, digging in some decayed manure, hops or old mushroom bed compost, together with some peat or leaf mould. If the soil is heavy, work in some grit or crushed brick to assist drainage. Excessive feeding, especially with artificial fertilisers should be guarded against and Mr Stanley Spencer, dahlia expert of Hockley has said '... over-feeding has been known to drive nearly all the colour from blooms formed on plants nearly twice their usual height.'

Wood ash, stored under cover, is valuable for the potash content will improve the colour and enhance the quality of the bloom. If this is not available, rake into the soil at planting time, 1 ounce per square yard of sulphate of potash.

For propagation, ground or pot tubers are usually purchased in November when lifted. They are packed into boxes and a mixture of peat and loam is packed around them, just covering the crown. Place in a temperature of 56°F (13°C) and keep the roots moist when after about three weeks the pale green shoots will be showing around the crown.

If no heat is available, store the tubers in boxes of peat or sand during winter, away from frost and box them early in April when the warmth of the sun will bring them into growth. They may be kept in a cold greenhouse or a closed frame simply constructed from old railway sleepers and frame lights made of laths and heavy grade polythene sheeting.

When the shoots are about 3 inches high, remove them with a sharp knife, and if possible with a small piece of tuber attached to the base and from which the roots will form more quickly. Insert the cuttings in a compost made up of sterilised loam, peat and sand in equal parts, spacing them 2 inches apart and keeping the compost moist but not wet. In a temperature of 55°F (13°C) they will root in three weeks when they will begin to form new growth at the top.

The cuttings should then be lifted with care so as not to break away the roots and they are then planted in small pots (Jiffy pots are suitable) containing a compost made up of loam, decayed manure, peat and sand in equal parts. They are grown on in a similar temperature until early May, giving plenty of moisture and fresh air, when they are moved to a frame to harden before planting out early in June.

Soil-heating cables will enable cuttings to be raised in a frame but failing this, if the tubers are planted in a frame in April, they may be divided into several pieces, each containing a shoot and a tuber, before planting out early in June.

To protect the cuttings and plants from 'damping off', dust them with sulphur when removed for rooting and again when in the pots. It is also advisable to shade them from strong sunlight in spring and especially is this necessary whilst rooting.

The plants must be thoroughly hardened before planting out about 1st June, about 10 days earlier in the south when late frosts should have ended. Plant the pompones 3 feet apart, just covering the small tuberous roots and water in. From now onwards they will require copious amounts of water whenever the weather is dry. As the plants will need supporting in all but the most sheltered gardens, it will be advisable to drive in a stout hardwood stake before planting so as not to damage the tuber. As the plants make growth, they should be tied loosely to the stakes with raffia. A well grown plant should be about 8 inches tall, bright green in colour whilst the soil ball should be a mass of white roots.

After planting, keep the hoe moving between the rows and early in August, as the first blooms are opening, give the plants a mulch of peat or decayed manure.

Growing for exhibition calls for disbudding and de-branching. A plant should not be expected to produce more than a limited number of stems and from these, all unwanted side growths must be removed by pinching them out as they form. This should continue until the first buds begin to form.

At the end of each shoot is found three buds as it is the centre or terminal bud that is retained, the others being pinched out. Each shoot is treated in this manner throughout the season, thus concentrating the energies of the plant into one main bud on each of several selected stems. The stems must be carefully tied in or as Turner said, 'tying "out" the stems rather than "in" like a wheat-sheaf for it is essential that sunlight and air be able to circulate around the stems.'

It may be necessary to shade the bloom from strong sunlight but if shaded too long before it is required to exhibit the blooms, those of pale colouring may lose colour and make them unsatisfactory for exhibition. Large cardboard 'dunce' caps fixed to the end of a cane will provide shading.

When the bloom is cut, the end of the stem should at once be immersed in boiling water for a few seconds to seal the stem, before plunging into a bucket of cold water almost up to the head. Exhibitors will often take their blooms to the show still in the buckets and if the pompones are to be shown, it is recommended that circles of plywood be cut so as to fit just inside the rim of the bucket and into the wood several holes are drilled through which the stems are placed. In this way, the blooms will rest on the wood whilst the stems are immersed in the water.

On the show bench, the blooms will be displayed in vases, arranged so that they are held well above the vase rim and so that their full beauty is displayed to the judges. A ball of wire netting placed in the vase will assist in the floral arrangement. The blooms should be just open with the petals in no way damaged.

CHAPTER XV

Miscellaneous Florists' Flowers

Double Daisy – Hollyhock – Hepatica – Pentstemon – Stock – Sweet
Rocket – Sweet William – Wallflower.

A number of the hardy plants which have remained as cherished
members of the cottage garden since earliest times, were also taken
up by the florists and brought to a perfection of beauty now rarely
to be seen in these flowers. They include the hollyhock and sweet
william, wallflower and double daisy, the double sweet rocket and
the hepatica, and latter being almost unknown to modern gardeners
though its flowers are amongst the most beautiful of all and it has
a neat, compact habit. Like the sweet william and double daisy,
its blooms are round, forming an unbroken circle, which was the
criterion of a true florist's flower. It was hardy and it was perennial
and though the number of varieties was limited, it received considerable attention from the florists.

DOUBLE DAISY

Bellis perennis, the Double Daisy, figures in the badge of Lady
Margaret Beaufort, mother of Henry VII by her marriage to
Edmund Tudor. She was founder of St John's College and Christ's
College, Cambridge and from Chaucer's time, this native flower has
been held in greater esteem by poets and nobility than any other
with the possible exception of the violet and primrose. Wrote
Chaucer in *The Legend of Good Women* :

> Of all the flowers in the meade
> Then love I most those floures white and redde,
> Such that men call daisies in our town . . .
> When it upriseth early by the morrow,
> That blissful sight softeneth all my sorrow.

Again, he alludes to its Anglo-Saxon name of 'daeyeseage', meaning
'the eye of the day' for it is the first flower to open each morning
and from this it takes its name. The French know it as Paquerette

because it is usually in fullness of bloom at the approach of Paques (Easter), but its botanical name comes from the Latin *bellus,* pretty.

Useful for spring bedding, to plant with violettas or primroses or in nooks about the rock garden, it requires an ordinary loamy soil. It is completely hardy anywhere but to be long living, it requires frequent division and enjoys best a position of semi-shade. 'Transplant them every year,' said one writer whilst Sir Thomas Hanmer said that they should be planted 'for edgings in poor soil'. Hanmer, who helped Evelyn devise the gardens as Sayes Court, grew eight kinds of the double daisy, including a 'green' one, possibly white shaded with green at the centre as sometimes seen in the double white primrose. The Rev. Hanbury (1770) grew 12 kinds, one of which he knew as the Double Painted Lady.

The pink double daisy is beautifully shown in a water colour of about 1570 attributed to Jaques le Moyne, who escaped the massacre of St Bartholomew and settled in England shortly afterwards. It is believed that he became tutor to the Sidney family at Penshurst. Several of his water colours have survived and are to be seen in the Victoria and Albert Museum. They are amongst the most botanically skilled of all flower paintings and most of them are enhanced by butterflies and moths most accurately depicted.

Several varieties of the double daisy dating from the early days of the 19th century survive, one of the loveliest being Dresden China with its tiny blooms of about the size of a sixpence, tightly packed with multitudes of quilled petals of a glorious shade of shell-pink. It is one of the most beautiful of all small plants. And of similar age is the scarlet Rob Roy which appeared shortly after the appearance of Scott's novel (possibly his best) of the same name which was published early in 1818 and which within a fortnight had sold the whole of the first edition of 10,000. The little scarlet buttons are borne on 3 inch stems and The Pearl, bearing equally small blooms of a lovely shade of pearly white acts as a pleasing contrast.

Nor should *Bellis prolifera,* the 'Hen and Childrens' of old cottage gardens be forgotten. Tiny flowerets develop from the main bloom and dangle around the plant like chickens around the mother hen. It is a delightful plant for a small pot in a sunny window. This and the named varieties of the double daisy require a soil which contains some humus for they are intolerant of dry conditions in summer. Prepare the soil as for pansies and primroses when they will prove most perennial.

HOLLYHOCK

Althaea rosea is its botanical name and exactly when the plant reached England it not known but it is mentioned in the 15th century poem of John (the) Gardener, and Turner spoke of it as a 'common' flower. As it is native of the Near East (where it is found in every garden), it may have come with the returning crusaders who gave it the name Holy-hock, which name was still in use in the 18th century when Mortimer published his works on husbandry (1707). Dr Prior Laveire, in his *Popular Names of British Plants,* believes the name to be from Colly, a cabbage, from the doubling of the flower.

Sir Thomas Hanmer writing in 1650 listed numerous varieties, including a double yellow raised, he tells us by the Duke of Orleans. By the beginning of the 19th century, Thomas Hogg, a nurseryman of Paddington Green, in his *Treatise* lists 80 named varieties and by that time the hollyhock had become a florists' flower. It remained so until the end of the century, the last to raise the hollyhock to the status of a florists' flower being William Chater of Saffron Walden whose double-flowering strain is still the best obtainable for it breeds remarkably true from seed.

The hollyhock is a perennial and is readily raised from seed which should be sown in drills in the open, during April. By early autumn, the plants will be large enough to transplant to the flowering position and they will bloom the following summer. To prolong the life of the plant, the stems should be removed as soon as they have flowered.

In early times, an infusion of the flowers was considered a valuable help towards relieving diseases of the lungs, bringing relief to those suffering from tuberculosis and to those who suffered from inflammation of the bladder. If only for its curative qualities, it may have been given the namy 'holy'.

It was given its botanical name *rosea* for its symmetrical flowers which measured about 3 inches across resembled those of *Rosa centifolia,* the Rose of a Thousand petals, so often depicted by the Dutch artists. The old florists exhibited the entire spike which often measured several feet in length and this was taken into consideration by the judges as well as the quality and arrangement of the individual flowers.

HEPATICA

A century ago it was known as *Anemone hepatica* and is native of the mountainous slopes of C. Europe. 'Next into the Winter Wolfesbane, these making their pride appear in winter are most welcome early guests,' wrote Parkinson of the plant and he grew ten kinds, including the double purple, 'sent from Alphonsus Pontius out of Italy as Clusius reporteth and which was also found in the woods near the Castle of Starnberg in Austria'. To be long living, it requires a well drained porous soil from which winter moisture can readily drain away. Like the primrose, it also enjoys semi-shaded conditions and ample supplies of moisture about its roots in summer. Though soon forming a clump, the hepatica resents transplanting more than most hardy plants. After moving, it may take two years to come into bloom again and so should be allowed to form a clump of 20 or more offsets, when after six years it may be lifted and divided which is done early in spring.

The soil should be of a fibrous nature, enriched with decayed manure and some peat or leaf mould for hepaticas are deeply rooting and are gross feeders, in this respect resembling the double primrose with which they may be grown.

Plant in spring, about 9 inches apart and with the crown just above soil level. They will appreciate a mulch given in autumn each year as the foliage begins to die back. This should consist of decayed manure mixed with some leaf mould and finely sifted turf loam. The mulch should be worked up to the crown of the plants as for primroses. They will also benefit from an occasional watering with dilute liquid manure. Van Osten in *The Dutch Gardener*, published in 1703 said : 'Plant them in sandy loam mixed with old dung and when not in flower, stand (or sit) over them and water them with human urine. If you do this they will so increase that you may fill your garden with them in a short time.' Hepaticas grow readily from seed freshly saved for if the seed becomes dry, it will take a year to germinate and must first be frosted. Harvest and sow the seed in July, using pans or boxes containing the John Innes compost and cover with a sheet of glass to hasten germination, or place the containers in a closed frame. The compost must be kept quite moist. When the seedlings have formed 2-3 leaves, transplant them to shaded beds, taking care not to injure the fleshy roots and do not expose them to a drying wind or to strong sunlight. Transplanting should be done in April during showery weather.

There are several handsome varieties still to be found in various gardens of England and Scotland. The best form is *H. angulosa*, Lodden Blue which in spring, bears large deep blue flowers on 6 inch stems. The true Hepatica, *H. triloba* which has 3-lobed leaves, bears large deep blue anemone-like flowers on 4 inch stems; whilst *alba* bears pure white flowers which act as a pleasing contrast. There is a single pink form, *rosea* and a mauve, *lilacina*. Double flowered varieties which bear blossoms like large double primroses may occasionally be found and until a year or so ago were listed in several plantsmen's catalogues at half a guinea each. The singles cost about £1 a dozen.

PENTSTEMON

It was one of the few plants of the New World taken up by the florist's for the handsome dangling tubular bells are circular at the mouth, the petals being slightly rolled back in a most attractive manner. *P. hartwegi*, discovered by Professor Humboldt in Mexico, growing at an elevation of more than 10,000 feet and introduced in 1828 is the chief parent of the florist's varieties. Several other species were discovered in N.W. America by David Douglas, the explorer who met with a cruel death early in 1835 when on an expedition to the Sandwich Islands. From *P. hartwegi* and other species, numerous hybrid varieties were introduced from 1835 onwards and came to be widely grown as bedding plants and to beautify the border. Hardy in the more favourably situated gardens, especially in the western parts of the British Isles where they may be permanent plants of the garden, they were especially cultivated by the Scottish growers who have maintained extensive collections up to the present time. In the colder parts, it is usual to lift the plants in November, to winter them under glass and to plant out again in May.

Cuttings, which form at the base of the plant are removed early in September and planted in boxes, pots or frames containing a sandy compost. Plant 2 inches apart and place in a frame or greenhouse, shading them from strong sunlight when they will root in about four weeks. The plants should not be disturbed until March when they are moved to small pots and grown on for 6-8 weeks in a frame or beneath barn cloches. They will have formed sturdy plants to be set out towards the end of spring.

The pentstemon requires a well drained sandy soil containing some decayed manure and peat or leaf mould. In a heavy, badly drained soil the plants may perish during winter. But this is an easily grown plant which blooms from July until November when, apart from chrysanthemums and michaelmas daisies, there is little other colour in the garden. At this time, no plant can match the pentstemon for brightness.

At least 50 varieties are obtainable, many dating from the mid-19th century and a specialist catalogue could be published by any-one who would take up their culture. Most are priced at about £1 a dozen and are obtainable in shades of pink, rose, purple, scarlet and crimson and intermediate shades. Amongst the finest is Coun-tess of Haddington, bearing large trumpets of rich crimson, veined with purple; and Countess of Dalkeith, the deep purple bells having a pure white throat. Lady Sherborne is of unusual colouring, bearing trumpets of shell pink margined with chocolate-brown around the edge; whilst Mrs J. Purser bears rose-pink flowers pencilled with darker rose. Two of the finest scarlet varieties are Thomas H. Cook and Chester Scarlet, both of which bear large stately spikes of the most intense red. Also good is Roderick Mac-kenzie with its large bells of richest purple and Lady Monckton, pale lilac with a white throat. Delightful too, is Lady Lloyd which forms a handsome spike of creamy white bells margined with rosy-pink.

STOCK

'Of all the flowers that have of late years been introduced into England' wrote Thomas Hogg, 'none seem to give greater pleasure than the different varieties of the 10-week stock; and none are sought after at the moment with greater avidity.' Hogg describes the colours of flowers he obtained from seed which had been sent to him from Denmark and calls them Danish Stocks. Amongst the colours he noticed were crimson, ruby, scarlet, mahogany, flesh, peach, ash, purple, blue, mulberry and black and they carried the warm, aromatic perfume of the wallflower.

All the garden stocks are descended from a single species, *Mat-thiola incana* and its variety *M. annua*, plants which are native of S. Europe though both forms were common in Elizabethan gardens. They were described by Lyte in his *New Herbal* as Stock Gilly-flowers and Gerard said that the plants 'were greatly esteemed for the beautie of the flowers and pleasant sweet perfume'. By the beginning of the 17th century, double stocks were known and as the plants grew only 12 inches tall were ideally suited to pot culture, they were later taken up by the florists, there being several classes for their exhibiting at the summer shows. 'The careful gardener,' wrote Hogg 'when in possession of a good double flowering scarlet, will not neglect to winter some plants in pots, either in frames or greenhouses, or hoops covered with mats during hard frosts.'

Stocks may be divided into four groups, one for each season of the year. First come the spring-flowering or Brompton Stocks, developed at the Brompton Road Nurseries of Messrs. London and Wise (who laid out the gardens at Blenheim Palace) early in the 18th century. The plants are true biennials, obtainable in white, purple-crimson and rose and should be sown early in July removing the dark green seedlings (as with all stocks) as these will give only single flowers. The seedlings should be transplanted in August and they may either be set out in their flowering quarters in October or wintered under a frame and planted out in March. Or they may be grown on in pots to bloom under glass early in the year. Lavender Lady and the crimson Queen Astrid are excellent varieties.

Henry Phillips has told of seeing the Carmine or Brompton stock exhibited at the London Horticultural Society's shows which were like 'ropes of roses'. He also tells of a plant growing in the garden of a Mr Stockdale at Notting Hill which in May, 1822 when in full bloom, measured 11 feet 9 inches in circumference.

The summer-flowering or Ten-week stocks are so called because they may be brought into bloom within ten weeks of sowing the seed in gentle heat early in March. Hansen's 100 per cent Double is a recommended strain for bedding, making branched plants only 9 inches tall and obtainable in all the stock shades including apple-blossom pink, light blue and yellow.

The Excelsior Mammoth Strain in a similar colour range, including blood red, grows 2 feet tall, the large densely packed spikes having a most majestic appearance in the border whilst they are valuable for cutting so that their delicious clove scent may be enjoyed indoors. Those Stocks known as Intermediate or East Lothian, discovered in a garden in Scotland, bloom in autumn. It was in 1868, that David Thomson, then head gardener to the Duke of Buccleuch, discovered the plants in a cottage garden where he was told, they had been growing for at least 300 years, since the time of Henry VIII. From a spring sowing, they will bloom in autumn or sown late in July, they will bloom early in spring in gentle heat under glass, or outdoors later in the year. Likewise the Winter-flowering stocks, the seed being sown in July for late winter flowering under glass. Making plants of vigorous branching habit, they grow 18 to 20 inches tall and produce their large dense spikes throughout winter under glass. Amongst the finest varieties are Mont Blanc (white); Queen Alexandra (rose-lilac); Crimson King and Salmon King. Under glass in a temperature of 50°F the perfume of the flowers is almost overpowering.

SWEET ROCKET

Hesperis matronalis or Dame's Violet is its botanical name for the flowers carry the unmistakable scent of the violet, much resembling the perfume of the wallflower to which it is closely related. Like the stock and wallflower, the scent has undertones of cloves which makes it more pleasing and more lasting.

Probably native of the British Isles as well as of Central Europe, it grows 3 feet tall with ovate lance-shaped leaves 'of a dark green colour, snipt about the edges,' wrote Gerard, 'the flowers come forth at the top of the branches, like those of the Stock gilly-flower . . .' The small white or purple cross-shaped flowers are borne during July and August and in the words of an early 19th century writer 'no flower garden ought to be without them; their neat habit, beauty, and particular fragrance, alike recommend them.'

But it was the double forms (in white and purple) that endeared the plant to early gardeners. They grew them in pots and in open ground beds, restricting the height by pinching out the leader shoot. The plants then grew only 20 inches tall and formed dense bushy growth composed of numerous basal shoots which were easily detached and grown on. Or where the plants were not to be propagated, they produced numerous flowering stems the following year and were a billowing mass of white (or purple) foam, scenting the air afar.

The plant requires a well drained sandy soil containing a little decayed manure and some peat or leaf mould. Plant in autumn for it is completely hardy and space 12 inches apart.

SWEET WILLIAM

Henry Phillips believed that the plant reached England with *Dianthus caryophyllus,* during the Norman Conquest for he says 'it grows on the hills of Normandy, west of Dieppe but the flowers are scarcely larger than those of London Pride'. The first writer to notice the plant was Dr Dodoens who, in 1554 when physician to the Emperor Charles V of Germany, published his *New Herbal* and though Turner does not mention it, Gerard writing some years later speaks of it as 'a common flower' and for the first time refers to it as the Sweet William, saying 'these plants are not used either in mete or medicine but are esteemed for their beauty, to deck up gardens and the bosoms of the beautiful' for which purpose they were used at the French Court early in the 19th century.

The flower, which came to be known as the auricula-eyed Sweet William was taken up by the Paisley weavers along with the pink for its inner circles of purple or crimson had an appeal similar to the lacing of the pinks. That held in most esteem however, was the double flowering form, known as King Willie. Until the ending of the second World War, it was to be found in cottage gardens everywhere. It is now rare though grows in several gardens in Northern Ireland. It is a handsome flower with several rows of petals and as it does not set seed must be propagated from cuttings or by layering as for carnations.

It requires a rich well drained soil but like all dianthus, requires lime in its diet, preferably in the form of lime rubble (mortar).

Rooted cuttings should be grown on in small pots during winter to be planted out in spring, spacing them 9 inches apart.

WALLFLOWER

Those who know only the single red and yellow wallflowers would find it hard to believe to what extent the plant was prized a century ago. In *The Floricultural Cabinet* for December, 1848 appeared a short piece on the culture of wallflowers, the writer saying that those 'having double flowers have been cultivated in Britain for three centuries; we have the blood-red, black, golden and pale yellow, and another which is nearly green. They are worthy of every attention and are so highly esteemed in some of the northern counties that they rank as prize (show) flowers and form

a class for competition. It is surprising to see the very large specimens which are produced, the spikes in bloom measuring from
18-24 inches long'.

The plant is a member of the same family with its four cross-
shaped petals that includes the Stock and Sweet Rocket, which also
endeared themselves to early gardeners on account of their delicious
scent. They were known as Gillyflowers and to Parkinson the wallflower was the wall-gillyflower. In the *Paradisus*, he described seven
kinds, including the double red and double yellow saying that 'the
sweetness of the flowers causeth them to be used for nosegays and
to deck up houses.' So often was the flower used as a nosegay that
it was for this reason given its botanical name *Cheiranthus*, meaning 'hand-flower', one held and carried in the hand for its perfume
'cheered' the spirits. To earlier gardeners it was known as the
chevisaunce which is an old English word meaning 'comforter',
because of its rich perfume. Spenser uses the word in his lines :

> The pretty paunce (pansy) and the chevisaunce
> Shall match with the fair flower-de-luce.

Native of S. Europe, it possibly reached England with the Norman
invasion for it was to be found on the walls of castles and
abbeys, probably rooted to stone sent over from France for their
building. Gerard spoke of the yellow Stock-gillyflower which was
that described by John Rea of Bewdley as being 'as broad as a
half-crown'. This was in 1665 and a century and a half later, a
writer said that 'in the last few years (about 1840) a number of
semi-double kinds have been imported from Germany . . . of
which there are striped kinds as well as self colours'. But it was
the double flowering wallflowers that interested the florists and as
they did not set seed, they were propagated by cuttings.

After flowering, the blooms were removed and the plants allowed
to remain in the beds. They would form an abundance of shoots
from the base which were removed when about 3 inches long. The
lower leaves are removed and the cuttings inserted in boxes of
sandy compost or around the side of a pot. Shade from the
sun and syringe if they wilt. They will root in 4 weeks when they
are moved to small pots and grown on in a frame until early
March, to be planted into their flowering quarters to bloom the
following year. In this way there will always be a stock of young
plants available.

Double wallflowers grow best in a well drained sandy soil, containing a little decayed manure and they require an open, sunny situation. During the summer, give the plants ample supplies of moisture to keep them growing.

Two of the oldest varieties are still occasionally to be found but the ease with which the single wallflower is raised from seed has, in this age of mass production, meant that the doubles which require vegetative propagation, have become more difficult to find. Parkinson's old double red, known as the Bloody Warrior is now almost extinct but the old double yellow, re-discovered in a Shropshire garden early in the century by Rev. Harpur Crewe, Rector of Drayton Beauchamp is still obtainable.

Index